Lords of the Sea

Lords of the Sea
Great Captains of the Royal Navy During the Age of Sail

A. T. Mahan

*Lords of the Sea: Great Captains of the Royal Navy
During the Age of Sail*
by A. T. Mahan

Originally published in 1896 in two volumes under the title
Types of Naval Officers Drawn from the History of the British Navy

Leonaur is an imprint of Oakpast Ltd

Material original to this edition and text in this form
copyright © 2009 Oakpast Ltd

ISBN: 978-1-84677-670-0 (hardcover)
ISBN: 978-1-84677-669-4 (softcover)

http://www.leonaur.com

Publisher's Note

The views expressed in this book are not necessarily
those of the publisher.

Contents

Preface	7
Naval Warfare in the Early 18th Century	15
Hawke: 1705-1781	63
Rodney: 1719-1792	111
Howe: 1726-1799	183
Jervis: 1735-1823	229
Saumarez: 1757-1836	273
Pellew: 1757-1833	305
Postscript	338

Preface

Although the distinguished seamen, whose lives and professional characteristics it is the object of this work to present in brief summary, belonged to a service now foreign to that of the United States, they have numerous and varied points of contact with America; most of them very close, and in some instances of marked historical interest. The older men, indeed, were during much of their careers our fellow countrymen in the colonial period, and fought, some side by side with our own people in this new world, others in distant scenes of the widespread strife that characterized the middle of the eighteenth century, the beginnings of "world politics;" when, in a quarrel purely European in its origin, "black men," to use Macaulay's words, "fought on the coast of Coromandel, and red men scalped each other by the great lakes of North America." All, without exception, were actors in the prolonged conflict that began in 1739 concerning the right of the ships of Great Britain and her colonies to frequent the seas bordering the American dominions of Spain; a conflict which, by gradual expansion, drew in the continent of Europe, from Russia to France, spread thence to the French possessions in India and North America, involved Spanish Havana in the western hemisphere and Manila in the eastern, and finally entailed the expulsion of France from our continent. Thence, by inevitable sequence, issued the independence of the United States. The contest, thus completed, covered forty-three years.

The four seniors of our series, Hawke, Rodney, Howe, and Jervis, witnessed the whole of this momentous period, and served conspicuously, some more, some less, according to their age and rank, during its various stages. Hawke, indeed, was at the time of the American Revolution too old to go to sea, but he did not die until October 16, 1781, three days before the surrender of Cornwallis at Yorktown, which is commonly accepted as the closing incident of our struggle for independence. On the other hand, the two younger men, Saumarez and Pellew, though they had entered the navy before the American Revolution, saw in it the beginnings of an active service which lasted to the end of the Napoleonic wars, the most continuous and gigantic strife of modern times. It was as the enemies of our cause that they first saw gunpowder burned in anger.

Nor was it only amid the commonplaces of naval warfare that they then gained their early experiences in America. Pellew in 1776, on Lake Champlain, bore a brilliant part in one of the most decisive—though among the least noted—campaigns of the Revolutionary contest; and a year later, as leader of a small contingent of seamen, he shared the fate of Burgoyne's army at Saratoga. In 1776 also, Saumarez had his part in an engagement which ranks among the bloodiest recorded between ships and forts, being on board the British flag-ship Bristol at the attack upon Fort Moultrie, the naval analogue of Bunker Hill; for, in the one of these actions as in the other, the great military lesson was the resistant power against frontal attack of resolute marksmen, though untrained to war, when fighting behind entrenchments,—a teaching renewed at New Orleans, and emphasized in the recent South African War. The well-earned honours of the comparatively raw colonials received generous recognition at the time from their opponents, even in the midst of the bitterness proverbially attendant upon family quarrels; but it is only just to allow that their endurance found its counterpart in the resolute and persistent valour of the assailants. In these two battles, with which the War of Independence may be said fairly to have begun, by land and by water, in the far North and in the far South, the men of the same stock, whose ancestors there met face to face as foes, have now in peace a common heritage of glory. If little of bitterness remains in the recollections which those who are now fellow-citizens retain of the struggle between the North and the South, within the American Republic, we of two different nations, who yet share a common tongue and a common tradition of liberty and law, may well forget the wrongs of the earlier strife, and look only to the common steadfast courage with which each side then bore its share in a civil conflict.

The professional lives of these men, therefore, touch history in many points; not merely history generally, but American history specifically. Nor is this contact professional only, devoid of personal tinge. Hawke was closely connected by blood with the Maryland family of Bladen; that having been his mother's maiden name, and Governor Bladen of the then colony being his first cousin. Very much of his early life was spent upon the American Station, largely in Boston. But those were the days of Walpole's peace policy; and when the maritime war, which the national outcry at last compelled, attained large dimensions, Hawke's already demonstrated eminence as a naval leader naturally led to his employment in European waters, where the more immediate dangers, if not the greatest interests, of Great Britain were then felt to be. The universal character, as well as the decisive issues of the opening struggle were as yet but dimly foreseen. Rodney also had family ties with America, though somewhat more remote. Caesar Rodney, a signer of the Declaration of Independence from Delaware, was of the same stock; their great-grandfathers were brothers. It was from the marriage of his ancestor with the daughter of a Sir Thomas Caesar that the American Rodney derived his otherwise singular name.

Howe, as far as known, had no relations on this side of the water; but his elder brother, whom he succeeded in the title, was of all British officers the one who most won from the colonial troops with whom he was associated a personal affection, the memory of which has been transmitted to us; while the admiral's own kindly attitude towards the colonists, and his intimacy with Franklin, no less than his professional ability, led to his being selected for the North American command at the time when the home country had not yet lost all hope of a peaceable solution of difficulties. To this the Howe tradition was doubtless expected to contribute. Jervis, a man considerably younger than the other three, by the accidents of his career came little into touch with either the colonies or the colonists, whether before or during the Revolutionary epoch; yet even he, by his intimate friendship with Wolfe, and intercourse with his last days, is brought into close relation with an event and a name indelibly associated with one of the great landmarks—crises—in the history of the American Continent. Although the issue of the strife depended, doubtless, upon deeper and more far-reaching considerations, it is not too much to say that in the heights of Quebec, and in the name of Wolfe, is signalized the downfall of the French power in America. There was prefigured the ultimate predominance of the traditions of the English-speaking races throughout this continent, which in our own momentous period stands mediator between the two ancient and contrasted civilizations of Europe and Asia, that so long moved apart, but are now brought into close, if not threatening, contact.

Interesting, however, as are the historical and social environments in which their personalities played their part, it is as individual men, and as conspicuous exemplars—types—of the varied characteristics which go to the completeness of an adequate naval organization, that they are here brought forward. Like other professions,—and especially like its sister service, the Army,—the Navy tends to, and for efficiency requires, specialization. Specialization, in turn, results most satisfactorily from the free play of natural aptitudes; for aptitudes, when strongly developed, find expression in inclination, and readily seek their proper function in the body organic to which they belong. Each of these distinguished officers, from this point of view, does not stand for himself alone, but is an eminent exponent of a class; while the class itself forms a member of a body which has many organs, no one of which is independent of the other, but all contributive to the body's welfare. Hence, while the effort has been made to present each in his full individuality, with copious recourse to anecdote and illustrative incident as far as available, both as a matter of general interest and for accurate portrayal, special care has been added to bring out occurrences and actions which convey the impression of that natural character which led the man to take the place he did in the naval body, to develop the professional function with which he is more particularly identified; for personality underlies official character.

In this sense of the word, types are permanent; for such are not the exclusive possession of any age or of any service, but are found and are essential in every period and to every nation. Their functions are part of the bed-rock of naval organization and of naval strategy, throughout all time; and the particular instances here selected owe their special cogency mainly to the fact that they are drawn from a naval era, 1739-1815, of exceptional activity and brilliancy.

There is, however, another sense in which an officer, or a man, may be accurately called a type; a sense no less significant, but of more limited and transient application. The tendency of a period,—especially when one of marked transition,—its activities and its results, not infrequently find expression in one or more historical characters. Such types may perhaps more accurately be called personifications; the man or men embodying, and in action realizing, ideas and processes of thought, the progress of which is at the time united, but is afterwards recognized as a general characteristic of the period. Between the beginning and the end a great change is found to have been effected, which naturally and conveniently is associated with the names of the most conspicuous actors; although they are not the sole agents, but simply the most eminent.

It is in this sense more particularly that Hawke and Rodney are presented as types. It might even be said that they complement each other and constitute together a single type; for, while both were men of unusually strong personality, private as well as professional, and with very marked traits of character, their great relation to naval advance is that of men who by natural faculty detect and seize upon incipient ideas, for which the time is ripe, and upon the practical realization of which the healthful development of the profession depends. With these two, and with them not so much contemporaneously as in close historical sequence, is associated the distinctive evolution of naval warfare in the eighteenth century; in their combined names is summed up the improvement of system to which Nelson and his contemporaries fell heirs, and to which Nelson, under the peculiar and exceptional circumstances which made his opportunity, gave an extension that immortalized him. Of Hawke and Rodney, therefore, it may be said that they are in their profession types of that element of change, in virtue of which the profession grows; whereas the other four, eminent as they were, exemplify rather the conservative forces, the permanent features, in the strength of which it exists, and in the absence of any one of which it droops or succumbs. It does not, however, follow that the one of these great men is the simple continuator of the other's work; rather it is true that each contributed, in due succession of orderly development, the factor of progress which his day demanded, and his personality embodied.

It was not in the forecast of the writer, but in the process of treatment he came to recognize that, like Hawke and Rodney, the four others also by natural characteristics range themselves in pairs,—presenting points of contrast, in deficiencies and in excellencies, which group them together, not by similarity chiefly, but as complementary. Howe and Jervis were both admirable general officers; but the strength of the one lay in his tactical acquirements, that of the other in strategic insight and breadth of outlook. The one was easy-going and indulgent as a superior; the other conspicuous for severity, and for the searchingness with which he carried the exactions of discipline into the minute details of daily naval life. Saumarez and Pellew, less fortunate, did not reach high command until the great days of naval warfare in their period had yielded to the comparatively uneventful occupation of girdling the enemy's coast with a system of blockades, aimed primarily at the restriction of his commerce, and incidentally at the repression of his navy, which made no effort to take the sea on a large scale. Under these circumstances the functions of an admiral were mainly administrative; and if Saumarez and Pellew possessed eminent capacity as general officers on the battle-field, they had not opportunity to prove it. The distinction of their careers coincides with their tenure of subordinate positions in the organisms of great fleets. With this in common, and differentiating them from Howe and Jervis, the points of contrast are marked. Saumarez preferred the ship-of-the-line, Pellew the frigate. The choice of the one led to the duties of a division commander, that of the other to the comparative independence of detached service, of the partisan officer. In the one, love of the military side of his calling predominated; the other was, before all, the seaman. The union of the two perfects professional character.

The question may naturally be asked,—Why, among types of naval officers, is there no mention, other than casual, of the name of Nelson? The answer is simple. Among general officers, land and sea, the group to which Nelson belongs defies exposition by a type, both because it is small in aggregate numbers, and because the peculiar eminence of the several members,—the eminence of genius,—so differentiates each from his fellows that no one among them can be said to represent the others. Each, in the supremacy of his achievement, stands alone,—alone, not only regarded as towering above a brilliant surrounding of distinguished followers, but alone even as contrasted with the other great ones who in their own day had a like supremacy. Such do not in fact form a class, because, though a certain community of ideas and principles may be traced in their actions, their personalities and methods bear each the stamp of originality in performance; and where originality is found, classification ceases to apply. There is a company, it may be, but not a class.

The last four biographies first appeared as contributions to the *Atlantic Monthly*, in 1893 and 1894. I desire to return to the proprietors my thanks for their permission to republish. The original treatment has been here considerably modified, as well as enlarged. I am also under special obligation to Mr. Fleetwood Hugo Pellew, who gave me the photograph of Lord Exmouth, with permission also to reproduce it. It represents that great officer at the age most characteristic of his particular professional distinction, as by me understood.

A. T. Mahan

Chapter 1

Naval Warfare in the Early 18th Century

The recent close of the nineteenth century has familiarized us with the thought that such an epoch tends naturally to provoke an estimate of the advance made in the various spheres of human activity during the period which it terminates. Such a reckoning, however, is not a mere matter of more and less, of comparison between the beginning and the end, regardless of intermediate circumstances. The question involved is one of an historical process, of cause and effect; of an evolution, probably marked, as such series of events commonly are, by certain salient incidents, the way-marks of progress which show the road traversed and the succession of stages through which the past has become the present. Frequently, also, such development associates itself not only with conspicuous events, but with the names of great men, to whom, either by originality of genius or by favouring opportunity, it has fallen to illustrate in action the changes which have a more silent antecedent history in the experience and reflection of mankind.

The development of naval warfare in the eighteenth century, its advance in spirit and methods, is thus exemplified in certain striking events, and yet more impressively is identified with the great names of Hawke and Rodney. The period of nearly half a generation intervened between their births, but they were contemporaries and actors, though to no large extent associates, during the extensive wars that occupied the middle of the century—the War of the Austrian Succession, 1739-1748, and the Seven Years War, 1756-1763. These two conflicts are practically one; the same characteristic jealousies and motives being common to both, as they were also to the period of nominal peace, but scarcely veiled contention, by which they were separated. The difference of age between the two admirals contributed not only to obviate rivalry, by throwing their distinctive activities into different generations, but had, as it were, the effect of prolonging their influence beyond that possible to a single lifetime, thus constituting it into a continuous and fruitful development.

They were both successful men, in the ordinary acceptation of the word success. They were great, not only in professional character, but in the results which do not always attend professional desert; they were great in achievement. Each name is indissolubly linked with a brilliant victory, as well as with other less known but equally meritorious actions; in all of which the personal factor of the principal agent, the distinctive qualities of the commander-in-chief, powerfully contributed and were conspicuously illustrated. These were, so to say, the examples, that enforced upon the men of their day the professional ideas by which the two admirals were themselves dominated, and upon which was forming a school, with professional standards of action and achievement destined to produce great effects.

Yet, while this is so, and while such emphatic demonstrations by deeds undoubtedly does more than any other teaching to influence contemporaries, and so to promote professional development, it is probably true that, as a matter of historical illustration, the advance of the eighteenth century in naval warfare is more clearly shown by two great failures, for neither of which were these officers responsible, and in one only of which in fact did either appear, even in a subordinate capacity. The now nearly forgotten miscarriage of Admiral Mathews off Toulon, in 1744, and the miserable incompetency of Byng, at Minorca, in 1756, remembered chiefly because of the consequent execution of the admiral, serve at least, historically, to mark the low extreme to which had then sunk professional theory and practice—for both were there involved. It is, however, not only as a point of departure from which to estimate progress that these battles—if they deserve the name—are historically useful. Considered as the plane to which exertion, once well directed and virile, had gradually declined through the prevalence of false ideals, they link the seventeenth century to the eighteenth, even as the thought and action—the theory and practice—of Hawke and Rodney uplifted the navy from the inefficiency of Mathews and Byng to the crowning glories of the Nile and Trafalgar, with which the nineteenth century opened. It is thus, as the very bottom of the wave, that those singular and signal failures have their own distinctive significance in the undulations of the onward movement. On the one hand they are not unaccountable, as though they, any more than the Nile and Trafalgar, were without antecedent of cause; and on the other they serve, as a background at least, to bring out the figures of the two admirals now before us, and to define their true historical import, as agents and as exponents, in the changes of their day.

It is, therefore, important to the comprehension of the changes effected in that period of transition, for which Hawke and Rodney stand, to recognize the distinctive lesson of each of these two abortive actions, which together may be said to fix the zero of the scale by which the progress of the eighteenth century is denoted. They have a relation to the past as well as to the future, standing far below the level of the one and of the other, through causes that can be assigned. Naval warfare in the past, in its origin and through long ages, had been waged with vessels moved by oars, which consequently, when conditions permitted engaging at all, could be handled with a scope and freedom not securable with the uncertain factor of the wind. The motive power of the sea, therefore, then resembled essentially that of the land,—being human muscle and staying power, in the legs on shore and in the arms at sea. Hence, movements by masses, by squadrons, and in any desired direction corresponding to a fixed plan, in order to concentrate, or to outflank,—all these could be attempted with a probability of success not predicable of the sailing ship. Nelson's remarkable order at Trafalgar, which may almost be said to have closed and sealed the record of the sail era, began by assuming the extreme improbability of being able at any given moment to move forty ships of his day in a fixed order upon an assigned plan. The galley admiral therefore wielded a weapon far more flexible and reliable, within the much narrower range of its activities, than his successor in the days of sail; and engagements between fleets of galleys accordingly reflected this condition, being marked not only by greater carnage, but by tactical combinations and audacity of execution, to which the sailing ship did not so readily lend itself.

When the field of naval warfare became extended beyond the Mediterranean,—for long centuries its principal scene,—the galley no longer met the more exacting nautical conditions; and the introduction of cannon, involving new problems of tactics and ship-building, accelerated its disappearance. The traditions of galley-fighting, however, remained, and were reinforced by the habits of land fighting,—the same men in fact commanding armies on shore and fleets at sea. In short, a period of transition ensued, marked, as such in their beginnings are apt to be, by an evident lack of clearness in men's appreciation of conditions, and of the path of development, with a consequent confusion of outline in their practice. It is not always easy to understand either what was done, or what was meant to be done, during that early sail era; but two things appear quite certainly. There is still shown the vehemence and determination of action which characterized galley fighting, visible constantly in the fierce effort to grapple the enemy, to break his ranks, to confuse and crush him; and further there is clear indication of tactical plan on the grand scale, broad in outline and combination, involving different—but not independent—action by the various great divisions of the fleet, each of which, in plan at least, has its own part, subordinate but contributory to the general whole.

The results, though not unimportant, were not satisfactory, for men were compelled to see that from various causes the huge numbers brought upon the field lapsed into confusion, and that battle, however well planned in large outline, resolved itself into a mere mass of warring units incoherently struggling one with another. There was lack of proportion between effort exerted and effect achieved. A period of systematization and organization set in. Unwieldy numbers were reduced to more manageable dimensions by excluding ships whose size and strength did not add to the efficiency of the order of battle; the powers and limitations of those which remained were studied, and certain simple tactical dispositions, fitted to particular emergencies, were recognized and adopted,—all tending to impart unity of movement and action, and to keep the whole in regulated order under the hand of the commander-in-chief, free from confusion.

To this point there was improvement; but reaction, as often, went too far. The change in accepted ideas is emphatically shown by a comparison of the Fighting Instructions of 1740 and 1756, when the crystallization of the system was complete but disintegration had not yet begun, with those issued in 1665 by the Duke of York, afterwards James II., at the beginning of the second of the three Anglo-Dutch Wars. His in turn are directly deducible from others framed shortly after the first war, in 1652-1654, when sail tactics had not passed the stage of infancy, and were still strongly affected by the galley tradition. There is here found, on the one hand, the prescription of the line of battle,—a single column of ships formed in each other's wake,—with the provision that if the enemy is to leeward, and awaits attack, the headmost squadron of the British shall steer for the headmost of the enemy's ships. This accords with the general tenor of the later Instructions; but there occurs elsewhere, and previously, the direction that, when the enemy is to windward, if the leading British Squadron finds it can weather any considerable part of them, it is to "tack and stand in, and strive to divide the enemy's body," and that, "being got to windward, is to bear down on those ships to leeward of them," which have thus been cut off.

The thing to be observed here is the separate, but positive, initiative prescribed for a portion of the fleet, with a view to divide the enemy, and then concentrate the whole fleet upon the fraction thus isolated. The British van takes a particular, but not an independent, action; for the other divisions contribute their part to the common purpose.

The middle squadron is to keep her wind, and to observe the motion of the enemy's van, which the last squadron—the rear—is to second; and both of these squadrons are to do their utmost to assist or relieve the first squadron, that divided the enemy's fleet.

Evidently here we have tactical combination in order to decisive action; clearly contemplated also beforehand, not merely by a capable individual general, but by the consensus of professional opinion which such a paper as the Fighting Instructions necessarily reflects. The stamp of the galley period is upon this: strenuous and close battle, the piercing of the enemy's order, the movement of the squadrons differentiated, in order that they may in a real and effective sense *combine*, instead of being merely *distributed*, as they afterwards were by both the letter of the later Instructions and the tradition by which these became encrusted. Nor should there be overlooked, in this connection, the discretion allowed the centre and rear. They are to "keep their wind;" an expression which leaves optional whether to tack, or stand as they are, whether to engage the separated enemies to windward or to leeward, as occasion may offer, in support of the van. The provisions of 1665 afterwards disappear. In 1740, and even as late as 1781, they are traceable only in certain colourless articles, suggestive of the atrophied organs of a body concerning whose past use physiologists may speculate.

As in the restoration of sounder methods, with which we shall be concerned, this degeneration of ideals was a work of time. In June, 1666, the British met with a severe check in the Four Days Battle, in which Monk, a soldier, commanded in chief. This reverse is chiefly to be attributed to antecedent strategic errors, which made a portion only of the available British force bear the brunt of the first three days; but, among the inevitable criticisms, we find stress laid upon fighting in line as essential to success. This insistence upon the line as an effective instrument proceeded, among others, from Sir William Penn, a seaman, and was at that time in the direction of professional advance. The line had not yet obtained the general professional acceptance needed to establish and utilize its indisputable value. This process was gradual, but when effected it followed the usual laws of human development; from a valuable means, it became in men's estimation an exaggerated necessity. It came to pass in time that the line no longer existed for tactics, but tactics for the line, in which they found their consummation and end.

There intervened, however, a happier period,—one of transition,—and in the third Anglo-Dutch war, 1672-1674, we seem to find a close approach to just proportion between regularity of formation and decisive tactical purpose; in which the principle of the line is recognized and observed, but is utilized by professional audacity for definite and efficient tactical action, aiming at conclusive results. The finest exponent of this, the culminating epoch of naval warfare in the seventeenth century, is the Dutchman Ruyter, who, taken altogether, was the greatest naval seaman of that era, which may be roughly identified with the reign of Charles II. After that, naval warfare was virtually suspended for fifteen years, and when resumed in the last decade of the century, the traces of incipient degeneracy can already be noted amid much brilliant performance. From that time completeness of military achievement became in men's minds less of an object than accurate observance of rule, and in practice the defensive consideration of avoiding disaster began to preponderate over offensive effort for the destruction of the enemy.

In the development of tactical science, the French had played a leading part, as they usually have where reflective mental processes and formal evolution of ideas are concerned. Among admirals, the greatest name of this later period is the French Tourville, a master of the science of his profession, and gifted with a personal courage of the heroic type; while the leading exponent of Tourville's ideas, as well as historian of his achievements, was the French priest Paul Hoste,—chaplain to his fleet, and the father of the systematic treatment of naval evolutions. But with Tourville's name is associated not only a high level of professional management, but a caution in professional action not far removed from timidity, so that an impatient Minister of Marine of his day and nation styled him "poltroon in head, though not in heart." His powers were displayed in the preservation and orderly movement of his fleet; in baffling, by sheer skill, and during long periods, the efforts of the enemy to bring him to action; in skilful disposition, when he purposely accepted battle under disadvantage; but under most favourable opportunities he failed in measures of energy, and, after achieving partial success, superfluous care of his own command prevented his blows from being driven home.

Tourville, though a brilliant seaman, thus not only typified an era of transition, with which he was contemporary, but foreshadowed the period of merely formal naval warfare, precise, methodical, and unenterprising, emasculated of military virility, although not of mere animal courage. He left to his successors the legacy of a great name, but also unfortunately that of a defective professional tradition. The splendid days of the French Navy under Louis XIV. passed away with him,—he died in 1701; but during the long period of naval lethargy on the part of the state, which followed, the French naval officers, as a class, never wholly lost sight of professional ideals. They proved themselves, on the rare occasions that offered, before 1715 and during the wars of Hawke and Rodney, not only gallant seamen after the pattern of Tourville, but also exceedingly capable tacticians, upon a system good as far as it went, but defective on Tourville's express lines, in aiming rather at exact dispositions and defensive security than at the thorough-going initiative and persistence which confounds and destroys the enemy. "War," to use Napoleon's phrase, "was to be waged without running risks." The sword was drawn, but the scabbard was kept ever open for its retreat.

The English, in the period of reaction which succeeded the Dutch wars, produced their own caricature of systematized tactics. Even under its influence, up to 1715, it is only just to say they did not construe naval skill to mean anxious care to keep one's own ships intact. Rooke, off Malaga, in 1704, illustrated professional fearlessness of consequences as conspicuously as he had shown personal daring in the boat attack at La Hougue; but his plans of battle exemplified the particularly British form of inefficient naval action. There was no great difference in aggregate force between the French fleet and that of the combined

Anglo-Dutch under his orders. The former, drawing up in the accustomed line of battle, ship following ship in a single column, awaited attack. Rooke, having the advantage of the wind, and therefore the power of engaging at will, formed his command in a similar and parallel line a few miles off, and thus all stood down together, the ships maintaining their line parallel to that of the enemy, and coming into action at practically the same moment, van to van, centre to centre, rear to rear. This ignored wholly the essential maxim of all intelligent warfare, which is so to engage as markedly to outnumber the enemy at a point of main collision. If he be broken there, before the remainder of his force come up, the chances all are that a decisive superiority will be established by this alone, not to mention the moral effect of partial defeat and disorder. Instead of this, the impact at Malaga was so distributed as to produce a substantial equality from one end to the other of the opposing fronts. The French, indeed, by strengthening their centre relatively to the van and rear, to some extent modified this condition in the particular instance; but the fact does not seem to have induced any alteration in Rooke's dispositions. Barring mere accident, nothing conclusive can issue from such arrangements. The result accordingly was a drawn battle, although Rooke says that the fight, which was maintained on both sides "with great fury for three hours, ... was the sharpest day's service that I ever saw;" and he had seen much,—Beachy Head, La Hougue, Vigo Bay, not to mention his own great achievement in the capture of Gibraltar.

This method of attack remained the ideal—if such a word is not a misnomer in such a case—of the British Navy, not merely as a matter of irreflective professional acceptance, but laid down in the official *Fighting Instructions*. It cannot be said that these err on the side of lucidity; but their meaning to contemporaries in this particular respect is ascertained, not only by fair inference from their contents, but by the practical commentary of numerous actions under commonplace commanders-in-chief. It further received authoritative formulation in the specific finding of the Court-Martial upon Admiral Byng, which was signed by thirteen experienced officers.

Admiral Byng should have caused his ships to tack together, and should immediately have borne down upon the enemy; his van steering for the enemy's van, his rear for its rear, each ship making for the one opposite to her in the enemy's line, under such sail as would have enabled the worst sailer to preserve her station in the line of battle.

Each phrase of this opinion is a reflection of an article in the Instructions. The line of battle was the naval fetish of the day; and, be it remarked, it was the more dangerous because in itself an admirable and necessary instrument, constructed on principles essentially accurate. A standard wholly false may have its error demonstrated with comparative ease; but no servitude is more hopeless than that of unintelligent submission to an idea formally correct, yet incomplete. It has all the vicious misleading of a half-truth unqualified by appreciation of modifying conditions; and so seamen who disdained theories, and hugged the belief in themselves as "practical," became *doctrinaires* in the worst sense.

It would seem, however, that a necessary antecedent to deliverance from a false conception,—as from any injurious condition,—is a practical illustration of its fallacy. Working consequences must receive demonstration, concrete in some striking disastrous event, before improvement is undertaken. Such experience is painful to undergo; but with most men, even in their private capacity, and in nearly all governmental action where mere public interests are at stake, remedy is rarely sought until suffering is not only felt, but signalized in a conspicuous incident. It is needless to say that the military professions in peace times are peculiarly liable to this apathy; like some sleepers, they can be awakened only by shaking. For them, war alone can subject accepted ideas to the extreme test of practice. It is doubtless perfectly true that acquaintance with military and naval history, mastery of their teachings, will go far to anticipate the penalty attaching to truth's last argument—chastisement; but imagination is fondly impatient of warning by the past, and easily avails itself of fancied or superficial differences in contemporary conditions, to justify measures which ignore, or even directly contravene, ascertained and fundamental principles of universal application.

Even immediate practical experience is misinterpreted when incidents are thus viewed through the medium of a precedent bias. The Transvaal War, for instance, has afforded some striking lessons of needed modifications, consequent upon particular local factors, or upon developments in the material of war; but does any thoughtful military man doubt that imagination has been actively at work, exaggerating or distorting, hastily waiving aside permanent truth in favour of temporary prepossessions or accidental circumstance? It is at least equally likely that the naval world at the present time is hugging some fond delusions in the excessive size and speed to which battle-ships are tending, and in the disproportionate weight assigned to the defensive as compared to the offensive factors in a given aggregate tonnage. Imagination, theory, *a priori* reasoning, is here at variance with rational historical precedent, which has established the necessity of numbers as well as of individual power in battle-ships, and demonstrated the superiority of offensive over defensive strength in military systems. These—and other—counterbalancing considerations have in past wars enforced the adoption of a medium homogeneous type, as conducive both to adequate numbers,—which permit the division of the fleet when required for strategic or tactical purposes,—and also directly to offensive fleet strength by the greater facility of manoeuvring possessed by such vessels; for the strength of a fleet lies not chiefly in the single units, but in their mutual support in elastic and rapid movement. Well tested precedent—experience—has here gone to the wall in favour of an untried forecast of supposed fundamental change in conditions. But experience is uncommonly disagreeable when she revenges herself after her own fashion.

The British Navy of the eighteenth century in this way received an unpleasant proof of the faultiness of its then accepted conclusions, in the miscarriages of Mathews off Toulon, in 1744, and of Byng off Minorca, in 1756. So fixed were men's habits of thought that the lessons were not at once understood. As evidenced by the distribution of censure, the results were attributed by contemporary judges to particular incidents of each battle, not to the erroneous underlying general plans, contravening all sound military precedent, which from the first made success improbable, indeed impossible, except by an inefficiency of the enemy which was not to be presumed. These battles therefore are important, militarily, in a sense not at all dependent upon their consequences, which were ephemeral. They are significant as extreme illustrations of incompetent action, deriving from faulty traditions; and they have the further value of showing the starting point, the zero of the scale, from which the progress of the century is to be measured. In describing them, therefore, attention will be given chiefly to those circumstances which exhibit the shackles under which fleet movements then laboured, not only from the difficulties inherent to the sea and sailing ships, but from the ideas and methods of the times. Those incidents also will be selected which show how false standards affected particular individuals, according to their personal characteristics.

In Admiral Mathews' action, in February, 1744, an allied fleet composed of sixteen French ships-of-the-line and twelve Spanish lay in Toulon, waiting to sail for a Spanish port. The British, in force numerically equal, were at anchor under the Hyères Islands, a few miles to the eastward. They got underway when the allied movement began on February 20th; but anchored again for the night, because the enemy that day came no farther than the outer road of Toulon. The next morning the French and Spaniards put to sea with a wind at first westerly, and stretched to the southward in long, single column, the sixteen French leading. At 10 a.m. the British followed, Vice-Admiral Lestock's division taking the van; but the wind, shifting to east, threw the fleet on the port tack, on which the rear under Rear-Admiral Rowley had to lead. It became necessary, therefore, for this division and the centre to pass Lestock, which took some time with the light airs prevailing. Two or three manoeuvres succeeded, with the object of forming the fighting order, a column similar and parallel to that of the enemy, and to get closer to him. When night fell a signal was still flying for the line abreast, by which, if completed, the ships would be ranged on a line parallel to the allies, and heading towards them; consequently abreast of each other. It would then need only a change of course to place them in column, sides to the enemy; which, as before said, was the fighting order—the "line of battle."

The line abreast, however, was not fully formed at dark. Therefore the admiral, in order to hasten its completion, soon afterwards made a night signal, with lanterns, for the fleet to bring-to,—that is, bring their sides to the wind, and stop. He intended thereby that the ships already in station should stand still, while the others were gaining their places, all which is a case of simple evolution, by land as by sea. It was contended by the admiral that Vice-Admiral Lestock's division was then too far to the right and rear, and hence too distant from the enemy, and that it was his duty first to get into his station and then to bring-to. To this the vice-admiral on his trial replied, first, that he was not out of his station; and, second, that if he were, the later signal, to bring-to, suspended the earlier, to form line abreast, and that it was therefore his business, without any discretion, to stop where he was. Concerning the first plea, a number of witnesses, very respectable in point of rank and opportunity for seeing, testified that the vice-admiral did bring-to three or four miles to the right and rear of his place in the line abreast, reckoning his station from the admiral's ship; yet, as the Court peremptorily rejected their evidence, it is probably proper to accept the contemporary decision as to this matter of fact.

But as regards the second plea, being a matter of military correctness, a difference of opinion is allowable. The Court adopted as its own the argument of the vice-admiral. Without entering here into a technical discussion, the Court's ruling, briefly stated, was that the second signal superseded the first, so that, if the vice-admiral was in the wrong place, it was not his duty to get into the right before stopping; and that this was doubly the case because an article of the Night Signals (7) prescribed that, under the conditions of the alleged offence, "a fleet sailing before the wind, or nearly so, if the admiral made the signal for the fleet to bring-to, the windward ships should bring-to first." Therefore, if Lestock was to windward, as the charge read, it was his duty to bring-to first and at once. It is evident, however, that even the Sailing Instructions, cast-iron as they were, contemplated a fleet in order, not one in process of forming order; and that to bring-to helter-skelter, regardless of order, was to obey the letter rather than the spirit. Muddle-headed as Mathews seems to have been, what he was trying to do was clear enough; and the duty of a subordinate was to carry out his evident aim. An order does not necessarily supersede its predecessor, unless the two are incompatible. The whole incident, from Lestock's act to the Court's finding, is instructive as showing the slavish submission to the letter of the Instructions; a submission traceable not to the law merely, but to the added tradition that had then fast hold of men's minds. It is most interesting to note that the unfortunate Byng was one of the signers of this opinion, as he was also one of the judges that sentenced Mathews to be dismissed from the navy, as responsible for the general failure.

During the night of the 21st the allies, who had stopped after dark, appear again to have made sail. Consequently, when day broke, the British found themselves some distance astern and to windward—northeast; the wind continuing easterly. Their line, indifferently well formed in van and centre, stretched over a length of nine miles through the straggling of the rear. Lestock's ship was six miles from that of Mathews, whereas it should not have been more than two and a half, at most, in ordinary sailing; for battle, the Instructions allowed little over a half-mile. Accepting the Court's finding that he was in position at dark, this distance can only be attributed, as Lestock argued and the Court admitted, to a current—that most convenient of scapegoats in navigation. The allies, too, had a lagging rear body, five Spanish ships being quite a distance astern; but from van to rear they extended but six miles, against the British nine. It was the distance of the British rear, not straggling in van or centre, that constituted this disadvantage.

Mathews wished to wait till Lestock reached his place, but the allies were receding all the time; and, though their pace was slackened to enable the five sternmost Spaniards to come up, the space between the fleets was increasing. It was the duty of the British admiral to force an action, on general principles; but in addition he believed that the French intended to push for Gibraltar, enter the Atlantic, and join their Brest fleet, in order to cover an invasion of England by an army reported to be assembling at Dunkirk. Clearly, therefore, something must be done; yet to enter into a general engagement with near a third of his command out of immediate supporting distance was contrary to the accepted principles of the day. The fleet was not extended with that of the enemy, by which is meant that the respective vans, centres, and rears were not opposed; the British van being only abreast of the allied centre, their centre of the allied rear, Lestock tailing away astern and to windward, while the dozen leading French were some distance ahead of both bodies. Now the Fighting Instructions required that—

> If the admiral and his fleet have the wind of the enemy, and they have stretched themselves in a line of battle, the van of the admiral's fleet is to steer with the van of the enemies, and *there* to engage them.

There was no alternative course laid down; just as there was no punishment alternative to death in the Article of War under which Byng was shot.

Yet the indications all were that to wait for this most formal and pedantic disposition, which ignored every principle of warfare, would be to throw away the chance of battle. The French, fresh from port and clean-bottomed, out-sailed the bulk of the British, as did the Spaniards, though to a less degree; and it was part of Lestock's defence, admitted by the Court, that, doing his utmost, his division, as a whole, certainly could not get abreast the allied rear. Lestock, indeed, directly submitted to the Court that the commander-in-chief was at fault in not waiting till his line was thus extended and formed, and then all bearing down together, in line abreast; although by his own contention no such issue could have been reached that day, unless the allies were obliging enough to wait.

> I aver, and I shall die in this opinion, that no man that is an officer, who knows his duty, will make the signal for line abreast to steer down upon an enemy, until the fleet

has been stretched and extended in a line of battle, according to the 19th Article of the Fighting Instructions. Can it be service to bear down so much unformed and in confusion, that the van cannot possibly join battle with, or engage the van of the enemy, the centre with the centre, and the rear with the rear?

Mathews not being then on trial, the Court in its finding did not reply directly to this question; but indirectly it left no doubt as to its opinion.

The Admiral, by bearing down as he did upon the rear division of the combined fleet, excluded the Vice-Admiral from any part of the engagement, if he could have come up; for if both lines had been closed, when the Admiral engaged the *Real*, there would have been no more than one ship of the enemy's fleet for the Vice-Admiral and his whole division to have engaged. It does not appear that the Vice-Admiral was in any part the cause of the miscarriage of his Majesty's fleet in the Mediterranean; the *bringing on of the general engagement according to the 19th Article* of the Fighting Instructions . . . . not depending upon him.

Sixteen officers of the rank of captain and above signed these opinions, and there is no denying the words of the 19th Article; yet one wonders to see no recognition of the necessity of using your opportunity as you find it, of the moral effect of an approaching reserve, which Lestock's division would have constituted, of the part it may take in improving or repairing the results of an action—taking the place of injured friends, preventing injured foes escaping, turning doubtful battle into victory. But no; these commonplaces of today and of all time were swamped by the Fighting Instructions. It will be seen in the sequel what a disastrous moral influence Lestock's aloofness exercised upon a few timid captains, and not improbably upon the entire subsequent course and worst errors of his unfortunate superior.

One of the witnesses in the ensuing Courts-Martial testified that the commander-in-chief, under these perplexing circumstances, went into the stern gallery of the flag-ship *Namur*, and called to Captain Cornwall of the *Marlborough*, next astern, asking what he thought. Cornwall replied he "believed they would lose the glory of the day, if they did not attack the Spaniards,"—*i.e.*, the allied rear-centre and rear,—"the Vice-Admiral—Lestock—being so far astern." To which the admiral said, "If you'll bear down and attack the *Real*,"—the *Real Felipe*, Spanish flag-ship,—"I'll be your second." This was about one o'clock, and the signal to engage had been made two hours earlier, probably with the double object of indicating the ultimate intention of the movements in hand, and the immediate urgency of forming the line. The admiral's words betray the indecision of an irresolute nature and of professional rustiness, but not of timidity, and Cornwall's words turned the scale. The course of the flag-ship *Namur* had hitherto been but a little off the wind, "lasking" down, to use the contemporary but long obsolete expression, in such manner as to show the admiral's desire to engage himself with the enemy's centre, according to the Fighting Instructions; but now, in hopelessness of that result, she kept broad off, directly for the nearest enemy, accompanied closely by the *Norfolk*, her next ahead, and by the *Marlborough*. Rear-Admiral Rowley, commanding the van, imitated the admiral's example, bringing the French ship abreast him to close action. He also was thoroughly supported by the two captains next astern of him, the second of whom was Edward Hawke,—afterwards the brilliant admiral,—in the *Berwick*. Two British groups, each of three ships, were thus hotly engaged; but with an interval between them of over half a mile, corresponding to the places open for six or seven other vessels. The conduct of the ships named, under the immediate influence of the example set by the two admirals, suggests how much the average man is sustained by professional tone; for a visible good example is simply a good standard, a high ideal, realized in action.

Unfortunately, however, just as Hawke's later doings showed the man able to rise above the level of prescribed routine duty, there was found in the second astern of the *Namur* a captain capable of exceptional backwardness, of reasoning himself into dereliction of clear duty, and thus effecting a demonstration that the example of timidity is full as contagious and more masterful than that of audacity. The flag-ships and their supporters ranged themselves along the hostile line to windward, within point-blank range; according to the 20th Article of the *Fighting Instructions*, which read:

> Every Commander is to take care that his guns are not fired till he is sure he can reach the enemy upon a point-blank; and by no means to suffer his guns to be fired over any of our own ships.

The point-blank is the range of a cannon laid level, and the requirement was necessary to efficient action in those days of crude devices for pointing, with ordnance material of inferior power. Even sixty years later Nelson expressed his indifference to improvements in pointing, on the ground that the true way of fighting was to get so close that you could not miss your aim. Thus Mathews' captain placed the *Namur*, of ninety guns, within four hundred yards—less than quarter of a mile—of the Spanish flag-ship, the *Real Felipe*, of one hundred and ten guns; and Cornwall brought the *Marlborough* immediately in the wake of the *Namur*, engaging the Spanish *Hercules*. But the *Dorsetshire*, which should have followed the *Marlborough*, was stopped by her commander, Captain George Burrish, at a distance which was estimated by several witnesses to be from half a mile to nearly a mile from the enemy, or, to use a very expressive phrase then current, "at random shot." The Court-Martial, however, in pronouncing upon this point, decided that inasmuch as a bar-shot came on board the *Dorsetshire* in this early part of the engagement, she must be construed to have brought to within extreme point-blank. In view of the mass of testimony to the greater distance, this seems to have been simply giving the benefit of a doubt.

Thus situated, the action between the *Namur* and *Marlborough* on the one side, and the *Real Felipe* and *Hercules* on the other, was for some time very hot; but the *Marlborough*, moving faster than the *Namur*, closed upon her, so that she had to get out of the way, which she did by moving ahead and at the same time hauling to windward, till she reached as far from the Spanish line as the *Dorsetshire* had remained. The Court in this matter decided that, after the admiral had thus hauled off, the *Dorsetshire* was in a line, or as far to leeward—towards the enemy—as the admiral. The *Marlborough* was thus left alone, exposed to the fire of a ship heavier than herself, and also to that of the *Hercules*, which was able to train upon her a considerable part of her battery. Under these circumstances, it was the duty of the *Dorsetshire*, as it was the opportunity of her commander, by attacking the *Hercules*, to second, and support, the engaged ship; but she continued aloof. After two hours—by 3 p.m.—the main and mizzen masts were cut out of the *Marlborough*, and she lost her captain with forty-two men killed, and one hundred and twenty wounded, out of a crew of seven hundred and fifty. Thus disabled, the sails on the foremast turned her head towards the enemy, and she lay moving sluggishly, between the fleets, but not under control. The admiral now sent an officer to Burrish—the second that morning—to order him into his station and to support the *Marlborough*; while to the latter, in response to an urgent representation by boat of her condition, and that she was threatened by the approach of the hitherto separated ships of the Spanish rear, he replied that the *Namur* was wearing and would come to her assistance.

When Burrish received his message, he sent for his lieutenants on the quarter-deck, and spoke to them words which doubtless reflect the reasoning upon which he was justifying to himself his most culpable inaction. "Gentlemen, I sent for you to show you the position of our ships to windward," (*i.e.* the ships of the centre division behind him, and Lestock's division), "likewise those five sail of the enemy that are astern of us. I have my orders to engage the *Real*, and you see I am bearing down for that purpose." The lieutenants remarked that he could do so with safety. To this he rejoined, with a curtness that testifies to the uneasiness of his mind, "I did not send for you to ask your opinions, but only to observe that not one of our ships is coming down to my assistance, in order to cut those five sail off, and in case those five sail should oblige me to haul my wind again, and leave the *Marlborough*, that you may be able to indemnify my conduct, if called in question." One witness also testified that he "was angry that Admiral Lestock's division did not bear down,"—which was just enough,—and that "he thought it most advisable to keep his station;" meaning by this, apparently, to remain where he was. His cross-examination of the evidence was directed to prove the danger to his ship from these remaining Spaniards. This anxiety was wholly misplaced, and professionally unworthy. Quite independent of orders by signal and message, he was bound, in view of the condition of the *Marlborough*, to go to her relief, and to assume that the three English ships of the centre division, in his rear, would surely sustain him. To base contrary action upon a doubt of their faithfulness was to condemn himself. Four ships to five under such conditions should be rather a spur than a deterrent to an officer of spirit, who understands the obligation of his calling.

Till this, the *Dorsetshire* had been under her three topsails only. She appears then to have stood down under more sail, but very slowly, and here occurred another disaster which was largely chargeable to her being out of her station. Seeing the desperate state of the *Marlborough*, Mathews, who throughout managed blunderingly, with the single exception of the original attack, had thought to aid her and divert the fire of the *Real* by sending against the latter a fire-ship. It was elementary that vessels of this class needed energetic support and cover in their desperate work. Small in size, of no battery-force except against boat attacks, loaded with combustibles and powder, success in the use of them under an enemy's guns required not only imperturbable coolness and nerve, but the utmost attainable immunity from the attention of the enemy. This could be secured only by a heavy and sustained fire from their own fleet. With the *Norfolk*, *Namur*, *Marlborough*, and *Dorsetshire* in close line, as they should have been, and heavily engaged, a fire-ship might have passed between them, and, though at imminent hazard even so, have crossed the four hundred yards of intervening water to grapple the hostile flag-ship; but with the *Marlborough* lying disabled and alone, the admiral himself acting with indecision, and the *Dorsetshire* hanging aloof, the attempt was little short of hopeless. Still it was made, and the *Anne Galley*—such was her odd name—bore down, passing close by the *Dorsetshire*.

It became doubly the duty of Burrish to act, to push home

whatever demonstration was in his power to make; the fire-ship, however, went by him and was permitted to pursue her desperate mission without his support. The *Real*, seeing the *Anne* approach, bore up out of her line, and at the same time sent a strongly-manned launch to grapple and tow her out of the way. This was precisely one of the measures that it was the business of supporting ships to repel. The captain of the fire-ship, thrown upon his own resources, opened fire, a most hazardous measure, as much of his priming was with loose powder; but the launch readily avoided injury by taking position directly ahead, where the guns would not bear. The crew of the *Anne* were now ordered into the boat, except the captain and five others, who were to remain to the last moment, and light the train; but from some cause not certainly demonstrated she exploded prematurely, being then within a hundred yards of the *Real*. It is necessary to say that the Court-Martial acquitted Burrish of blame, because he "had no orders to cover the fire-ship, either by signal or otherwise." Technically, the effect of this finding was to shift an obvious and gross blunder from the captain to some one else; but it is evident that if the *Dorsetshire* had occupied her station astern of the *Marlborough*, the fire-ship's attempt would have been much facilitated.

The Court decided unanimously that Burrish "ought to have borne down as far to leeward as where the admiral first began to engage, notwithstanding that the admiral might be hauled off before the *Dorsetshire* got so far to leeward." The point upon which the line should have been formed was thus established by the Court's finding. The subsequent proceedings of this ship need not be related. She now came slowly into close action, but that part of the enemy's order was already broken, and their rear vessels, the fear of which had controlled her captain, passed by as they came up without serious action.

How far Burrish's example influenced the captains immediately behind him cannot certainly be affirmed. Such shyness as he displayed is not only infectious, but saps that indispensable basis upon which military effectiveness reposes, namely, the certainty of co-operation and support, derived from mutual confidence, inspired by military discipline, obedience, and honour. It is well to note here that the remoteness of Lestock's division thus affected Burrish, who evidently could not understand either its distance or its failure to approach, and who, being what he was, saw himself threatened with want of that backing which he himself was refusing to the *Marlborough*. While he was blaming Lestock, hard things were being said about him in Lestock's division; but the lesson of Lestock's influence upon Burrish is not less noteworthy because the latter forfeited both duty and honour by his hesitation. It is to be feared that the captain of the *Essex*, following the *Dorsetshire*, was a coward; even so Burrish, an old captain, certainly did not cheer his heart by good example, but rather gave him the pretext for keeping still farther off. The rearmost two ships of the division but confirm the evidences of demoralization, and the more so that their captains seem from the evidence to have been well-disposed average men; but the five Spanish vessels approaching, with the *Dorsetshire* and the *Essex* holding aloof, was too much for their resolution—and not unnaturally. The broad result, however, was lamentable; for four British ships feared to come to the aid of an heroic and desperately injured consort, in deadly peril, because five enemies were drawing nigh.

Upon these four therefore fell, and not unjustly, the weight of national anger. Burrish was cashiered, and declared forever incapable of being an officer in the Navy. Norris, of the *Essex*, absconded to avoid trial. The two others were pronounced unfit to command, but, although never again employed, mitigating circumstances in their behaviour caused them to be retained on the lists of the Navy. It is not too much to say that they were men just of the stamp to have escaped this shame and ruin of reputation, under more favourable conditions of professional tone.

Concerning the vice-admiral's action at this time, which had its share in the ruin of these captains, another curious instance of men's bondage to the order of battle transpires. The three rear ships of his squadron were clean, that is, relatively fast; and they were rearmost for this very reason of speed, because, when the division led on the other tack, they, as headmost ships of the fleet, would be ready to chase. Nevertheless, when the admiral sent to Lestock in the forenoon to hurry him into line, no order was given to these ships to press ahead. Why? Lestock answers that to send those ships ahead, out of the place in the line prescribed to them by the commander-in-chief, was breaking the line, which should expose him to condign punishment; and this opinion the Court also adopts:

> The messages sent to the Vice-Admiral by the Admiral's two lieutenants were to make what sail he possibly could, and to close the line with his division; no signal was made for him to chase with his division, or send ships of his division to chase; without which, *while the signal for the line of battle was flying*, and more especially after the messages brought him, he could not, *without breach of duty*, either have chased or sent ships to chase out of the line.

It is to be noted that the word "chase" is here used in the strictest technical sense, not merely to exclude Lestock from diverting a ship to some other purpose than that of the engagement, but even from shifting her place in the general order in the view of furthering the engagement; for the Court says again:

> The Vice-Admiral could not send any ships of his division to the relief of the *Namur* and *Marlborough without breaking the order of battle*, there being four ships of the Admiral's division" (to wit, the *Dorsetshire* and that crowd) "stationed between the Vice-Admiral's division and the *Marlborough*, which four ships might have gone to the assistance of the *Marlborough*.

The second in command thus had no liberty to repair either the oversights of his superior, or the results of obvious bad conduct in juniors; for Burrish's backwardness was observed throughout the rear. There was a long road yet to travel to Nelson's personal action at St. Vincent and Copenhagen, or to his judicious order at Trafalgar, "The Second in command will, after my intentions are made known to him, have the entire direction of his line." Even that great officer Hood, off the Chesapeake in 1781, felt himself tied hand and foot by the union flag at the mizzen peak,—the signal for the line. Only the commander-in-chief could loose the bonds; either by his personal initiative alone, and vigilant supervision, as did Hawke and Rodney, or by adding to this the broad view of discretion in subordinates which Nelson took. Before leaving this subject, note may be taken of a pettifogging argument advanced by Lestock and adopted by the Court, that orders to these three ships to press ahead would have resulted in nothing, because of the lightness of the wind then and afterwards. True, doubtless, and known after the fact; but who before the event could predict the uncertain Mediterranean breeze, or how much each foot gained might contribute to the five minutes which measure the interval between victory and defeat. It is not by such lagging hesitations that battles are won.

It is a trivial coincidence, though it may be noted in passing, that as it was the second astern of the commander-in-chief on whom fell the weight of the disgrace, so it was the second astern of the commander of the van who alone scored a distinct success, and achieved substantial gain of professional reputation. Hawke, at first bearing down, had come to close action with the Spanish *Neptuno*, a vessel nominally of less force than his own ship, the *Berwick*. The *Neptuno* was at length driven out of her line, with a loss of some two hundred killed and wounded. Thus left without an immediate antagonist, Hawke's attention was attracted by another Spanish vessel, the *Poder*, of the same nominal force as the *Neptuno*, and following her in the order; with which four or five of the seven British ships, that should have closed the interval between Mathews and Rowley, were carrying on a distant and circumspect engagement, resembling in caution that of the *Dorsetshire* and her followers. He carried the *Berwick* close alongside the new enemy, dismasted her, and after two hours compelled her to strike her flag; the only vessel in either fleet that day to surrender, and then only after a resistance as honourable to Spain as that of the *Marlborough* had been to Great Britain. Her commander refused to yield his sword to any but Hawke, who also took possession of the prize with a party from his own ship; thus establishing beyond dispute, by all customary formalities, his claim to the one trophy of the day. The occurrences through which she was afterwards lost to the

British, so that only the honour of the capture remained, and that to Hawke alone, must be briefly told; for they, too, are a part of the mismanagement that has given to this battle its particular significance in naval history.

As the unlucky fire-ship bore down, Mathews began wearing the *Namur*,—turning her round, that is, from the wind, and therefore towards the *Marlborough* and her opponents. In this he seems to have had first in view supporting the fire-ship and covering the *Marlborough*. Boats were ahead of the latter towing her from the enemy. As she was thus being dragged off, but after the fire-ship blew up, the *Namur* passed between her and the hostile line; then, hauling to the wind on the starboard tack, she stood north towards Lestock's division. This movement to the rear was imitated by the British ships of the centre,—the *Dorsetshire* and others,—and, beyond a brush with the rear five Spanish vessels as they came up, the action in the centre here ceased.

This retrograde movement of Mathews and his division drew the centre away from the van. At about the same time the allied van, composed wholly of French ships, seeing the straits of the *Poder* and the *Real*, tacked—turned round—to come down to their assistance. This imposed a like movement upon the British van, lest it should be engaged apart from the rest of the fleet, and perhaps doubled on, by a number of perfectly fresh ships. The *Poder*, having lost her chief spars, could not be carried off, nor was Hawke able even to remove the men he had thrown on board. She was therefore retaken by the French. Lieutenant Lloyd, the officer in charge, escaped with a part of the prize crew, taking with him also a number of Spanish prisoners; but a junior lieutenant and some seamen were left behind and captured. The *Berwick* being compelled to follow her division, Lloyd could not rejoin her till the following day, and sought refuge for that night on board another ship.

The next day, February 23rd, Mathews had another chance. As he did not pursue during the night, while the allies continued to retire, he was a long way off at daylight; but his fleet was now united, and the enemy retreating. He need therefore have no anxiety about the crippled *Marlborough*, but could follow freely;

whereas, the enemy being pursued, their injured ships both retarded the movement and were endangered. In the course of the day, the *Poder* had lagged so far behind that Admiral Rowley, who had recognized Hawke's enterprise the day before, directed him to move down upon her. As he approached, the French ship in company abandoned her, but in taking possession Hawke was anticipated by the *Essex*, which Mathews himself had ordered to do so. The captain of the *Essex* got hold of the Spanish flag, with some other small trophies, which he afterwards refused to give up unless compelled; and, as Mathews would not give an order, Hawke never got them. Thus curiously it came to pass that the one man who above several misdemeanants distinguished himself by bad conduct, amounting to cowardice, and who ran away to escape trial, kept the tokens of the single achievement of the day from him whose valour had won them. The *Poder* herself was set on fire, and destroyed.

The British fleet continued to follow during the 23rd, and at nightfall was within three or four miles of the enemy, when Mathews again stopped. The allies, continuing to withdraw, were next morning nearly out of sight, and further pursuit was abandoned.

Thus ended this almost forgotten affair, which in its day occasioned to an unusual degree the popular excitement and discussion which always follow marked disaster, and but rarely attend success. Besides the particular missteps of Lestock and the individual captains, which have been mentioned, Mathews's conduct was marked by serious failures in professional competency. The charge preferred against him which seems most to have attracted attention, and to have been considered most damaging, was taking his fleet into action in a confused and disorderly manner. It is significant of professional standards that this should have assumed such prominence; for, however faulty may have been his previous management, the most creditable part of his conduct was the manner of his attack. He did not wait for a pedantically accurate line, but by a straightforward onslaught, at a favourable moment, upon a part of the enemy,—and that the rear,—set an example which, had it been followed by all who could do so, would probably have resulted in a distinct and brilliant success. He was justified—if he reasoned at all—in expecting that Lestock could get into action as soon as the French van; or, at the least, before it could reverse the conditions which would have ensued from a vigorous encounter upon the lines of Mathews's attack. It is most doubtful, indeed, whether the French van would have ventured to engage, in the case supposed; for the French admiral, writing to the French ambassador in Spain, used these words:

> It is clear, in the situation I was in, it could not be expected that a French admiral should go to the assistance of the Spaniards; neither could the vanguard of the fleet do it without running the hazard of being surrounded by the vanguard of the English, which had the wind of them; but *as soon as the English left me* I drew together all the ships of both squadrons, and sailed immediately to the assistance of the *Real Felipe*, in doing which I was exposed to the fire of the whole English line; but happily the English did not punish my *rashness* as it deserved.

Evidently De Court shared to the full the professional caution which marked the French naval officers, with all their personal courage; for if it was rash to pass the hostile line after it wore, it would be reckless to do so before.

Considered simply as a tactical situation, or problem, quite independent of any tactical forethought or insight on the part of the commander-in-chief,—of which there is little indication,—the conditions resulting from his attack were well summed up in a contemporary publication, wholly adverse to Mathews in tone, and saturated with the professional prepossessions embodied in the Fighting Instructions. This writer, who claims to be a naval officer, says:

> The whole amount of this fight is that the centre, consisting of eleven ships-of-the-line, together with two of-the-line and two fifty-gun ships of the Rear-Admiral's division *were able to destroy* the whole Spanish squadron, much more so as three of those ships went on with the French, and four of the sternmost did not get up with their ad-

miral before it was darkish, long after the fire-ship's misfortune, so that the whole afternoon there were only five, out of which the *Constante* was beat away in less than an hour; what then fifteen ships could be doing from half an hour past one till past five, no less than four hours, and these ships not taken, burnt, and destroyed, is the question which behoves them to answer.

In brief, then, Mathews's attack was so delivered that the weight of thirteen of-the-line fell upon five Spanish of the same class, the discomfiture of which, actually accomplished even under the misbehaviour of several British ships, separated the extreme rear, five other Spanish vessels, from the rest of the allies. Whatever the personal merit or lack of merit on the part of the commander-in-chief, such an opportunity, pushed home by a "band of brothers," would at the least have wiped out these rear ten ships of the allies; nor could the remainder in the van have redeemed the situation. As for the method of attack, it is worthy of note that, although adopted by Mathews accidentally, it anticipated, not only the best general practice of a later date, but specifically the purpose of Rodney in the action which he himself considered the most meritorious of his whole career,— that of April 17, 1780. The decisive signal given by him on that occasion, as explained by himself, meant that each ship should steer, not for the ship corresponding numerically to her in the enemy's order, but for the one immediately opposite at the time the signal was made. This is what Mathews and his seconds did, and others should have imitated. Singularly enough, not only was the opportunity thus created lost, but there is no trace of its existence, even, being appreciated in such wise as to affect professional opinion. As far as Mathews himself was concerned, the accounts show that his conduct, instead of indicating tactical sagacity, was a mere counsel of desperation.

But after engaging he committed palpable and even discreditable mistakes. Hauling to windward—away—when the *Marlborough* forced him ahead, abandoned that ship to overwhelming numbers, and countenanced the irresolution of the *Dorsetshire* and others. Continuing to stand north, after wearing on the evening of the battle, was virtually a retreat, unjustified by the conditions; and it would seem that the same false step gravely imperilled the *Berwick*, Hawke holding on, most properly, to the very last moment of safety, in order to get back his prize-crew. Bringing-to on the night of the 23rd was an error of the same character as standing north during that of the 22nd. It was the act of a doubtful, irresolute man,—irresolute, not because a coward, but because wanting in the self-confidence that springs from conscious professional competency. In short, the commander-in-chief's unfitness was graphically portrayed in the conversation with Cornwall from the quarter gallery of the flag-ship. "If you approve and will go down with me, I will go down." Like so many men, he needed a backer, to settle his doubts and to stiffen his backbone. The instance is far from unique.

In the case of Byng, as of Mathews, we are not concerned with the general considerations of the campaign to which the battle was incidental. It is sufficient to note that in Minorca, then a British possession, the French had landed an army of 15,000 men, with siege artillery sufficient to reduce the principal port and fortress, Port Mahon; upon which the whole island must fall. Their communications with France depended upon the French fleet cruising in the neighbourhood. Serious injury inflicted upon it would therefore go far to relieve the invested garrison.

Under these circumstances the British fleet sighted Minorca on the 19th of May, 1756, and was attempting to exchange information with the besieged, when the French fleet was seen in the southeast. Byng stood towards it, abandoning for the time the effort to communicate. That night both fleets manoeuvred for advantage of position with regard to the wind. The next day, between 9 and 10 a.m., they came again in view of each other, and at 11 were about six miles apart, the French still to the southeast, with a breeze at south-southwest to southwest. The British once more advanced towards them, close hauled on the starboard tack, heading south-easterly, the enemy standing on the opposite tack, heading westerly, both carrying sail to secure the weather gage (B1, F1). It appeared at first that the French would pass ahead of the British, retaining the windward posi-

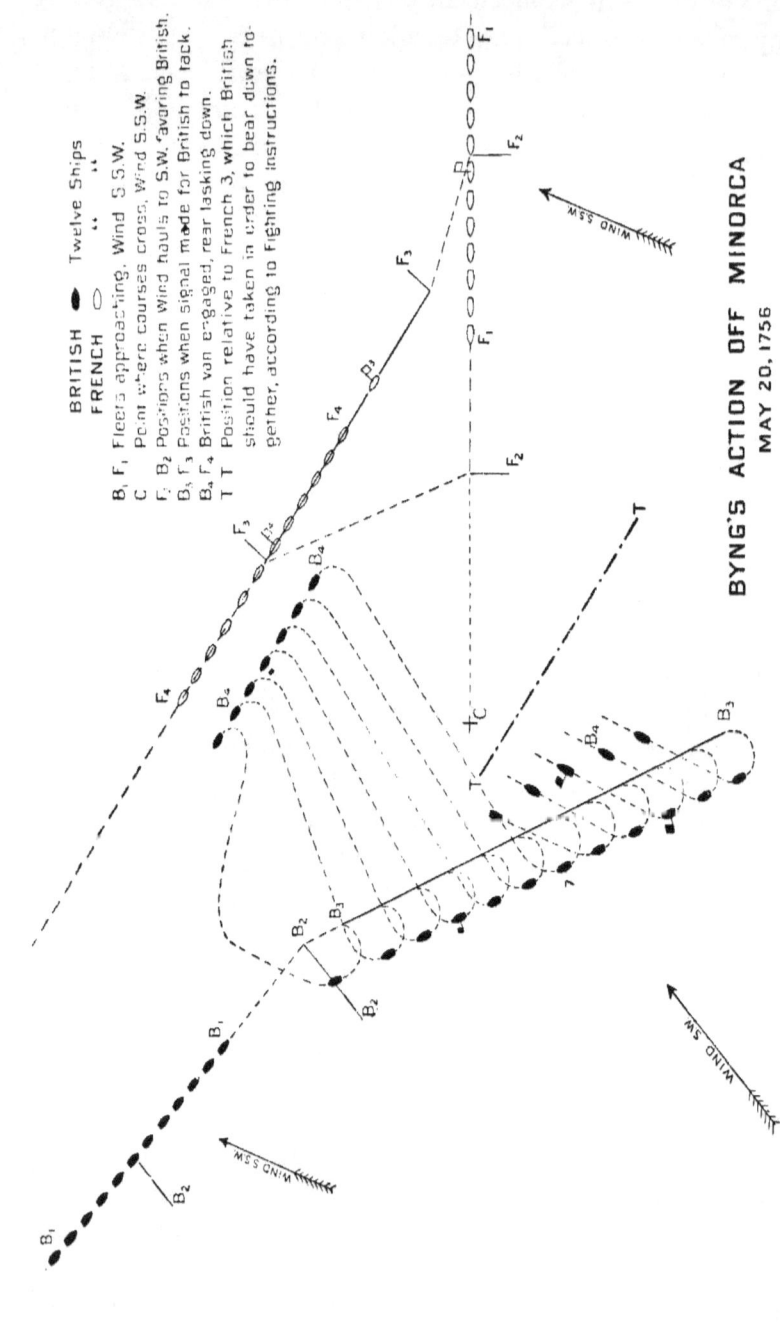

BYNG'S ACTION OFF MINORCA
MAY 20, 1756

tion; but towards noon the wind changed, enabling the latter to lie up a point or two higher (B2). This also forced the bows of the several French vessels off their course, and put them out of a regular line of battle; that is, they could no longer sail in each other's wake (F2). Being thus disordered, they reformed on the same tack, heading northwest, with the wind very little forward of the beam. This not only took time, but lost ground to leeward, because the quickest way to re-establish the order was for the mass of the fleet to take their new positions from the leewardmost vessel. When formed (F3), as they could not now prevent the British line from passing ahead, they hove-to with their main-topsails aback,—stopped,—awaiting the attack, which was thenceforth inevitable and close at hand.

In consequence of what has been stated, the British line (B2-B3)—more properly, column—was passing ahead of the French (F2-F3), steering towards their rear, in a direction in a general sense opposite to theirs, but not parallel; that is, the British course made an angle, of between thirty and forty-five degrees, with the line on which their enemy was ranged. Hence, barring orders to the contrary,—which were not given,—each British ship was at its nearest to the enemy as she passed their van, and became more and more distant as she drew to the rear. It would have been impossible to realize more exactly the postulate of the 17th Article of the Fighting Instructions, which in itself voiced the ideal conditions of an advantageous naval position for attack, as conceived by the average officer of the day; and, as though most effectually to demonstrate once for all how that sort of thing would work, the adjunct circumstances approached perfection. The admiral was thoroughly wedded to the old system, without an idea of departing from it, and there was a fair working breeze with which to give it effect, for the ships under topsails and foresail would go about three knots; with top-gallant sails, perhaps over four. A fifty-gun ship, about the middle of the engagement, had to close her lower deck ports when she set her top-gallant sails on the wind, which had then freshened a little.

The 17th Article read thus:

If the admiral see the enemy standing towards him, and he has the wind of them, the van of the fleet is to make sail till they come the length of the enemy's rear, and our rear abreast of the enemy's van; then he that is in the rear of our fleet is to tack first, and every ship one after another as fast as they can throughout the whole line; and if the admiral will have the whole fleet to tack together, the sooner to put them in a posture of engaging the enemy, he will hoist (a prescribed signal) and fire a gun; and whilst they are in fight with the enemy the ships will keep at half a cable's length—one hundred yards—one of the other.

All this Byng aimed to do. The conditions exactly fitted, and he exactly followed the rules, with one or two slight exceptions, which will appear, and for which the Court duly censured him. When thus much had been done, the 19th Article in turn found its postulate realized, and laid down its corresponding instruction:

If the admiral and his fleet have the wind of the enemy, and they have stretched themselves in a line of battle, the van of the admiral's fleet is to *steer with* the van of the enemy's, and there to engage with them.

The precise force of "steer with" is not immediately apparent to us today, nor does it seem to have been perfectly clear then; for the question was put to the captain of the flag-ship,—the heroic Gardiner,—"You have been asked if the admiral did not express some uneasiness at Captain Andrews"—of the van ship in the action—"not seeming to understand the 19th Article of the Fighting Instructions; Do not you understand that article to relate to our van particularly when the two fleets are in a parallel line of battle to each other?" (As TT, F3).

Answer. "I apprehended it in the situation we were in[1] if the word *For* were instead of the word *With*, he would, I apprehend, have steered directly *for* the van ship of the Enemy."

Question. "As the 19th Article expresses to steer with the van of the enemy, if the leading ship had done so, in the oblique line we were in with the enemy, and every ship had observed it the

---

1. This wording and punctuation is exact from the text.

same, would it not have prevented our rear coming to action at all, at least within a proper distance?"

Answer. "Rear, and van too."

"Steer with" therefore meant, to the Court and to Gardiner, to steer parallel to the enemy,—possibly likewise abreast,—and if the fleets were already parallel the instruction would work; but neither the articles themselves, nor Byng by his signals, did anything to effect parallelism before making the signal to engage.

The captain of the ship sternmost in passing, which became the van when the fleet tacked together according to the Instructions and signals, evidently shared Gardiner's impression; when about, he steered parallel to—"with"—the French, who had the wind nearly abeam. The mischief was that the ships ahead of him in passing were successively more and more distant from the enemy, and if they too, after tacking, steered with the latter, they would never get any nearer. The *impasse* is clear. Other measures doubtless would enable an admiral to range his fleet parallel to the enemy at any chosen distance, by taking a position himself and forming the fleet on his ship; or, in this particular instance, Byng being with the van as it, on the starboard tack, was passing the enemy (B3 B3), could at any moment have brought his fleet parallel to the French by signalling the then van ship to keep away a certain amount, the rest following in her wake. Nothing to that effect being in the Instructions, it seems not to have occurred to him. His one idea was to conform to them, and he apprehended that after tacking, as they prescribed, the new van ship would bear down and engage without further orders, keeping parallel to the French when within point-blank, the others following her as they could; a process which, from the varying distances, would expose each to a concentrated fire as they successively approached. Byng's action is only explicable to the writer by supposing that he thus by "steer with" understood "steer for;" for when, after the fleet tacked together, the new van ship (formerly the rear) did not of her own motion head for the leading enemy, he signalled her to steer one point, and then two points, in that direction. This, he explained in his defence, was "to put the leading captain in mind of his Instructions, who

I perceived did not steer away with the enemy's leading ship agreeable to the 19th Article of the Fighting Instructions." The results of these orders not answering his expectations, he then made the signal to engage, as the only remaining way perceptible to him for carrying out the Instructions.

To summarize the foregoing, up to the moment the signal for battle was made: While the fleets were striving for the weather gage, the wind had shifted to the southwest. The French, momentarily disordered by the change, had formed in line ahead about noon, heading northwest, westerly, so as just to keep their main topsails aback and the ships with bare steerage way, but under command (F3). The British standing south-southeast, by the wind, were passing (B2-B3) across the head of the enemy's fleet at a distance of from three to two miles—the latter being the estimate by their ships then in the rear. The French having twelve vessels in line and the British thirteen, the gradual progress of the latter should bring their then van "the length of the enemy's rear," about the time the rear came abreast of his van. When this happened, the Instructions required that the fleet tack together, and then stand for the enemy, ship to ship, number one to number one, and so along the line till the number twelves met.[2]

This Byng purposed to do, but, unluckily for himself, ventured on a refinement. Considering that, if his vessels bore down when abreast their respective antagonists, they would go bows-on, perpendicularly, subject to a raking—enfilading—fire, he deferred the signal to tack till his van had passed some distance beyond the French rear, because thus they would have to approach in a slanting direction. He left out of his account here the fact that all long columns tend to straggle in the rear; hence, although he waited till his three or four leading ships had passed the enemy before making signal to tack, the rear had got no farther than abreast the hostile van. Two of the clearest witnesses, Baird of the *Portland*, next to the then rear ship, and Cornwall of the *Revenge*, seventh from it, testified that, after tacking together,

---

2. So far was literalism carried, that, before the signal for battle, Byng evened numbers with his opponent by directing his weakest ship to leave the line, with no other orders than to be ready to take the place of a disabled vessel.

to the port tack, when they kept away for the enemy in obedience to the signal for battle, it was necessary, in order to reach their particular opponents, to bring the wind not only as far as astern, but on the starboard quarter, showing that they had been in rear of their station before tacking, and so too far ahead after it; while Durell of the *Trident*, ninth from rear and therefore fifth from van, asserted that at the same moment the British van, which after tacking became the rear, had overpassed the enemy by five or six ships. This may be an exaggeration, but that three or four vessels had gone beyond is proved by evidence from the ships at that end of the line. The Court therefore distinctly censured the admiral for this novelty:

> Unanimously, the Court are of opinion that when the British fleet on the starboard tack were stretched abreast, *or about the beam* of the enemy's line, the admiral should have tacked the fleet all together, and immediately have conducted it on a direct course for the enemy, the van steering for the enemy's van, etc.

The instructive point, however, is not Byng's variation, nor the Court's censure, but the idea, common to both, that the one and only way to use your dozen ships under the conditions was to send each against a separate antagonist. The highest and authoritative conception of a fleet action was thus a dozen naval duels, occurring simultaneously, under initial conditions unfavourable to the assailant. It is almost needless to remark that this is as contrary to universal military teaching as it was to the practice of Rodney, Howe, Jervis, and Nelson, a generation or two later.

This is, in fact, the chief significance of this action, which ratified and in a measure closed the effete system to which the middle eighteenth century had degraded the erroneous, but comparatively hearty, tradition received by it from the seventeenth. It is true, the same blundering method was illustrated in the War of 1778. Arbuthnot and Graves, captains when Byng was tried, followed his plan in 1781, with like demonstration of practical disaster attending false theory; but, while the tactical inefficiency was little less, the evidence of faint-hearted professional incompetency, of utter personal inadequacy, was at least not so glaring. It is the combination of the two in the person of the same commander that has given to this action its pitiful pre-eminence in the naval annals of the century.

It is, therefore, not so much to point out the lesson, as to reinforce its teaching by the exemplification of the practical results, that there is advantage in tracing the sequel of events in this battle. The signal to tack was made when the British van had reached beyond the enemy's rear, at a very little after 1 p.m. (B3). This reversed the line of battle, the rear becoming the van, on the port tack. When done, the new van was about two miles from that of the French (F4); the new rear, in which Byng was fourth from sternmost, was three and a half or four from their rear. Between this and 2 p.m. came the signals for the ship then leading to keep two points, twenty-five degrees, more to starboard,—towards the enemy; a measure which could only have the bad effect of increasing the angle which the British line already made with that of the French, and the consequent inequality of distance to be traversed by their vessels in reaching their opponents. At 2.20 the signal for battle was made, and was repeated by the second in command, Rear-Admiral Temple West, who was in the fourth ship from the van. His division of six bore up at once and ran straight down before the wind, under topsails only, for their several antagonists; the sole exception being the van-most vessel, which took the slanting direction desired by Byng, with the consequence that she got ahead of her position, had to back and to wear to regain it, and was worse punished than any of her comrades. The others engaged in line, within point-blank, the rear-admiral hoisting the flag for close action (B4). Fifteen minutes later, the sixth ship, and rearmost of the van, the *Intrepid*, lost her foretopmast, which crippled her.

The seventh ship, which was the leader of the rear, Byng's own division, got out of his hands before he could hold her. Her captain, Frederick Cornwall, was nephew to the gallant fellow who fell backing Mathews so nobly off Toulon, and had then succeeded to the command of the *Marlborough*, fighting her till himself disabled. He had to bring the wind on the starboard quarter of his little sixty-four, in order to reach the seventh in the enemy's line, which was an eighty-gun ship, carrying the flag of the French admiral. This post, by professional etiquette, as by evident military considerations, Byng owed to his own flag-ship, of equal force.

The rest of the rear division the commander-in-chief attempted to carry with himself, slanting down; or, as the naval term then had it, "lasking" towards the enemy. The flag-ship kept away four points—forty-five degrees; but hardly had she started, under the very moderate canvas of topsails and foresail, to cover the much greater distance to be travelled, in order to support the van by engaging the enemy's rear, when Byng observed that the two ships on his left—towards the van—were not keeping pace with him. He ordered the main and mizzen topsails to be backed to wait for them. Gardiner, the captain, "took the liberty of offering the opinion" that, if sail were increased instead of reduced, the ships concerned would take the hint, that they would all be sooner alongside the enemy, and probably receive less damage in going down. It was a question of example.

The admiral replied, "You see that the signal for the line is out, and I am ahead of those two ships; and you would not have me, as admiral of the fleet, run down as if I was going to engage a single ship. It was Mr. Mathews's misfortune to be prejudiced by not carrying his force down together, which I shall endeavour to avoid."

Gardiner again "took the liberty" of saying he would answer for one of the two captains doing his duty. The incident, up to the ship gathering way again, occupied less than ten minutes; but with the van going down headlong—as it ought—one ceases to wonder at the impression on the public produced by one who preferred lagging for laggards to hastening to support the forward, and that the populace suspected something worse than pedantry in such reasoning at such a moment. When way was resumed, it was again under the very leisurely canvas of topsails and foresail.

By this had occurred the incident of the *Intrepid* losing her foretopmast. It was an ordinary casualty of battle, and one to be expected; but to such a temper as Byng's, and under the cast-iron regulations of the Instructions, it entailed consequences fatal to success in the action,—if success were ever attainable under such a method,—and was ultimately fatal to the admiral himself. The wreck of the fallen mast was cleared, and the foresail set to maintain speed, but, despite all, the *Intrepid* dropped astern in the line. Cornwall in the *Revenge* was taking his place at the moment, and fearing that the *Intrepid* would come back upon him, if in her wake, he brought up first a little to windward, on her quarter; then, thinking that she was holding her way, he bore up again. At this particular instant he looked behind, and saw the admiral and other ships a considerable distance astern and to windward; much Lestock's position in Mathews's action. This was the stoppage already mentioned, to wait for the two other ships. Had Cornwall been Burrish, he might in this have seen occasion for waiting himself; but he saw rather the need of the crippled ship. The *Revenge* took position on the *Intrepid*'s lee quarter, to support her against the enemy's fire, concentrated on her when her mast was seen to fall. As her way slackened, the *Revenge* approached her, and about fifteen minutes later the ship following, the *Princess Louisa*,—one of those for which Byng had waited,—loomed up close behind Cornwall, who expected her to run him on board, her braces being shot away. She managed, however, with the helm to back her sails, and dropped clear; but in so doing got in the way of the vessel next after her, the *Trident*, which immediately preceded Byng. The captain of the *Trident*, slanting down with the rest of the division, saw the situation, put his helm up, ran under the stern of the *Louisa*, passed on her lee side,—nearest the enemy,—and ranged up behind the *Revenge*; but in doing this he not only crossed the stern of the *Louisa*, but the bow of the admiral's ship—the *Ramillies*.

Under proper management the *Ramillies* doubtless could have done just what the *Trident* did,—keep away with the helm, till the ships ahead of her were cleared; she would be at least hasting towards the enemy. But the noise of battle was in the air, and the crew of the *Ramillies* began to fire without orders, at an improper distance. The admiral permitted them to continue, and the smoke enveloping the ship prevented fully noting the incidents just narrated. It was, however, seen before the firing that the *Louisa* was come up into the wind with her topsails shaking, and the *Trident* passing her to leeward. There should, therefore, have been some preparation of mind for the fact suddenly reported to the admiral, by a military passenger on the quarter deck, that a British ship was close aboard, on the lee bow. It was the *Trident* that had crossed from windward to leeward for the reasons given, and an instant later the *Louisa* was seen on the weather bow. Instead of keeping off, as the *Trident* had done, the admiral ordered the foresail hauled up, the helm down, luffed the ship to the wind, and braced the fore-topsail sharp aback; the effect of which was first to stop her way, and then to pay her head off to leeward, clear of the two vessels. About quarter of an hour elapsed, by Captain Gardiner's evidence, from the time that the *Ramillies*'s head pointed clear of the *Trident* and *Louisa* before sail was again made to go forward to aid the van. The battle was already lost, and in fact had passed out of Byng's control, owing to his previous action; nevertheless this further delay, though probably due only to the importance attached by the admiral to regularity of movement, had a discreditable appearance.

The Court held that the admiral was justified in not trying to go to leeward of the two ships, under the circumstances when they were seen; but blamed him for permitting the useless cannonade which prevented seeing them sooner. The results at this moment in other parts of the field should be summarized, as they show both the cause and the character of the failures due to faulty management.

The five ships of the British van had already seen their adversaries withdraw after a sharp engagement. This seems to have been due to the fact that two were individually overmatched and driven off; whereupon the other three retired because unable to contend with five. But no support reached the British van at this important moment; on the contrary, the British rear was now two or three miles distant, astern and to windward. The lagging of the crippled *Intrepid* held back the *Revenge*. Cornwall was detained some time by the old idea that he needed a signal to pass her, because to do so was breaking the order established by the admiral; but concluding at last that Byng was unaware of the conditions, and seeing that his immediate opponent—

the French admiral—was drawing ahead, he sent word to the *Intrepid* to hold her fire for a few moments till he could go by. He then made sail.

The French rear with its commander-in-chief had been watching the incidents narrated: the crippling of the *Intrepid*, the consequent disorder in the British rear, and the increasing distance between it and the van. When the *Revenge*, however, passed ahead, and Byng disentangled his flag-ship, the moment for a decisive step arrived. The French rear vessels were nearer the British van than Byng's division was. They now filled their topsails, made more sail, stood for the British leading ships, already partially unrigged, passed by, and in so doing gave them the fire of a number of substantially fresh vessels, which had undergone only a distant and ineffective cannonade. Byng saw what was about to happen, and also set more canvas; but it was no longer possible to retrieve the preceding errors. The French admiral had it in his power very seriously to damage, if not to destroy the hostile van; but in accordance with the tradition of his nation he played an over-prudent game, strictly defensive, and kept too far off. After exchanging distant broadsides, he steered northwest towards Mahon, satisfied that he had for the time disabled his opponent. The British that evening tacked off-shore and stood to the southeast. Four days later they abandoned the field, returning to Gibraltar. The fall of Minorca followed.

Nothing could have been much worse than the deplorable management of this action on the part of the commander-in-chief. It is a conspicuous instance of weak and halting execution, superimposed upon a professional conception radically erroneous; and it reflected throughout the timid hesitancy of spirit which dictated the return to Gibraltar, under the always doubtful sanction of a Council of War. But the historical value of the lesson is diminished if attention is confined to the shortcomings of the admiral, neglectful of the fact that his views as to the necessity to observe the routine of the Fighting Instructions are reproduced in the evidence of the captains; and that the finding of the Court censures, not the general idea, but certain details, important yet secondary. Durell, being asked whether the admiral could not have passed under the stern of the *Trident*, as the *Trident* had under that of the *Louisa*, replies, "Yes, but she would have been to leeward of those ships ahead;" that is, to leeward of the line. Gardiner "knows no other method than what the admiral took, for preserving the line regular." Cornwall cannot pass the *Intrepid* without a signal, because it would be breaking the order. These were all good men.

The Court, composed of four admirals and nine captains, the junior of whom had over ten years seniority, give in their finding no shadow of disapproval to the broad outlines of the action. There can be, therefore, no doubt about service standards. The questions put to the witnesses reveal indeed a distinct preference for forming the line of battle *parallel* to that of the enemy before bearing down, so that all the ships may have the same distance to go, have a clear field ahead of each, and the comparatively simple mutual bearing of "abeam" to observe; but it refrains from censuring the admiral for forming on a line very oblique to that of the enemy, which entailed the burden of changing the relative positions during standing down, so as to arrive all together, on a line parallel to his; while the course itself being oblique alike to their own front and the enemy's, each preceding ship was liable to get in the way, "to prove an impediment," to its follower,—as actually happened. It was indeed impossible to fault the commander-in-chief in this particular, because his action was conformable to the letter of the Instructions, with which he was evidently and subserviently eager to comply.

The decision of the Court therefore was, in substance, that in bearing down upon the enemy Byng did not do wrong in starting upon a line oblique to them; but that he should have steered such a course, and maintained such spread of sail, graduated to the speed of the slowest ship in the fleet, that all should reach point-blank range at the same time, and be then ranged on a line parallel to that of the enemy.

When on the starboard tack, the admiral should have tacked the fleet all together and immediately conducted it on a direct course for the enemy; .... each ship steering for her opposite ship in the enemy's line, and under such sail as might have enabled the worst sailing ship, under all her plain sail, to preserve her station.

It is needless to insist with any naval man, or to any soldier, that such an advance, in orderly fashion, oblique to the front, is unattainable except by long drill, while this fleet had been but a few weeks assembled; and the difficulty is enhanced when each ship has not only to keep its station in line, but to reach a particular enemy, who may not be just where he ought, having respect to the British order. The manoeuvre favoured by the Court for the fleet as a whole was in fact just that which Byng attempted for his own division, with the results that have been narrated. These were aggravated by his mismanagement, but did not originate from it.

The invariable result of an attack thus attempted, however vigorously made, was that the van of the assailant got into action first, receiving the brunt of the enemy's fire without proper support. Not infrequently, it also underwent a second hammering from the enemy's rear, precisely in the same way as occurred in Byng's action; and whether this happened or not depended more upon the enemy than upon the British rear. In ignoring, therefore, the idea of combining an attack in superior numbers upon a part of the enemy, and adopting instead that of an onslaught upon his whole, all along the line, the British practice of the eighteenth century not only surrendered the advantage which the initiative has, of effecting a concentration, but subjected their own fleets to being beaten in detail, subject only to the skill of the opponent in using the opportunity extended to him. The results, at best, were indecisive, tactically considered. The one apparent exception was in June, 1794, when Lord Howe, after long vainly endeavouring a better combination with a yet raw fleet, found himself forced to the old method; but although then several ships were captured, this issue seems attributable chiefly to the condition of the French Navy, greatly fallen through circumstances foreign to the present subject. It was with this system that Rodney was about to break, the first of his century formally to do so. A false tactical standard, however, was not the only drawback under which the British Navy laboured in 1739. The prolonged series of wars, which began when the establishment of civil order under Cromwell permitted the nation to turn from internal strife to external interests, had been for England chiefly maritime. They had recurred at brief intervals, and had been of such duration as to insure a continuity of experience and development. Usage received modification under the influence of constant warlike practice, and the consequent changes in methods, if not always thoroughly reasoned, at the least reflected a similar process of professional advance in the officers of the service. This was consecutively transmitted, and by the movement of actual war was prevented from stagnating and hardening into an accepted finality. Thus the service and its officers, in the full performance of their functions, were alive and growing. Nor was this all. The same surroundings that promoted this healthful evolution applied also a continual test of fitness to persons. As each war began, there were still to be found in the prime of vigour and usefulness men whose efficiency had been proved in its predecessor, and thus the line of sustained ability in leadership was carried on from one naval generation to another, through the sixty-odd years, 1652-1713, over which these conditions extended.

The peace of Utrecht in 1713 put an end to this period. A disputed succession after the death of Queen Anne, in 1714, renewed the condition of internal disquietude which had paralyzed the external action of England under Charles I.; and this co-operated with the mere weariness of war, occasioned by prolonged strife, to give both the country and the navy a temporary distaste to further military activity. The man of the occasion, who became the exponent and maintainer of this national inclination, was Sir Robert Walpole; to whom, during his ministry of over twenty years, can fairly be applied Jefferson's phrase concerning himself, that his "passion was peace." But, whatever the necessity to the country of such a policy, it too often results, as it did in both these cases, in neglect of the military services, allowing the equipment to decay, and tending to sap the professional interest and competency of the officers.

From this last evil the United States Navy in Jefferson's day was saved by the simple fact that the officers were young men, or at the most in the early prime of life,—the Navy itself, in 1812, being less than twenty years old as a corporate organization. The British Navy of 1739 was in very different case. For a quarter of a century the only important military occurrence had been the Battle of Cape Passaro, in 1718, where the British fleet in a running fight destroyed a much inferior Spanish force; and the occasion then was not one of existent war, but of casual hostilities, which, precipitated by political conditions, began and ended with the particular incident, as far as the sea was concerned. Back of this lay only Malaga, in 1704; for the remaining years of war, up to 1713, had been unmarked by fleet battles. The tendency of this want of experience, followed by the long period—not of peace only, but—of professional depression resultant upon inactivity and national neglect, was to stagnation, to obviate which no provision existed or was attempted. Self-improvement was not a note of the service, nor of the times. The stimulus of occupation and the corrective of experience being removed, average men stuck where they were, and grew old in a routine of service, or, what was perhaps worse, out of the service in all but name. In naval warfare, the Battle of Malaga, the last point of performance, remained the example, and the Fighting Instructions the passively accepted authority. The men at the head of the Navy, to whom the country naturally looked, either had no record—no proof of fitness—because but youths in the last war, or else, in simple consequence of having then had a chance to show themselves, were now superannuated. This very fact, however, had the singular and unfortunate result that, because the officers of reputation were old, men argued, by a curious perversion of thought, that none but the old should be trusted.

Of this two significant cases will tell more than many words. Mathews, who commanded at Toulon in 1744, was then sixty-seven years old, and had not been at sea between 1724 and 1742. Hawke, in 1747, when he had already established an excellent reputation as a captain, and for enterprise in recent battle, was thought young to be entrusted with a squadron of a dozen ships-of-the-line, although he was forty-two,—two years older than Nelson at the Nile, but four years younger than Napoleon and Wellington at Waterloo, and one year less in age than Grant at the close of the American Civil War. Such instances are not of merely curious interest; they are symptoms of professional states of mind, of a perplexity and perversion of standards which work disastrously whenever war succeeds to a prolonged period of peace, until experience has done its work by sorting out the unsound from among the fair-seeming, and has shown also that men may be too old as well as too young for unaccustomed responsibility. The later prevalence of juster views was exemplified in the choice of Wolfe, who was but thirty-two when he fell before Quebec in 1759, charged with one of the most difficult enterprises that had then been entrusted to a British general.

It is these two factors, therefore, an erroneous standard and a lethargic peace, which principally caused the weakness of the British official staff for battle service at the period of lowest descent, which was reached in the first quarter of the eighteenth century, but was prolonged and intensified by a protracted interval of professional apathy. Other grievous evils doubtless existed, serious defects in administration, involving indifferent equipment, bad and scanty provisions, inferior physique in the ships' companies, and wretched sanitary arrangements; but while all these unquestionably gravely affected general efficiency for war, they belonged rather to the civil than the military side of the profession. In the hour of battle it was not these, but the tone and efficiency of the officers, that chiefly told. A false pattern of action had been accepted at a moment favourable to its perpetuation, when naval warfare on the grand scale had ceased, owing to the decline of the principal enemy, the navy of France; while the average competency of naval officers had been much lowered through want of professional incentive, and the absence of any sifting process by which the unfit could be surely eliminated. That plenty of good material existed, was sufficiently shown by the number of names, afterwards distinguished, which soon began to appear. Weeding went on apace; but before its work was done, there had to be traversed a painful period, fruitful of evidences of unfitness, of personal weakness, of low or false professional ideas.

It is with this period that we have first had to do as our point of departure, by which not only to estimate the nature and degree of the subsequent advance, but to illustrate also the part specifically contributed to it by Hawke and Rodney, through their personal and professional characteristics. While types, they are more than mere exponents of the change as a whole, and will be found to bear to it particular relations,—its leaders in fact, as well as in name. It is not merely fanciful to say that Hawke stands for and embodies the spirit of the new age, while Rodney rather exemplifies and develops the form in which that spirit needed ultimately to cloth itself in order to perfect its working. The one is a protest in act against the professional faintheartedness, exaggerated into the semblance of personal timidity, shown by the captains off Toulon in 1774; the other, in the simple but skilful methods and combinations adopted by him, both represents and gives effect to a reaction against the extravagant pedantry, which it fell to Byng, in all the honesty of a thoroughly commonplace man, to exhibit in unintentional caricature.

In thus ascribing to these great men complementary parts in leading and shaping the general movement, it is not meant that either is deficient on the side attributed to the other. Hawke showed by his actions that he was by no means indifferent to tactical combinations, which is another way of saying that he appreciated the advantage of form in warfare; while Rodney, though a careful organizer and driller of fleets, and patient in effort to obtain advantage before attacking, exhibited on occasion headlong, though not inconsiderate, audacity, and also tenacious endurance in fight. Still, it will probably be admitted by the student of naval biography that to him Hawke suggests primarily the unhesitating sudden rush—the swoop—upon the prey, while Rodney resembles rather the patient astute watcher, carefully keeping his own powers in hand, and waiting for the unguarded moment when the adversary may be taken suddenly at unawares. Certain it is that, with opportunities much more numerous than were permitted to Hawke, his successes would have been far greater but for an excess of methodical caution. There was a third, who combined in due proportion, and possessed to an extraordinary degree, the special qualities here assigned to each. It is one of the ironies of history that the first Sir Samuel Hood should have had just opportunity enough to show how great were his powers, and yet have been denied the chance to exhibit them under conditions to arrest the attention of the world; nay, have been more than once compelled to stand by hopelessly, and see occasions lost which he would unquestionably have converted into signal triumphs. In him, as far as the record goes, was consummated the advance of the eighteenth century. He was the greatest of the sewers. It fell to Nelson, his pupil,—in part at least,—to reap the harvest.

Before closing this part of our subject, the necessary preliminary to understanding the progress of naval warfare in the eighteenth century, it is pertinent to note the respect in which advance there differs from that of the nineteenth, and in some degree, though less, from that of the seventeenth centuries. The period was not one of marked material development. Improvements there were, but they were slow, small in ultimate extent, and in no sense revolutionary. Ships and guns, masts and sails, grew better, as did also administrative processes; it may indeed be asserted, as an axiom of professional experience, that as the military tone of the sea-officers rises, the effect will be transmitted to those civil functions upon which efficiency for war antecedently depends. Still, substantially, the weapons of war were in principle, and consequently in general methods of handling, the same at the end of the period as at the beginning. They were intrinsically more efficient; but the great gain was not in them, but in the spirit and intellectual grasp of the men who wielded them. There was no change in the least analogous to that from oars to sails, or from sails to steam.

Under such conditions of continued similarity in means, advance in the practice of any profession is effected rather in the realm of ideas, in intellectual processes; and even their expert application involves mind rather than matter. In the nineteenth century such intellectual processes have been largely devoted to the purposes of material development, and have found their realization, in the navy as elsewhere, in revolutionizing instruments, in providing means never before attainable. The railroad, the steamer, the electric telegraph, find their counterpart in the heavily armoured steamship of war. But in utilizing these new means the navy must still be governed by the ideas, which are, indeed, in many ways as old as military history, but which in the beginning of the eighteenth century had passed out of the minds of naval men. It was the task of the officers of that period to recall them, to formulate them anew, to give them a living hold upon the theory and practice of the profession. This they did, and they were undoubtedly helped in so doing by the fact that their attention was not diverted and absorbed, as that of our day very largely has been, by decisive changes in the instruments with which their ideas were to be given effect. Thus they were able to make a substantial and distinctive contribution to the art of naval warfare, and that on its highest side. For the artist is greater than his materials, the warrior than his arms; and it was in the man rather than in his weapons that the navy of the eighteenth century wrought its final conspicuous triumph.

Hawke: 1705-1781

Chapter 2

Hawke: 1705–1781

The first great name in British naval annals belonging distinctively to the eighteenth century rather than to the seventeenth, is that of Edward Hawke. He was born in 1705, of a family of no marked social distinction, his father being a barrister, and his grandfather a London merchant. His mother's maiden name was Bladen. One of her brothers held an important civil office as Commissioner of Trade and Plantations, and was for many years a member of Parliament. Under the conditions which prevailed then, and for some generations longer, the influence attaching to such positions enabled the holder to advance substantially the professional interests of a naval officer. Promotion in rank, and occupation both in peace and war, were largely a matter of favour. Martin Bladen naturally helped his nephew in this way, a service especially valuable in the earlier part of a career, lifting a man out of a host of competitors and giving him a chance to show what was in him. It may readily be believed that Hawke's marked professional capacity speedily justified the advantage thus obtained, and he seems to have owed his promotion to post-captain to a superior officer when serving abroad; though it is never possible to affirm that even such apparent official recognition was not due either to an intimation from home, or to the give and take of those who recognized Bismarck's motto, *Do ut des*.

However this may have been, the service did not suffer by the favours extended to Hawke. Nor was his promotion unduly rapid, to the injury of professional character, as often happened when rank was prematurely reached. It was not till March 20,

1734, that he was "made post," as the expression went, by Sir Chaloner Ogle into the frigate *Flamborough*, on the West India Station. Being then twenty-nine years old, in the prime of life for naval efficiency, he had reached the position in which a fair opportunity for all the honours of the profession lay open to him, provided he could secure occupation until he was proved to be indispensable. Here also his uncle's influence stood good. Although the party with which the experienced politician was identified had gone out of power with Sir Robert Walpole, in 1742, his position on the Board dealing with Colonial affairs left him not without friends. "My colleague, Mr. Cavendish," he writes, "has already laid in his claim for another ship for you. But after so long a voyage" (he had been away over three years) "I think you should be allowed a little time to spend with your friends on shore. It is some consolation, however, that I have some friends on the new Board of Admiralty."

"There has been a clean sweep," he says again, "but I hope I may have some friends amongst the new Lords that will upon my account afford you their protection."

This was in the beginning of 1743, when Hawke had just returned from a protracted cruise on the West India and North American stations, where by far the greater part of his early service was passed. He never again returned there, and very shortly after his uncle's letter, just quoted, he was appointed to the *Berwick*, a ship-of-the-line of seventy guns. In command of her he sailed in September, 1743, for the Mediterranean; and a few months after, by his decided and seamanlike course in Mathews's action, he established his professional reputation and fortunes, the firm foundations of which had been laid during the previous years of arduous but inconspicuous service. Two years later, in 1746, Martin Bladen died, and with him political influence, in the ordinary acceptation, departed from Hawke. Thenceforth professional merit, forced upon men's recognition, stood him in stead.

He was thirty-nine when he thus first made his mark, in 1744. Prior to this there is not found, in the very scanty records that remain of his career, as in that of all officers of his period while in subordinate positions, any certain proof that he had ever been seriously engaged with an enemy. War against Spain had been declared, October 19, 1739. He had then recently commissioned a fifty-gun ship, the *Portland*, and in her sailed for the West Indies, where he remained until the autumn of 1742; but the inert manner in which Spain maintained the naval contest, notwithstanding that her transmarine policy was the occasion of the quarrel, and her West Indian possessions obviously endangered, removed all chance of active service on the large scale, except in attacking her colonies; and in none of those enterprises had the *Portland* been called upon to share.

Meantime, a general European war had begun in 1740, concerning the succession to the Austrian throne; and, in the political combinations which followed, France and Great Britain had as usual ranged themselves on opposite sides, though without declaring war upon each other. Further, there had existed for some time a secret defensive alliance between France and Spain, binding each party to support the other, under certain conditions, with an effective armed force, to be used not for aggressive purposes, but in defence only. It was claimed, indeed, that by so doing the supporting country was not to be considered as going to war, or even as engaged in hostilities, except as regarded the contingent furnished. This view received some countenance from international law, in the stage of development it had then reached; yet it is evident that if a British admiral met a Spanish fleet, of strength fairly matching his own, but found it accompanied by a French division, the commander of which notified him that he had orders to fight if an attack were made, friendly relations between the two nations would be strained near to the breaking point. This had actually occurred to the British Admiral Haddock, in the Mediterranean, in 1741; and conditions essentially similar, but more exasperated, constituted the situation under which Hawke for the first time was brought into an action between two great fleets.

On the 11th of January, 1744, when the *Berwick* joined the British fleet, it had rendezvoused at the Hyères Islands, a little east of Toulon, watching the movements of twelve Spanish ships-of-the-line, which had taken refuge in the port. As these were unwilling to put to sea trusting to their own strength, the French Admiral De Court was ordered to accompany and protect them when they sailed. This becoming known, Admiral Mathews had concentrated his fleet, which by successive reinforcements—the *Berwick* among others—numbered twenty-eight of-the-line when the allies, in about equal force, began to come out on the 20th of February.

The action which ensued owes its historical significance wholly to the fact that it illustrated conspicuously, and in more than one detail, the degenerate condition of the official staff of the British navy; the demoralization of ideals, and the low average of professional competency.[3] That there was plenty of good metal was also shown, but the proportion of alloy was dangerously great. That the machinery of the organization was likewise bad, the administrative system culpably negligent as well as inefficient, had been painfully manifested in the equipment of the ships, in the quality of the food, and in the indifferent character of the ships' crews; but in this respect Hawke had not less to complain of than others, having represented forcibly to the Admiralty the miserable unfitness of the men sent him. Nevertheless, despite all drawbacks, including therein a signalling system so rudimentary and imperfect as to furnish a ready excuse to the unwilling, as well as a recurrent perplexity to those honestly wishing to obey their orders, he showed that good will and high purpose could not only lead a man to do his full duty as directed, but guide him to independent initiative action when opportunity offered. Under all external conditions of difficulty and doubt, or even of cast-iron rule, the principle was as true then as when Nelson formulated it, that no captain when in doubt could do very wrong if he placed his ship alongside an enemy. That Hawke so realized it brought out into more glaring relief the failure of so many of his colleagues on this occasion.

But the lesson would be in great part lost, if there were to be seen in this lapse only the personal element of the delinquents, and not the widespread decline of professional tone. Undoubt-

---

3. For the account of Mathews's action, including Hawke's personal share in it, see *ante*, pp. 21-47.

edly, of course, it is true that the personal equation, as always, made itself felt, but here as intensifying an evil which had its principal source elsewhere.

Hawke carried Nelson's maxim into effect. Upon the signal for battle he took his own ship into close action with the antagonist allotted to him by the order of the fleet; but after beating her out of the line he looked round for more work to do. Seeing then that several of the British vessels had not come within point-blank, but, through professional timidity, or over-cautious reverence for the line of battle, were engaging at long range a single Spaniard, he quitted his own position, brought her also to close quarters, and after an obstinate contest, creditable to both parties, forced her to surrender. She was the only ship to haul down her flag that day, and her captain refused to surrender his sword to any but Hawke, whom alone he accepted as his vanquisher.

A generation or two later Hawke's conduct in this matter would have drawn little attention; it would not have been exceptional in the days of St. Vincent and Nelson, nor even in that of Howe. At the time of its occurrence, it was not only in sharp contrast with much that happened on the same field of battle, but it was somewhat contrary to rule. It possessed so far the merit of originality; and that on the right side,—the side of fighting. As in all active life, so in war a man is more readily pardoned for effecting too much than too little; and it was doubly so here, because it was evident from the behaviour of his peers that he must expect no backing in the extra work he took upon himself. Their aloofness emphasized his forwardness; and the fact that through the withdrawal of his admiral for the night, the prize was ultimately retaken, together with an officer and seamen he had placed on board, fixed still further attention upon the incident, in which Hawke's action was the one wholly creditable feature.

The effect of the battle upon his fortunes was summed up in a phrase. When his first lieutenant was sent to report the loss of the prize-crew to Rear-Admiral Rowley, the commander of the division, the latter replied, among other things, that "he had not been well acquainted with Captain Hawke before, but he should now be well acquainted with him from his behaviour."

Like Nelson at St. Vincent, Hawke was now revealed, not to the navy only but to the nation,—"through his behaviour." Somewhat exceptionally, the king personally took knowledge of him, and stood by him. George II. paid most interested attention to the particulars elicited by the Courts-Martial,—a fact which doubtless contributed to make him so sternly unyielding in the case of Byng, twelve years later. To the king Hawke became "my captain;" and his influence was directly used when, in a flag promotion in 1747, some in the Admiralty proposed to include Hawke in the retirement of senior captains, which was a common incident in such cases. "I will not have Hawke 'yellowed,'" was the royal *fiat*; a yellow admiral being the current phrase for one set aside from further active employment.

Such were the circumstances under which Hawke first received experience of the fighting conditions of the navy. Whatever his previous attitude towards accepted traditions of professional practice, this no doubt loosened the fetters; for they certainly never constrained him in his subsequent career. He remained in the Mediterranean fleet, generally upon detached services in command of divisions of ships, until the end of 1745. Returning then to England, he saw no further active service until he became a Rear-Admiral—of the White—on July 15, 1747.

The promotions being numerous, Hawke's seniority as captain carried him well up the list of rear-admirals, and he was immediately employed; hoisting his flag July 22nd. He then became second to Sir Peter Warren, commander-in-chief of the "Western Squadron." This cruised in the Bay of Biscay, from Ushant to Finisterre, to intercept the naval divisions, and the accompanying convoys of merchant and transport ships, with which the French were then seeking to maintain their colonial empire in North America and in India: an empire already sorely shaken, and destined to fall finally in the next great war.

Hawke was now in the road of good luck, pure and unadulterated. His happy action in capturing the *Poder* illustrates indeed opportunity improved; but it was opportunity of the every day sort, and it is the merit that seized it, rather than the opportunity itself, that strikes the attention. The present case was different.

A young rear-admiral had little reason to hope for independent command; but Warren, a well-tried officer, possessing the full confidence of the First Lord, Anson, himself a master in the profession, was in poor health, and for that reason had applied for Hawke to be "joined with him in the command," apparently because he was the one flag-officer immediately available. He proposed that Hawke should for the present occasion take his place, sail with a few ships named, and with them join the squadron, then at sea in charge of a captain. Anson demurred at first, on the ground of Hawke's juniority,—he was forty-two,—and Warren, while persisting in his request, shares the doubt; for he writes:

> I observe what you say about the ships abroad being under so young an officer. I am, and have been uneasy about it, though I hope he will do well, *and it could not then be avoided*.

Anson, however, was not fixed in his opposition; for Warren continued:

> From your letter I have so little reason to doubt his being put under my command, that I have his instructions all ready; and he is prepared to go at a moment's notice.

The instructions were issued the following day, August 8th, and on the 9th Hawke sailed. But while there was in this so much of luck, he was again to show that he was not one to let occasion slip. Admiral Farragut is reported to have said, "Every man has *one* chance." It depends upon himself whether he is by it made or marred. Burrish and Hawke toed the same line on the morning of February 22nd, and they had had that day at least equal opportunity.

Hawke's adequacy to his present fortune betrayed itself again in a phrase to Warren:

> I have nothing so much at heart as the faithful discharge of my duty, and in such manner as will give satisfaction both to the Lords of the Admiralty and yourself. This shall ever be my utmost ambition, and *no lucre of profit, or other views*, shall induce me to act otherwise.

Not prize-money; but honour, through service. And this in

fact not only ruled his thought but in the moment of decision inspired his act. Curiously enough, however, he was here at odds with the spirit of Anson and of Warren. The latter, in asking Hawke's employment, said the present cruise was less important than the one to succeed it, "for the galleons"—the Spanish treasure-ships—"make it a general rule to come home late in the fall or winter." Warren by prize-money and an American marriage was the richest commoner in England, and Anson it was that had captured the great galleon five years before, to his own great increase; but it was Hawke who, acknowledging a letter from Warren, as this cruise was drawing to its triumphant close, wrote:

> With respect to the galleons, as it is uncertain when they will come home and *likewise impossible for me to divide my force in the* present necessitous condition of the ships under my command, I must lay aside all thoughts of them during this cruise.

In this unhesitating subordination of pecuniary to military considerations we see again the temper of Nelson, between whom and Hawke there was much community of spirit, especially in their independence of ordinary motives and standards. "Not that I despise money," wrote Nelson near the end of a career in which he had never known ease of circumstances; "quite the contrary, I wish I had a hundred thousand pounds this moment;" but "I keep the frigates about me, for I know their value in the day of battle, and compared with that day, what signifies any prizes they might take?" Yet he had his legal share in every such prize.

The opening of October 14th, the eighth day after Hawke's letter to Warren just quoted, brought him the sight of his reward. At seven that morning, the fleet being then some four hundred miles west of La Rochelle in France, a number of sails were seen in the southeast. Chase was given at once, and within an hour it was evident, from the great crowd of vessels, that it was a large convoy outward-bound which could only be enemies. It was in fact a fleet of three hundred French merchantmen, under the protection of eight ships-of-the-line and one of fifty guns, commanded by Commodore L'Etenduère. The force then with

Hawke were twelve of-the-line and two of fifty guns. Frigates and lighter vessels of course accompanied both fleets. The average size and armament of the French vessels were considerably greater than those of the British; so that, although the latter had an undoubted superiority, it was far from as great as the relative numbers would indicate. Prominent British officers of that day claimed that a French sixty-gun ship was practically the equal of a British seventy-four. In this there may have been exaggeration; but they had good opportunity for judging, as many French ships were captured.

When L'Etenduère saw that he was in the presence of a superior enemy, he very manfully drew out his ships of war from the mass, and formed them in order of battle, covering the convoy, which he directed to make its escape accompanied by one of the smaller ships-of-the-line with the light cruisers. He contrived also to keep to windward of the approaching British. With so strong a force interposed, Hawke saw that no prize-money was easily to be had, but for that fortune his mind was already prepared. He first ordered his fleet to form order of battle; but finding time was thereby lost he changed the signal to that for a general chase, which freed the faster sailers to use their utmost speed and join action with the enemy, secure of support in due time by their consorts as they successively came up.

Half an hour before noon the leading British reached the French rear, already under short canvas. The admiral then made signal to engage, and the battle began. As the ships under fire reduced sail, the others overtook them, passed by the unengaged side and successively attacked from rear to van. As Hawke himself drew near, Rodney's ship, the *Eagle*, having her wheel and much of her rigging shot away, was for the time unmanageable and fell twice on board the flag-ship, the *Devonshire*, driving her to leeward, and so preventing her from close action with the French flag-ship *Tonnant*, of eighty guns, a force far exceeding that of the *Devonshire*, which had but sixty-six.

> This prevented our attacking *Le Monarque*, 74, and the *Tonnant*, within any distance to do execution. However we attempted both, especially the latter. While we were engaged

with her, the breechings of all our lower-deck guns broke, and the guns flew fore and aft, which obliged us to shoot ahead, for our upper guns could not reach her.

The breaking of the breechings—the heavy ropes which take the strain of the guns' recoil—was doubtless accelerated by the undue elevation necessitated by the extreme range. The collision with the *Eagle* was one of the incidents common to battle, but it doubtless marred the completeness of the victory. Of the eight French ships engaged, six were taken; two, the *Tonnant* and her next astern, escaped, though the former was badly mauled.

Despite the hindrance mentioned, Hawke's personal share in the affair was considerable, through the conspicuous activity of the flag-ship. Besides the skirmish at random shot with the *Tonnant*, she engaged successively the *Trident*, 64, and the *Terrible*, 74, both which were among the prizes. He was entirely satisfied also with the conduct of all his captains,—save one. The freedom of action permitted to them by the general chase, with the inspiring example of the admiral himself, was nobly used.

> Captain Harland of the *Tilbury*, 60, observing that the *Tonnant* fired single guns at us in order to dismast us, stood on the other tack, between her and the *Devonshire*, and gave her a very smart fire.

It was no small gallantry for a 60 thus to pass close under the undiverted broadside of an 80,—nearly double her force,—and that without orders; and Hawke recognized the fact by this particular notice in the despatch. With similar initiative, as the *Tonnant* and *Intrépide* were seen to be escaping, Captain Saunders of the Yarmouth, 64, pursued them on his own motion, and was accompanied, at his suggestion, by the sixty-gun ships of Rodney and of Saumarez. A detached action of an hour followed, in which Saumarez fell. The enemy escaped, it is true; but that does not impeach the judgment, nor lessen the merits, of the officers concerned, for their ships were both much smaller and more injured than those they attacked. Harland and Saunders became distinguished admirals; of Rodney it is needless to say the same.

In his report of the business, Hawke used a quaint but very expressive phrase:

> As the enemy's ships were large, *they took a great deal of drubbing*, and (consequently) lost all their masts, except two, who had their foremasts left. This has obliged me to lay-to for these two days past, in order to put them into condition to be brought into port, as well as our own, which have suffered greatly.

Ships large in tonnage were necessarily also ships large in scantling, heavy ribbed, thick-planked, in order to bear their artillery; hence also with sides not easy to be pierced by the weak ordnance of that time. They were in a degree armoured ships, though from a cause differing from that of today; hence much "drubbing" was needed, and the prolongation of the drubbing entailed increase of incidental injury to spars and rigging, both their own and those of the enemy. Nor was the armour idea, directly, at all unrecognized even then; for we are told of the *Real Felipe* in Mathews's action, that, being so weakly built that she could carry only twenty-four-pounders on her lower deck, she had been "fortified in the most extraordinary surprising manner; her sides being lined four or five foot thick everywhere with junk or old cables to hinder the shot from piercing."

It has been said that the conduct of one captain fell under Hawke's displeasure. At a Council of War called by him after the battle, to establish the fitness of the fleet to pursue the convoy, the other captains objected to sitting with Captain Fox of the *Kent*, until he had cleared himself from the imputation of misbehaviour in incidents they had noticed. Hawke was himself dissatisfied with Fox's failure to obey a signal, and concurred in the objection. On the subsequent trial, the Court expressly cleared the accused of cowardice, but found him guilty of certain errors of judgment, and specifically of leaving the *Tonnant* while the signal for close action was flying. As the *Tonnant* escaped, the implication of accountability for that result naturally follows. For so serious a consequence the sentence only was that he be dismissed his ship, and, although never again employed, he was retired two years after as a rear-admiral. It was becoming increasingly evident that error of judgment is an elastic phrase which can be made to cover all degrees of faulty action, from the mistakes to which every man is liable and the most faithful cannot always escape, to conduct wholly incompatible with professional efficiency or even manly honour.

The case of Fox was one of many occurring at about this period, which, however differing in detail between themselves, showed that throughout the navy, both in active service before the enemy, and in the more deliberate criteria of opinion which influence Courts-Martial, there was a pronounced tendency to lowness of standard in measuring officer-like conduct and official responsibility for personal action; a misplaced leniency, which regarded failure to do the utmost with indulgence, if without approval. In the stringent and awful emergencies of war too much is at stake for such easy tolerance. Error of judgment is one thing; error of conduct is something very different, and with a difference usually recognizable. To style errors of conduct "errors of judgment" denies, practically, that there are standards of action external to the individual, and condones official misbehaviour on the ground of personal incompetency. Military standards rest on demonstrable facts of experience, and should find their sanction in clear professional opinion. So known, and so upheld, the unfortunate man who falls below them, in a rank where failure may work serious harm, has only himself to blame; for it is his business to reckon his own capacity before he accepts the dignity and honours of a position in which the interests of the nation are entrusted to his charge.

An uneasy consciousness of these truths, forced upon the Navy and the Government by widespread shortcomings in many quarters—of which Mathews's battle was only the most conspicuous instance—resulted in a very serious modification of the Articles of War, after the peace. Up to 1748 the articles dealing with misconduct before the enemy, which had been in force since the first half of the reign of Charles II., assigned upon conviction the punishment of "death, or other punishment, as the circumstances of the offence shall deserve and the Court-

Martial shall judge fit." After the experiences of this war, the last clause was omitted. Discretion was taken away. Men were dissatisfied, whether justly or not, with the use of their discretion made by Courts-Martial, and deprived them of it. In the United States Navy, similarly, at the beginning of the Civil War, the Government was in constant struggle with Courts-Martial to impose sentences of severity adequate to the offence; leaving the question of remission, or of indulgence, to the executive. These facts are worthy of notice, for there is a facile popular impression that Courts-Martial err on the side of stringency. The writer, from a large experience of naval Courts, upon offenders of many ranks, is able to affirm that it is not so. Marryat, in his day, midway between the two periods here specified, makes the same statement, in "Peter Simple."

"There is an evident inclination towards the prisoner; every allowance and every favour granted him, and no legal quibbles attended to." It may be added that the inconvenience and expense of assembling Courts make the executive chary of this resort, which is rarely used except when the case against an accused is pretty clear,—a fact that easily gives rise to a not uncommon assertion, that Courts-Martial are organized to convict.

This is the antecedent history of Byng's trial and execution. There had been many examples of weak and inefficient action— of distinct errors of conduct—such as Byng was destined to illustrate in the highest rank and upon a large scale, entailing an unusual and conspicuous national disaster; and the offenders had escaped, with consequences to themselves more or less serious, but without any assurance to the nation that the punishment inflicted was raising professional standards, and so giving reasonable certainty that the like derelictions would not recur. Hence it came to pass, in 1749, not amid the agitations of war and defeats, but in profound peace, that the article was framed under which Byng suffered:

> Every person in the fleet, who through cowardice, negligence, or disaffection, shall in time of action, ... not do his utmost to take or destroy every ship which it shall be his duty to engage; and to assist all and every of His

Majesty's ships, or those of His allies, which it shall be his duty to assist and relieve, ... being convicted thereof by sentence of a Court-Martial, shall suffer death.

Let it therefore be observed, as historically certain, that the execution of Byng in 1757 is directly traceable to the war of 1739-1747. It was not determined, as is perhaps generally imagined, by an obsolete statute revived for the purpose of a judicial murder; but by a recent Act, occasioned, if not justified, by circumstances of marked national humiliation and injury. The offences specified are those of which repeated instances had been recently given; and negligence is ranked with more positive faults, because in practice equally harmful and equally culpable. Every man in active life, whatever his business, knows this to be so.

At the time his battle with L'Etenduère was fought, Hawke was actually a commander-in-chief; for Warren, through his disorder increasing upon him, had resigned the command, and Hawke had been notified of the fact. Hence there did not obtain in his case the consideration, so absurdly advanced for limiting Nelson's reward after the Nile, that he was acting under the orders of a superior several hundred miles away. Nevertheless, Hawke, like Nelson later, was then a new man,—"a young officer;" and the honour he received, though certainly adequate for a victory over a force somewhat inferior, was not adequate when measured by that given to Anson, the First Lord of the Admiralty, for a much less notable achievement six months before. Anson was raised to the peerage; Hawke was only given the Order of the Bath, the ribbon which Nelson coveted, because a public token, visible to all, that the wearer had done distinguished service. It was at that period a much greater distinction than it afterwards became, through the great extension in numbers and the division into classes. He was henceforth Sir Edward Hawke; and shortly after the Peace of Aix-la-Chapelle, signed April 30, 1748, another flag-promotion raised him to the rank of Vice-Admiral, of the Blue Squadron.

Such rank, accompanied by such recognized merit, insured that he should thenceforth always command in chief; and so it was, with a single brief interval due to a very special and exceptional cause to be hereafter related. During the years of peace, from 1748 to 1755, his employment was mainly on shore, in dockyard command, which carried with it incidentally a good deal of presiding over Courts-Martial. This duty, in his hands, could hardly fail to raise professional standards, with all the effect that precedents, established by the rulings and decisions of Courts, civil and military, exert upon practice. Such a period, however, affords but little for narration, either professional or personal, except when the particular occupations mentioned are the subject of special study. General interest they cannot be said to possess.

But while thus unmarked on the biographical side, historically these years were pregnant with momentous events, which not only affected the future of great nations then existing, but were to determine for all time the extension or restriction of their social systems and political tendencies in vast distant regions yet unoccupied by civilized man, or still in unstable political tenure. The balance of world power, in short, was in question, and that not merely as every occurrence, large or small, contributes its something to a general result, but on a grand and decisive scale. The phrase "world politics," if not yet invented, characterizes the issues then eminently at stake, though they probably were not recognized by contemporaries, still blinded by the traditions which saw in Europe alone the centre of political interests.

To realize the conditions, and their bearing upon a future which has become our present, we should recall that in 1748 the British Empire, as we understand the term, did not exist; that Canada and Louisiana—meaning by the latter the whole undefined region west of the Mississippi—were politically and socially French; that between them the wide territory from the Alleghenies to the Mississippi was claimed by France, and the claim vigorously contested not only by Great Britain herself, but by the thirteen British colonies which became the United States of America; that in India the representatives of both mother countries were striving for mastery, not merely through influence in the councils of native rulers, but by actual territorial sway, and that the chances seemed on the whole to favour France.

In the great struggle for Anglo-Saxon predominance, which

had begun under William III., but was now approaching its crisis and final decision in the Seven Years War, the determining factor was to be the maritime strength of Great Britain. It is, therefore, the distinctive and distinguished significance of Hawke's career that during so critical a period he not only was the most illustrious and able officer of her navy—the exponent of her sea-power—but that by the force of his personality he chiefly shaped the naval outcome. He carried on the development of naval warfare, revolutionized ideas, raised professional standards, and thereby both affected the result in his own time, and perpetuated an influence, the effect of which was to be felt in the gigantic contests of later days. In this eminent particular, which involves real originality, no sea officer of the eighteenth century stands with him; in this respect only he and Nelson, who belongs rather to the nineteenth, are to be named together.

In the years of nominal peace, 1748-1755, the Navy of Great Britain was permitted by a politically cautious Government to decline much in power; but there was compensation in the fact that that of France drooped equally. In both countries there was then, as there has been ever since, a party opposed to over-sea enterprise. "The partisans of the Ministry," wrote Walpole in 1755, "d———n the Plantations and ask if we are to involve ourselves in a war for them." The French government underwent a like revulsion of feeling as regarded India, and in 1754 recalled Dupleix in mid-career, in order to quiet the remonstrances of Great Britain. It would be irrelevant, were it not signally instructive, to remark that both nations passed under the influence of the same ideas a hundred years later. In the middle of the nineteenth century, the preponderant expression in England was that the colonies were unprofitable encumbrances, and, if occasion arose, should be encouraged to separate rather than urged to remain; while France, through whatever motive, at a critical moment abandoned the field in Egypt, by refusing joint action. It is, therefore, probably the result of a true national genius, asserting itself above temporary aberrations, that the close of the nineteenth century saw France wholly excluded, politically, from Egypt, as she had before been from India, and Great Britain involved in an expensive war, the aim of which was the preservation of the imperial system, in the interest not only of the mother country, but of the colonies as well.

And that it was in the interest of her colonies was precisely the all important part which differentiated the Seven Years War in its day, and the South African War in our day, from the struggle, so disastrous to the Empire, that is known as the American Revolution. "There is no repose for our thirteen colonies," wrote Franklin a hundred and fifty years ago, "so long as the French are masters of Canada."

"There is no repose for British colonists in South Africa," was the virtual assertion of Natal and the Cape Colony, "so long as the Boer political methods are maintained in the Transvaal with the pledged support of the Orange Free State." Irreconcilable differences of political and social systems, when brought into close contact, involve irrepressible conflict, and admit of no lasting solution except the subjugation and consequent submersion of one or the other.

Such a final settlement was attained in North America and in India by the Seven Years War. The full results thereof even we of this day have not yet seen; for who can yet predict the effect upon the question of the Pacific and of China, that by this war was assured the dominance of the Anglo-Saxon political and legal tradition over the whole American continent north of the tropics, and that the same tradition shall, for a future yet indeterminate, decisively shape the course of India and the Philippines? The preceding war, 1739-1748, had been substantially inconclusive on the chief points at issue, because European questions intervening had diverted the attention of both France and Great Britain from America and from India; and the exhaustion of both had led to a perfunctory compact, in which the underlying contention was substantially ignored in order to reach formal agreement. That the French conquest of Madras, in India, was yielded in exchange for Louisburg and Cape Breton Island, which the American colonists had won for England, typifies concisely the *status quo* to which both parties were willing momentarily to revert, while they took breath before the inevitable renewal of the strife, with added fury, a few years later; but then upon its proper scene, the sea and the over-sea regions in dispute.

In this great arbitrament Hawke was at once called forth to play his part. In 1754 diplomatic contention had become acrimonious, and various events showed that the moment of open conflict was approaching. The squadron in India was then considerably increased. In the beginning of 1755 Hawke was again afloat to command the Channel Fleet, the operations of which extended ordinarily from the Channel, over the Bay of Biscay, to Cape Finisterre. A naval force was collecting at the same time at Portsmouth, under Boscawen, to counteract the preparations the French were known to be making in North America. It sailed soon afterwards, with orders to intercept a squadron convoying reinforcements for Canada; and on the 8th of June two of these ships were captured off the mouth of the St. Lawrence, the remainder escaping under cover of a fog. In July Hawke went out, with instructions to take any French ships-of-the-line that he might meet; and in August he was further directed to send into port French ships of every kind, merchant and other, that he might encounter. Before the end of the year three hundred trading vessels, valued at $6,000,000, had been thus seized. War had not yet been declared, but the captured vessels were held, as on other occasions before and after, as hostages to await the settlement of existing difficulties.

The French government protested of course, and recalled its ambassador, but it did not proceed to formal hostilities. A great stroke was in preparation at Toulon, which could be covered for a while by diplomatic correspondence, coupled with angry demonstrations on the Atlantic and Channel coasts. On the 10th of April, 1756, twelve French ships-of-the-line and fifteen thousand troops sailed for Minorca, then a British possession, and in the absence of a hostile fleet effected a landing without opposition. The British cabinet having taken alarm too late, Admiral Byng had sailed from Portsmouth, with ten ships, only three days before the French left Toulon; when he arrived off Port Mahon, six weeks later, a practicable breach in the works had already been made. The French fleet was cruising outside in support of the siege, and Byng, whose force had been increased to thirteen ships, engaged it on May 20. The action was in itself indecisive; but, upon the opinion of a council of war that nothing more could be done, Byng retired to Gibraltar. The result to him personally is well known. Port Mahon surrendered on June 28. War had by this been declared; by Great Britain on the 17th of May, and by France June 20, 1756.

When the news of Byng's retreat was received in England, Hawke was sent out to supersede him. He went only personally, accompanied by a second in command, but with no fleet, and with sealed instructions. Opening these when he reached Gibraltar, he found orders to send home Byng and his second in command, and to institute an inquiry into the conduct of the captains, suspending any one found "not to have acted with due spirit and vigour." An investigation of this kind would enable him to form an opinion of Byng's own conduct even more exact and authentic than his other official opportunities for personal intercourse with the chief actors, but he must have refrained with much discretion from expressing his judgment on the affair in such way as to reach the public ear. It was stated in the *Gentleman's Magazine*, in 1766, that an inquiry was provoked in the House of Commons, shortly after these events, by Pitt, who took Byng's side; but that Hawke, being a member of the House, denied some of Pitt's allegations as to the inadequacy of Byng's fleet, on the strength of his own personal observation after taking over the command. Thereupon, so the account says, the categorical test question, the *argumentum ad hominem*, was put to him whether with Byng's means he could have beat the enemy; and the manner of the first Pitt, in thus dealing with an opponent in debate, can be imagined from what we know of him otherwise. Whether the story be true or not, Hawke was not a man to be so overborne, and the reply related is eminently characteristic, "By the grace of God, he would have given a good account of them." Whatever the reason, there seems little doubt that Pitt did not like Hawke; but the latter was at once too independent to care, and too necessary to be discarded.

He remained in the Mediterranean only six months, returning to England in January, 1757. His tenure of this command was marked by an incident which exemplifies the vigorous exercise of power frequent in naval commanders, in the days when neither steam nor telegraph existed to facilitate reference home for instructions; when men with their strong right arms redressed on the spot what they thought a wrong. A British ship carrying supplies to Gibraltar, where Hawke was then lying, was captured by a French privateer and taken into the Spanish port of Algeciras, on the opposite side of the bay. Her surrender was demanded from the governor of the port, Spain being then neutral; but, being refused, the admiral sent the boats of the squadron and cut her out. This being resisted by the Spanish forts, a hundred British seamen were killed or wounded. On the admiral's return home, Pitt is reported to have told him that he thought he would himself have acted in the same way, but would have made some concession afterwards. Hawke replied that his duty, having the country's force in his hands, was to act as he had,—not to make concessions; but that the Ministry could deal with the case subsequently as it thought fit. In other words, as in joint operations with the army, later in the year, he took the ground that the land officers were the judges of their own business, but that he would see them put safe on shore, as a first step; so in a matter affecting national honour, as he conceived it, he would do the seaman's part and redress the injury, after which the civil authority could arrange with the other party. The known details of this transaction are not full enough to permit a decided opinion as to how far the admiral was justified in his action, judged even by the international law of the day. It was not necessarily a breach of neutrality to admit a belligerent with her prize; but it would have been, had the French ship gone out from Algeciras, seized her prey, and returned with it. Whatever the facts, however, the episode illustrates interestingly the spirit of Hawke himself, and of the service of that day, as well as his characteristic independence towards superiors when he felt himself right.

From this time forward Hawke's service was confined to the Channel Fleet. This was, during that war, the post for the most capable of British officers; for, while the matter at stake was oversea predominance and conquest, yet both these depended upon the communications of the French colonies and distant possessions with the mother country. The source of all their strength, the one base indispensable to their operations, was the coast of France; to close exit from this was therefore to strike at the root. This was much less true for the colonies of Great Britain, at least in America; their numbers, and resources in every way, were so far superior to those of Canada that they needed only to be preserved from interference by the navy of France,—an end also furthered by the close watch of the French ports. This blockade, as it is often, but erroneously, styled, Hawke was the first to maintain thoroughly and into the winter months; and in so doing he gave an extension to the practice of naval warfare, which amounted to a veritable revolution in naval strategy. The conception was one possible only to a thorough seaman, who knew exactly and practically what ships could do; one also in whom professional knowledge received the moral support of strong natural self-confidence,—power to initiate changes, to assume novel responsibility, through the inner assurance of full adequacy to bear it.

All this Hawke had. The method, therefore, the holding the sea, and the exposure of heavy ships to weather before thought impossible, was well within the range of his ability,—of his native and acquired faculties; but it is due to him to recognize the intellectual force, the originality, which lifted him above the accepted tradition of his predecessors, and by example transmitted to the future a system of warfare that then, as well as in his own hands, was to exercise a decisive effect upon the course of history. It is also to be remembered that he took this weighty step with instruments relatively imperfect, and greatly so. The bottoms of ships were not yet coppered; in consequence they fouled very rapidly, the result of which was loss of speed. This meant that much greater power, press of canvas, was needed to force them through the water, and that they had to be sent frequently into port to be cleaned. Thus they were less able than ships of later days to overtake an enemy, or to keep off a lee shore, while more intricate administration and more ships were required to maintain the efficiency of the squadron by a system of reliefs. Hawke noted also another difficulty,—the fatigue of the crews in cleaning their ships' bottoms. It was even more important to success, he said, to restore the seaman, worn by cruising, by a few days quiet and sleep in port, than to clean thoroughly at the expense of exhausting them. "If the enemy should slip out and run," he writes, "we must follow as fast as we can." Details such as these, as well as the main idea, must be borne in mind, if due credit is to be given to Hawke for one of the most decisive advances ever made in the practice of naval campaigning.

Some time, however, was to elapse before the close watch of the French ports became a leading feature in the naval policy of the government. The early disasters of the war had forced the king, after much resistance, finally to accept the first Pitt as the leading minister of the Crown, in June, 1757. Pitt's military purpose embraced two principal objects: 1, the establishment of the British colonial system by the destruction of that of France, which involved as a necessary precedent the control of the sea by a preponderant navy; and, 2, the support of Frederic of Prussia, then engaged in his deadly contest with the combined armies of France, Austria, and Russia. Frederic's activity made a heavy drain upon the troops and the treasure of France, preventing her by just so much from supporting her colonies and maintaining her fleet; but, heavily outnumbered as he was, it was desirable to work all possible diversion in his favour by attacks elsewhere. This Pitt proposed to do by a series of descents upon the French coast, compelling the enemy to detach a large force from before the Prussian king to protect their own shores.

As far as the home naval force was concerned, the years 1757 and 1758 were dominated by this idea of diversion in favour of Frederic the Great. From the general object of these enterprises, the army was necessarily the principal agent; but the navy was the indispensable auxiliary. Hawke's association with them is interesting chiefly as illustrative of professional character; for there was little or no room for achievement of naval results. The first expedition in which he was concerned was that against Rochefort in 1757. This, though now long forgotten, occasioned by its failure a storm of contemporary controversy. Whatever chances of success it may under any circumstances have had were lost beforehand, owing to the lateness of the season—June—in which Pitt took office. Preparation began at the moment when execution was due. The troops which should have sailed in early summer could not, from delays apparently unavoidable under the conditions, get away before September 10. Hawke himself hoisted his flag—assumed active command—only on August 15. The previous administration was responsible for whatever defect in general readiness increased this delay; as regards the particular purpose, Pitt's government was at fault in attempting at all an undertaking which, begun so late in the year, could not expect success under the notorious inadequacy of organization bequeathed to him by his predecessors. But there will always be found at the beginning of a war, or upon a change of commanders, a restless impatience to do something, to make a showing of results, which misleads the judgment of those in authority, and commonly ends, if not in failure, at least in barren waste of powder and shot.

Not the least of the drawbacks under which the enterprise laboured was extremely defective information—especially hydrographic. The character of the coast, the places suited for landing, the depths of water, and the channels, were practically unknown. Hence a necessity for reconnoissances, pregnant of indefinite delay, as might have been foreseen. Among Hawke's memoranda occur the words, "Not to undertake anything without good pilots." The phrase is doubly significant, for he was not a man to worry needlessly about pilots, knowing that pilots look not to military results, but merely to their own responsibility not to take the ground; and it shows the total ignorance under which laboured all who were charged with an undertaking that could only succeed as a surprise, executed with unhesitating rapidity. Hawke himself was astounded at finding in Basque Roads, before Rochefort—

> .... a safe spacious road in which all the navy of England, merchant ships included, may ride without the least an-

noyance. Before I came here, the place was represented as very difficult of access, and so narrow that ships could not lie in safety from the forts—nay, *the pilots made many baulks before we came in.*

In fact, want of good pilotage summed up the fault of the expedition, from its inception in the Cabinet throughout all the antecedent steps of consultation and preparation. Pitt's impetuosity doubtless acted as a spur to laggards, but it was accompanied by a tendency to overbearing insolence that not infrequently browbeats cautious wisdom. When applied to a man like Hawke, strong in natural temper and in conscious mastery of his profession, the tone characteristic of Pitt provokes an equally resolute self-assertion, as far removed from subjection as it is from insubordination; but friendship becomes impossible, and even co-operation difficult.

Throughout all Hawke kept his head, and made no serious mistake; but he accepts no unmerited censures. Seeing that the transports are not enough for the healthful carriage of the troops, he so represents it. The government, already impatient at any report of defects, hopes that things are now arranged to his *satisfaction*. He says:

> I am astonished at this expression, it is my duty to represent defects, but I am *satisfied* with any decision *you* make. I have received your letter signifying His Majesty's directions to use the utmost diligence in embarking the troops and getting to sea. As I cannot doubt my letter of Sunday being immediately communicated to you, I should have expected that *before yours was sent* His Majesty would have been fully satisfied that I needed no spur in executing his orders.

As Hawke and Anson—the First Lord—were friends, there can be little doubt that we see here a firm protest against the much lauded tone to which the efficiency of the British army and navy under Pitt has been too exclusively attributed. It was in the civil administration, the preparation that underlies military success, which being at home was under his own eye, that Pitt's energy was beneficially felt, and also in his prompt recognition of fit instruments; but he had no need to discover Hawke or Boscawen. He might as well be thought to have discovered the sun.

In discharging his part of the expedition Hawke's course is consistent and clear. It must in the first place be recognized that such enterprises are of secondary importance, and do not warrant the risks which are not only justifiable but imperative when a decisive issue is at stake. Hawke's heroic disregard of pilotage difficulties at Quiberon, in 1759, would have been culpable temerity at Basque Roads, in 1757. But, save delays on this account, no time is lost by him. When the decision to land is reached, he is clear as to the possibility of landing; but when the generals think it impossible to effect certain results, he replies that is their business, on which he does not pretend to judge. In his evidence before the Court afterwards, he said, "Whether they should land or not, he constantly thought it the part of the generals to determine. He could not but suppose they were infinitely better judges of their own business than he could be." Their conduct was marked by vacillations strange to him, and which apparently displeased him; the troops being, on one occasion, embarked in the boats for some hours, and yet returning to the ships without proceeding. He then addressed a formal letter to the commanding general, saying that if he had no further operation to propose the fleet would return at once to England, and he declined to attend a Council of War to decide either of these points. The Army should decide, alone, whether it could effect anything by landing; if not, he, without asking counsel, would stay no longer. On October 7th he reached Spithead.

Pitt, who had espoused Byng's cause against the previous administration, followed its precedent in throwing the blame on the military and naval leaders. In Parliament, he "declared solemnly his belief that there was a determined resolution, both in the naval and military commanders, against any vigorous exertion of the national power." For far less than this accusation Byng had been condemned; but in fact the fault at Rochefort lay clearly on those who issued the orders,—upon the Cabinet; upon the character of the expedition itself,—a great risk for a secondary and doubtful object; upon the inconsiderate haste which disregarded alike the season and the inadequate knowledge; upon defective preparation in the broadest sense of the words. Diversions, in truth, are feints, in which the utmost smoke with the least fire is the object. Carried farther, they entail disaster; for they rest on no solid basis of adequate force, but upon successful deception. Pitt's angry injustice met with its due rebuke the next year at St. Cas. It can scarcely be doubted that words such as those quoted were responsible, in part at least, for the disastrous issue of that diversion, the story of which belongs, if to the navy at all, to the life of Howe.

That Hawke resented this language can scarcely be doubted, and none the less that he evidently himself felt that something might have been attempted by the troops. He was clear of fault in his own consciousness; but in the general censure he was involved with his associates—known, so to say, by his friends, implicated in the meshes of a half-truth, where effort to clear one's self results in worse entanglement. He had the manly cast of character which will not struggle for self-vindication; but his suppressed wrath gathered force, until a year later it resulted, upon occasion of official provocation, in an explosion that has not a close parallel in naval history.

He had hoisted his flag again on February 28, 1758. His first service was directed against a French squadron of five ships-of-the-line, fitting at Rochefort to convoy troops for the relief of Louisburg, in Cape Breton Island, then about to be besieged by British and colonial forces. Hawke's observations of the previous year had ascertained the hitherto unknown facilities of Basque Roads for occupation by a fleet and consequent effectual interception of such an expedition. Upon making the land the French vessels were found already in the Roads, therefore soon to sail; but before this superior force of seven ships they cut their cables, and fled across the shoals up the river Charente, on which Rochefort lies. Hawke, instructed by his previous experience, had earnestly but fruitlessly demanded fire-ships and bomb-vessels to destroy the enemy in case they grounded on the flats; which they did, and for some hours lay exposed to such an attack. Not having these means, he had to watch helplessly the process of lightening and towing by which they at last made their escape. He then returned to England, having frustrated the relief expedition but, through defective equipment, not destroyed the vessels. The Admiralty, upon receiving his report of the transaction, made no acknowledgments to him.

Pitt had profited by Hawke's ineffectual request for small vessels and his suffering from the want of them; but he utilized the suggestions in a manner that robbed their author of any share in the results. A squadron of that sort was to be constituted, to operate on the French coast in diversions like that of 1757; but it was to be an independent command, under an officer chosen by the Government without consulting the admiral. To the main fleet was assigned the necessary, but in credit very secondary, office of cruising off Brest, to prevent interruption by the French ships there; to play, in short, the inconspicuous role of a covering force, while the light squadron had the brilliant part of fighting. The officer selected for the latter was Howe, deservedly a favourite of Hawke's, but not therefore acceptable to him as a supplanter in his honours.

The admiral had been for some time superintending the equipment of the vessels for the light division, when, on May 10, 1758, Howe reported to him, bringing his orders. Hawke boiled over at once; and, in a heat evidently beyond his will to control, despatched the following letter, three hours after Howe's arrival.

Portsmouth
7 o'clock p.m. 10th May, 1758

Sir,—About 4 o'clock arrived here Captain Howe, and delivered me their Lordships' order of the 9th. In last September I was sent out to command an expedition under all the disadvantages one could possibly labour under, arising chiefly from my being under the influence of land-officers in Councils of War at sea.[4] Last cruise (March-April, 1758) I went out on a particular service, almost without the least means of performing it. Now every means to ensure success is provided; another is to reap the credit; while it is probable

---

4. By express orders from the Ministry Councils of War had to be held.

that I, with the capital ships, might be ordered to cruise in such a manner as to prevent his failing in this attempt. To fit out his ships for this service I have been kept here,[5] and even now have their Lordships' directions, at least in terms, to obey him. He is to judge of what he wants for his expedition; he is to make his demands, and I am to comply with them. I have therefore directed my flag immediately to be struck, and left their Lordships' orders with Vice-Admiral Holburne. For no consequence that can attend my striking it without orders shall ever outbalance with me the wearing it one moment with discredit. I am, etc.

E. Hawke

It is impossible to justify so extreme a step as abandoning one's command without permission, and especially under circumstances that permitted the orderly course of asking for detachment. Nevertheless, Hawke did well to be angry; and, as is sometimes the case, an injudicious and, in point of occasion, unseemly loss of temper, doubtless contributed to insure for him in the future, to a degree which forbearance or mere remonstrance would not have assured, the consideration essential to his duties. Many will remember the effect produced by Plimsoll's unparliamentary outbreak. The erroneous impression, that admirals and generals fit to be employed at all were to be ridden booted and spurred, needed correction. Hawke had misapprehended the intention of the Government, in so far as believing that the light squadron was to be employed in Basque Roads, the scene of last year's failure; but he was right in thinking that intrusting the enterprise to another, on that occasion his junior, would be a reflection upon himself, intensified by making the command practically independent, while he was limited to the covering duty. Under these circumstances, erroneously imagined by him, the squadron should have been attached to his command, and the particular direction left to him; the Government giving to him, instead of to Howe, the general orders which it issued, and arranging with him beforehand as to the command of the detached squadron.

---

5. An application for four days' leave for private business had been refused.

But even under the actual conditions, of an intention to operate on the western Channel coast of France, it would have been graceful and appropriate to recognize Hawke's eminent past, and recent experience, by keeping under his command the ships he had himself fitted for the service, and directing him to despatch Howe with the necessary instructions. It was as in the Nile campaign, where the general directions were sent to St. Vincent, with a clear expression of the Government's preference for Nelson as the officer to take charge. The intended scene of Howe's operations, if not formally within Hawke's district, was far less distant from Brest than Toulon and Italy were from Cadiz, where St. Vincent covered Nelson's detachment. In the wish for secrecy, perhaps, or perhaps through mere indifference to the effect produced upon Hawke, as a man assumed to need curb and spur, he was left in ignorance, to imagine what he pleased; and this action, succeeding previous neglects and Pitt's imputations of the previous year, elicited an outburst which, while it cannot be justified in its particular manifestation, was in spirit inevitable. A man submissive to such treatment as he had good cause to suspect, would be deficient in the independence of character, and sensitive regard to official reputation, without which he was unfit to command the Channel Fleet.

Hawke was summoned at once to the Admiralty, and in the interview which ensued, as shown by the minutes endorsed on his own letter, his misconception as to the quarter in which Howe was to act afforded standing ground for a compromise. Hawke having committed himself officially, and upon a mistaken premise, the Admiralty had him technically at their mercy; but such a triumph as they could win by disciplining him would be more disastrous than a defeat. He disclaimed resentment towards any person, and reiterated that his action was intended merely to defend his character and honour, which he said—to quote the minute exactly:

> .... were not *so much* touched as he apprehended when the suspicion he had of Mr. Howe's going to Basque Roads arose—from the Lords asking him some days since for a draft of the Roads.

The italics are the present writer's; but the words as they stand would indicate that he did not yield his view of the matter in general, nor leave hearers under any doubt as to how far he could safely be treated with contumely or slight. There can be little doubt that the substantial result was to strengthen his position in the exacting duty that lay before him in the following year.

The whole business was then salved over by the First Lord, Anson, taking command of the Channel Fleet for the particular occasion. Hawke accompanied him as second in command, while Howe went his way with the light squadron and the troops. Both divisions sailed on the 1st of June. On the 18th our admiral was so unwell with a severe fever and cold—a complaint to which he was much subject—that he had to ask to be sent into port. He went ashore before the end of the month, and remained unemployed till the following May.

The year 1759 is the culminating epoch of Hawke's career. In it occurred the signal triumph of Quiberon Bay, the seal of his genius, significant above all as demonstrating that the ardour of the leader had found fulfilment in his followers, that the spirit of Hawke had become the spirit of the Navy. This year also yielded proof of his great capacity as a seaman and administrator, in the efficient blocking of Brest, prolonged through six months of closest watching into the period of the winter gales, in face of which it had hitherto been thought impossible to keep the sea with heavy ships massed in fleets; for, as he most justly said, in explaining the necessity of maintaining the rendezvous fixed by him, "A single ship may struggle with a hard gale of wind when a squadron cannot. In working against a strong westerly gale in the Channel, where it cannot make very long stretches,"—because it finds shores and shoals on either side,—"it must always by wearing lose ground, but more especially if it should so blow as to put it past carrying sail." The method used by Hawke was not only an innovation on all past practice, but, as has before been said, constituted the pattern whereon were framed the great blockades of the Napoleonic period, which strangled both the naval efficiency and the commercial and financial resources of the Empire. These were but developments of Hawke's fine achievement of 1759; the prestige of originality belongs to him. Even their success, with better ships and the improvement of detail always accompanying habit, is foreshadowed by his.

I may safely affirm that, except the few ships that took refuge in Conquet, hardly a vessel of any kind has been able to enter or come out of Brest for four months (ending October 10th). They have been obliged to unload near forty victuallers at Quimperley and carry their cargoes by land to Brest. It must be the fault of the weather, not ours, if any of them escape.

It was suitable indeed that so strenuous and admirable an exhibition of professional ability,—of naval generalship,—alike in strategic combination, tactical disposition, and administrative superintendence, should terminate in a brilliant triumph, at once its fruit and its crown; wherein sedulous and unremittent readiness for instant action, comprehended by few, received a startling demonstration which none could fail to understand. As Nelson was pursued by ignorant sneers before the Nile, so Hawke was burned in effigy by the populace, at the very moment when laborious effort was about to issue in supreme achievement. The victory in either case is less than the antecedent labour, as the crown, after all, is less than the work, the symbol than the fact symbolized.

A brief account of preceding conditions, and of the dispositions maintained to meet them, is therefore necessary to due appreciation of the victory of Quiberon Bay. Although the diversions of 1758 had not very materially aided Frederic of Prussia, they had inflicted distinct humiliation and harassment upon France. This, added to defeat upon the Continent and in North America, had convinced the French Government, as it convinced Napoleon a half-century later, that a determined blow must be struck at England herself as the operative centre upon which rested, and from which proceeded, the most serious detriment to their cause and that of their allies. It was resolved, therefore, to attempt an invasion of England; to the threat of which the English people were always extremely sensitive.

From local conditions the French preparations had to be

made in several separate places; it was the task of the British Navy to prevent the concentration of these different detachments in a joint effort. The troops must embark, of course, from some place near to England; their principal points of assembly were on the Channel, whence they were to cross in flat-boats, and in the Biscay ports, from Brest to the mouth of the Loire. The Bay of Quiberon, from which Hawke's action takes its name, lies between the two latter points. It is sheltered from the full force of the Atlantic gales by a peninsula of the same name, and by some shoals which prolong the barrier to the southward of the promontory.

To cross safely, it was necessary to provide naval protection. To this end squadrons were equipped in Toulon and in Brest. Combined at the latter point, and further strengthened by divisions expected to return from North America, they would constitute a force of very serious consideration in point of numbers. Rochefort also was an element in the problem, though a minor one; for either the small force already there might join the concentration, or, if the port were unwatched, the American or other divisions might get in there, and be at least so much nearer to Brest, or to a neighbouring point of assembly, as Quiberon Bay.

As the French Navy was essential to the French crossing, as its junction was essential to action, as the point of junction was at or near Brest—for there was the district near which the troops were assembling—and as by far the largest detachment was already in Brest, that port became the important centre upon blocking which depended primarily the thwarting of the invasion. If the French Navy succeeded in concentrating at Brest, the first move in the game would be lost. Hawke therefore had the double duty of not allowing the squadron there to get out without fighting, and of closing the entrance to reinforcements. The latter was far the more difficult, and could not be assured beyond the chance of failure, because an on-shore gale, which would carry his fleet into the Channel to avoid being driven on the French coast, would be fair for an outside enemy to run into the port, friendly to him. This actually occurred at a most critical moment, but it could only happen by a combination of circumstances; that is, by the hostile squadron chancing to arrive at a moment when the British had been blown off. If it approached under ordinary conditions of weather it would run into the midst of foes.

The great names of the British Navy were then all afloat in active command. Rodney was before Havre, which he bombarded in the course of the summer, doing a certain amount of damage, harassing the local preparations for invasion, and intercepting vessels carrying supplies to the Brest fleet and coastwise. Boscawen, second only to Hawke, was before Toulon, to hold there the dozen ships-of-the-line under De la Clue, as Hawke was charged to stop the score under Conflans.

In broad conception, Hawke's method was simple and can be easily stated; the difficulty lay in carrying it out. The main body of his force had a rendezvous, so chosen that in violent weather from the westward it could at worst drift up Channel, but usually would have a fair wind for Torbay, a roadstead on the British coast about a hundred miles distant. To the rendezvous the fleet was not tied under ordinary circumstances; it was merely a headquarters which admitted of cruising, but where despatches from home would always find the admiral in person, or news of his whereabouts. Near Brest itself was kept an inshore squadron of three or four ships, which under ordinary circumstances could see the enemy inside, noting his forwardness; for the cannon of the day could not molest a vessel more than a mile from the entrance, while the conditions within of spars and sails indicated to a seaman the readiness or intention to move, to a degree not ascertainable with ships dependent on steam only.

With these dispositions, if a westerly gale came on, the fleet held its ground while it could, but when expedient to go put into Torbay. Owing to the nearness of the two places, the weather, when of a pronounced character, was the same at both. While the wind held to the westward of south, or even at south-southeast, a ship-of-the-line could not beat out from Brest; much less a fleet. The instant the wind went east, fair for exit, the British left Torbay, with certainty of not being too late; for, though the enemy might get out before their return, the east wind would not suffer them to close with the French coast at another point soon enough to avoid a meeting. While in Torbay the time was improved by taking on board stores and provisions; nor was the night's rest at anchor a small consideration for seamen worn with continual cruising.

The practical merits displayed by Hawke in maintaining this simple but arduous service were, first and supremely, the recognition of its possibility, contrary to a tradition heretofore as commonly and as blindly accepted as those of the line-of-battle, and of the proper methods for fleet attack before described. It must be remembered also that in these wars, 1739-1763, for the first time the British Navy found the scene of action, in European waters, to be the Biscay coast of France. In the former great wars of the seventeenth century, French fleets entered the Channel, and pitched battles were fought there and in the North Sea. Thence the contest shifted to the Mediterranean, where the great fleets operated in the later days of William III., and the reign of Anne. Then, too, the heavy ships, like land armies, went into winter quarters. It was by distinguished admirals considered professionally criminal to expose those huge yet cumbrous engines of the nation's power to the buffetings of winter gales, which might unfit them next year to meet the enemy, snugly nursed and restored to vigour in home ports during the same time. The need of periodical refitting and cleaning the bottoms clinched the argument in favour of this seasonable withdrawal from the sea.

With this presumed necessity, attention had not been paid to developing a system of maintenance and refit adapted to the need of a fleet performing what Hawke undertook. In this, of course, there cannot be assigned to him the individuality of merit that may belong to a conception, and does belong to the man who initiates and assumes, as he did, the responsibility for a novel and hazardous course of action. Many agents had to contribute to the forwarding of supplies and repairs; but, while singleness of credit cannot be assumed, priority is justly due to him upon whose shoulders fell not only all blame, in case his enterprise failed, but the fundamental difficulty of so timing the reliefs of the vessels under his command, so arranging the order of rotation in their going and coming as to keep each, as well as the whole body, in a constant condition of highest attainable efficiency—in numbers, in speed, and in health—for meeting the enemy, whose time of exit could not be foreknown. Naturally, too, the man on whom all this fell, and who to the nation would personify success or failure, as the event might be,—terms which to him would mean honour or ruin,—that man, when professionally so competent as Hawke, would be most fruitful in orders and in suggestions to attain the desired end. In this sense there can be no doubt that he was foremost, and his correspondence bears evidence of his preoccupation with the subject.

Into particulars it is scarcely necessary to go. Administrative details are interesting only to specialists. But one quality absolutely essential, and in which most men fail, he manifested in high degree. He feared no responsibility, either towards the enemy, or towards the home authorities. Superior and inferior alike heard plainly from him in case of defects; still more plainly in case of neglect. "It is a matter of indifference to me whether I fight the enemy, should they come out, with an equal number, one ship more, or one ship less."

"I depend not on intelligence from the French ports; what I see I believe, and regulate my conduct accordingly;" a saying which recalls one of Farragut's—

> The officers say I don't believe anything. I certainly believe very little that comes in the shape of reports. They keep everybody stirred up. I mean to be whipped or to whip my enemy, and not to be scared to death.

Agitation, to a very considerable degree, was the condition of Hawke's superiors; to say the least, anxiety strained to the point of approaching panic. But Hawke could have adopted truly as his own Farragut's other words, "I have full confidence in myself and in my judgment,"—that is, of course, in professional matters; and he spoke reassuringly out of the firmness of his self-reliance. "Their Lordships will pardon me for observing that from the present disposition of the squadron I think there is little room for alarm while the weather continues tolerable." Again, a few days later, "Their Lordships may rest assured there is little foundation for the present alarms. While the wind is fair for the enemy's coming out, it is also favourable for our keeping them in; and while we are obliged to keep off they cannot stir." This was in October, when the weather was already wild and the days shortening.

With equally little hesitancy, though without breach of subordination, he overbears the Admiralty when they wish to pay what he considers exaggerated care to cleaning the bottoms, traceable, no doubt, to the prejudices of the Sea Lords.

> If the ships take up a month by cleaning, from the time they leave me to their return, it will be impossible for me to keep up the squadron. The only practicable way is to heel, etc., and confine them to ten days in port for the refreshment of their companies in case they should miss the spring tide.
>
> Their Lordships will give me leave to observe that the relief of the squadron depends more on the refreshment of the ships' companies than on cleaning the ships. By the hurry the latter must be performed in, unless the ship continues a month or five weeks in port, which the present exigency will by no means admit of, the men would be so harassed and fatigued that they would return to me in a worse condition than when they left me. . . . However, I shall endeavour to comply with all their Lordships' directions in such manner as, *to the best of my judgment, will answer their intentions in employing me here.*

The words italicized strike the true note of subordination duly tempered with discretion.

To the Navy Board, a civil adjunct to the Admiralty, but possessed of considerable independent power to annoy officers in active military service, he took a more peremptory tone. He had discharged on his own authority, and for reasons of emergency, a mutinous surgical officer. For this he was taken to task, as Nelson a generation later was rebuked by the same body. "I have to acquaint you," he replied, "that there was no mistake in his being ordered by me to be discharged." He then gives his reasons, and continues:

For the real good of the service I ordered him to be discharged, and his crime noted on his list of pay, for your information. I shall not enter into any dispute with you about my authority as a Commanding Officer, neither do I ever think of inconveniences or prejudices to myself, as a party, according to your insinuations, where the good of the service is concerned.

It must be added that to subordinates he was as liberal with praise as he was with censure, where either was merited; nor did he fail in kindly personal intervention upon due occasion for deserving or unfortunate men. More reserved, apparently, than Nelson, he seems to have been like him sympathetic; and hence it was that, as before observed, it was his spirit that he communicated to the navy rather than a system, admirable as was the strategic system embodied in his methods of blockade. It was by personal influence rather than by formulated precept that Hawke inspired his service, and earned a just claim to be reckoned the greatest force of his century in naval development.

The general conditions being as described, the fighting in the naval campaign of 1759 began in the Mediterranean. On June 8th Boscawen, having driven two French frigates into a fortified bay near Toulon, attacked them with three ships-of-the-line. The attack failed, and the British ships were badly injured; a timely lesson on the general inexpediency of attacking shore batteries with vessels, unless for special and adequate reasons of probable advantage. In July he returned to Gibraltar, to refit and for provisions. In the absence of details, positive criticism is unwarranted; but it is impossible not to note the difference between this step, during summer weather, and the Toulon blockades of Lord St. Vincent, who, when before Brest, modelled his course upon that of Hawke. The port being thus left open, De la Clue sailed on the 5th of August for Brest. On the 17th he was near the straits of Gibraltar, hugging the African coast, and falling night gave promise of passing unseen, when a British lookout frigate caught sight of his squadron. She hauled in for Gibraltar at once, firing signal guns. Boscawen's ships were in the midst of repairs, mostly dismantled; but, the emergency not being unforeseen, spars and sails were sent rapidly aloft, and within three hours they were underway in pursuit. The French division separated during the night. Five ships put into Cadiz. The British next morning caught sight of the remaining seven, among which was the admiral, and a sharp chase resulted in the destruction of five. From August 18th the Toulon fleet was eliminated from the campaign; though the vessels in Cadiz remained to the end a charge upon Hawke's watchfulness, similar to that caused by the enemy's divisions expected from America.

That one of the latter was already on its way home, under the command of Commodore Bompart, was notified to our admiral on September 21st by a despatch from England. He immediately sent a division of heavy ships to reinforce the light squadron to the southward. "If the alarm is great now," he said, "it will be much greater if he get into Rochefort." Further information from the West Indies contradicted the first report, and on October 10th Hawke recalled the ships-of-the-line, apparently at the wish of the Admiralty; for he expresses his regret at doing so, and asks for more of the "many ships" then in England, that Rochefort may be blocked as well as Brest. The incident has now little importance, except as indicating the general national nervousness, and the difficulty under which he laboured through force inadequate to the numerous and exacting duties entailed by constant holding the sea in war. From this point of view it bears upon his conduct.

That Bompart was coming proved to be true. On November 10th Hawke anchored with the fleet in Torbay, after three days of struggle against a very heavy westerly storm. "Bompart, if near, may get in," he wrote the Admiralty, "but no ship can get out from any port in the Bay." The weather had then moderated, but was still too rough for boating, even in the sheltered roadstead; hence he could get no reports of the state of the ships, which shows incidentally the then defective system of signalling. On the 12th he sailed, on the 13th was again forced into Torbay by a south-wester, but on the 14th got away finally. On the afternoon of the 16th the fleet was twenty-five miles from the Island of Ushant, near Brest, and there learned from transports, returning from the light division off Quiberon, that the French fleet had been seen the day before, seventy-five miles northwest of Belleisle; therefore some fifty or sixty miles southeast of the point where this news was received. Conflans had sailed the same day that the British last left Torbay, but before his departure Bompart had opportunely arrived, as Hawke had feared. His ships were not able to go at once to sea on so important a mission, but their seasoned crews were a welcome reinforcement and were distributed through the main fleet, which numbered twenty-one ships-of-the-line. Hawke had twenty-three.

Concluding that the enemy were bound for Quiberon, Hawke carried a press of sail for that place. He knew they must be within a hundred miles of him and aimed to cut them off from their port. During the 17th the wind, hanging to the south and east, was adverse to both fleets, but on the 18th and 19th it became more favourable. At half-past eight on the morning of the 20th, one of the lookout frigates ahead of the British made the signal for sighting a fleet. It was then blowing strong from the west-northwest, and Belleisle, which is ten miles west of Quiberon Bay, and south of which the fleets must pass, was by the English reckoning forty miles distant. A course of some fifty or sixty miles was therefore to be run before the enemy could close the land, and there remained about eight hours of sun.

Hawke's day had come. Towards ten o'clock he had the enemy sufficiently in view to see that they were intent upon securing their arrival, rather than fighting. He therefore made signal for the seven ships nearest them "to chase and draw into a line-of-battle ahead of me, and endeavour to stop them till the rest of the squadron should come up, who also were *to form as they chased that no time might be lost* in the pursuit." The French "kept going off under such sail as all their squadron could carry and *yet keep together*, while we crowded after him *with every sail our ships could bear.*" The words italicized sum up the whole philosophy of a general chase. The pursued are limited to the speed of the slowest, otherwise he who cannot but lag is separated and lost; the pursuer need slacken no whit, for his friends are ever coming up to his aid. Overtaking is inevitable, unless the distance is too short.

At half-past two firing began between the French rear and the leading British. Of the two foremost in the chase, who thus opened the fight, one was the same *Dorsetshire* which in Mathews's battle had played the laggard. Her captain, who thus rose to his opportunity, was one of the two to whom Hawke addressed the enthusiastic compliment that they had "behaved like angels." Hawke himself was at this moment south of Belleisle, with several ships ahead of him; while the French admiral was leading his fleet, in order better to pilot them over dangerous ground, and by his own action show more surely than was possible by signal what he wished done from moment to moment. At the southern extreme of the shoals which act as a breakwater to Quiberon Bay are some formidable rocks, known as the Cardinals. Around these M. de Conflans passed soon after the firing began, his rear being then in hot action.

Hawke himself was without a pilot, as were most of his captains. The sailing master of the flag-ship was charged with that duty for the fleet, but had of the ground before him no exact personal knowledge; nor could reliance be placed upon the imperfect surveys of a locality, which it was not the interest of an almost constant enemy to disclose. Enough, however, was known to leave no doubt of the greatness of the risks, and it was the master's part to represent them. The occasion, however, was not one of a mere diversion, of a secondary operation, but of one vital to the nation's cause; and Hawke's reply, stamped with the firmness of a great officer, showed how little professional timidity had to do with his laudable care of his fleet in Basque Roads two years before. "You have done your duty in warning me," he replied; "now lay us alongside the French Commander-in-chief." So amid the falling hours of the day the British fleet, under the unswerving impulse of its leader, moved steadfastly forward, to meet a combination of perils that embraced all most justly dreaded by seamen,—darkness, an intricate navigation, a lee shore fringed with outlying and imperfectly known reefs and shoals, towards which they were hurried by a fast-rising wind and sea, that forbade all hope of retracing their steps during the long hours of the night.

"Had we but two hours more daylight," wrote Hawke in his official report, "the whole had been totally destroyed or taken; for we were almost up with their van when night overtook us." His success would have been greater, though not more decisive of issues than the event proved it; but nothing could have added to the merit or brilliancy of his action, to which no element of grandeur was wanting. This was one of the most dramatic of sea fights. Forty-odd tall ships, pursuers and pursued, under reefed canvas, in fierce career drove furiously on; now rushing headlong down the forward slope of a great sea, now rising on its crest as it swept beyond them; now seen, now hidden; the helmsmen straining at the wheels, upon which the huge hulls, tossing their prows from side to side, tugged like a maddened horse, as though themselves feeling the wild "rapture of the strife" that animated their masters, rejoicing in their strength and defying the accustomed rein.

The French admiral had flattered himself that the enemy, ignorant of the ground, would not dare to follow him round the Cardinals. He was soon undeceived. Hawke's comment on the situation was that he was "for the old way of fighting, to make downright work with them." It was an old way, true; but he had more than once seen it lost to mind, and had himself done most to restore it to its place,—a new way as well as an old. The signals for the general chase and for battle were kept aloft, and no British ship slacked her way. Without ranged order, save that of speed, the leaders mingled with the French rear; the roar and flashes of the guns, the falling spars and drifting clouds of smoke, now adding their part to the wild magnificence of the scene. Though tactically perfect in the sole true sense of tactics, that the means adopted exactly suited the situation, this was a battle of incidents, often untold,—not one of manoeuvres. As the ships, rolling heavily, buried their flanks deeply in the following seas, no captain dared to open his lower tier of ports, where the most powerful artillery was arrayed—none save one, the French *Thésée*, whose rashness was rebuked by the inpouring waters, which quickly engulfed both ship and crew. The *Superbe* met a like fate, though not certainly from the same cause. She sank under the broadside of the *Royal George*, Hawke's flag-ship. An eye witness wrote:

> The *Royal George*'s people gave a cheer, but it was a faint one; the honest sailors were touched at the miserable state of so many hundreds of poor creatures.

Americans and English can couple this story of long ago with Philip's ejaculation off Santiago de Cuba, but three years since: "Don't cheer, boys, those poor devils are dying."

By five o'clock two French ships had struck, and two had been sunk. Hawke wrote:

> Night was now come and being on a part of the coast, among islands and shoals of which we were totally ignorant, without a pilot, as was the greatest part of the squadron, and blowing hard on a lee shore, I made the signal to anchor.

The day's work was over, and doubtless looked to him incomplete, but it was effectually and finally done. The French Navy did not again lift up its head during the three years of war that remained. Balked in their expectation that the foe's fear of the beach would give them refuge, harried and worried by the chase, harnessed to no fixed plan of action, Conflans's fleet broke apart and fled. Seven went north, and ran ashore at the mouth of the little river Vilaine which empties into Quiberon Bay. Eight stood south, and succeeded in reaching Rochefort. The fate of four has been told. Conflans's flagship anchored after night among the British, but at daybreak next morning cut her cables, ran ashore, and was burned by the French. One other, wrecked on a shoal in the bay, makes up the tale of twenty-one. Six were wholly lost to their navy; the seven that got into Vilaine only escaped to Brest by twos, two years later, while the Rochefort division was effectually blocked by occupying Basque Roads, the islands of which and of Quiberon were cultivated as kitchen gardens for the refreshment of British crews.

Of the British, one ship went on a shoal during the action, and on the following day another coming to her assistance also grounded. Both were lost, but most of their people were saved. Beyond this Hawke's fleet suffered little, he wrote:

> As to the loss we have sustained, let it be placed to the account of the necessity I was under of running all risks to break this strong force of the enemy.

A contemporary witness assigns to Hawke's own ship a large individual share in the fighting. Of this he does not himself speak, nor is it of much matter. That all was done with her that could be done, to aid in achieving success, is sufficiently assured by his previous record. Hawke's transcendent merit in this affair was that of the general officer, not of the private captain. The utmost courage shown by the commander of a single ship before the enemy's fire cannot equal the heroism which assumes the immense responsibility of a doubtful issue, on which may hang a nation's fate; nor would the admiral's glory be shorn of a ray, if neither then nor at any other time had a hostile shot traversed his decks.

The night of the 20th passed in anxieties inseparable from a situation dangerous at best, but still more trying to an admiral upon whom, after such a day, night had closed without enabling him to see in what case most of his ships were. "In the night," he reports, "we heard many guns of distress fired, but, blowing hard, want of knowledge of the coast, and whether they were fired by a friend or an enemy, prevented all means of relief." In the morning he resumed his activity. Little, however, could be done. The continuing violence of the wind, and ignorance of the ground, prevented approach within gun-shot to the ships at the mouth of the Vilaine, while they, by lightening and favour of the next flood tide, warped their way inside through the mud flats.

Hawke remained nearly two months longer, returning to England January 17, 1760. He had then been thirty-five weeks on board, without setting foot on shore. At the age of fifty-four, and amid such manifold cares, it is not to be wondered at that he should need relief. Rather must he be considered fortunate that his health, never robust in middle life, held firm till his great triumph was achieved. Boscawen succeeded him temporarily in the command.

He was received in England with acclamations and with honours; yet the most conspicuous mark of approval conferred on admirals before and after, the grant of the peerage, was not given to him, who had wrought one of the very greatest services ever done for the country. Recent precedent—that of Anson—demanded such recognition; and popular enthusiasm would have applauded, although the full military merit of the man could scarcely be appreciated by the standards of his generation. That no such reward was bestowed is most probably attributable to Hawke's own indifference to self-advancement. If demanded by him, it could scarcely have been refused; but he never pushed his own interests. His masculine independence in professional conduct, towards superiors and inferiors, found its root and its reflection in personal unconcern—as well antecedent as subsequent—about the results from his actions to his fortunes. To do his own part to the utmost, within the lines of the profession he knew, was his conception of duty. As he would not meddle with the land officers' decision as to what they should or should not do, so he left to the politicians, in whose hands the gifts lay, to decide what they would, or should, accord to a successful admiral. Pitt, the Great Commoner, left Hawke a commoner. Possibly he recognized that only by stretch of imagination could Hawke be reckoned one of the creations of a great Minister's genius.

Little remains to tell. On September 3, 1762, the admiral's flag was hauled down for the last time. He never went to sea again. In 1766, when Pitt came back to power as Lord Chatham, Hawke became First Lord of the Admiralty, and so remained till 1771. It was a time of unbroken peace, succeeding a period of continuous wars extending over a quarter of a century; consequently there was in naval and military matters the lassitude usual to such a period. Hawke is credited with formulating the principle that "the British fleet could only be termed considerable in the proportion it bore to that of the House of Bourbon;" that is, to the combined navies of France and Spain, over which that House then reigned. The maxim proves that he had some claim to statesmanship in his view of affairs outside his service; and his manifested freedom from self-seeking is the warrant that no secondary political motives would divert his efforts from this aim. That he succeeded in the main, that he was not responsible for the fallen condition of the fleet when war again arose in 1778, is evidenced by a statement, uncontradicted, in the House of Lords in 1779, that when he left office the navy had 139 ships-of-the-line, of which 81 were ready for sea.

In 1765 Hawke, who was then already a full admiral, wearing his flag at the mainmast head, was made Vice-Admiral of Great Britain; an honorary position, but the highest in point of naval distinction that the nation had to give. As one who held it three-quarters of a century later wrote, "It has ever been regarded as the most distinguished compliment belonging to our profession." The coincidence is significant that upon Hawke's death Rodney succeeded him in it; affirming, as it were, the consecutiveness of paramount influence exercised by the two on the development of the Navy. In 1776 the peerage was at last conferred; seventeen years after his great victory, and when, having passed three score and ten, a man who had ever disdained to ask must have felt the honour barren to himself, though acceptable for his son.

His last recorded professional utterances are in private letters addressed in the summer of 1780 to the commander-in-chief of the Channel Fleet—Francis Geary—who had served with him in the Bay of Biscay, though he missed Quiberon. He recommends the maintenance of his old station off Brest, and says—

> For God's sake, if you should be so lucky as to get sight of the enemy, get as close to them as possible. Do not let them shuffle with you by engaging at a distance, but get within musket shot if you can. This will be the means to make the action decisive.

In these words we find an unbroken chain of tradition between Hawke and Nelson. One of Hawke's pupils was William Locker; and Locker in turn, just before Hawke's death, had Nelson for a lieutenant. To him Nelson in after years, in the height of his glory, wrote:

> To you, my dear friend, I owe much of my success. It was you who taught me,—'Lay a Frenchman close and you will beat him.'

Hawke died October 16, 1781. On his tomb appear these words, "Wherever he sailed, victory attended him." It is much to say, but it is not all. Victory does not always follow desert. "It is not in mortals to command success,"—a favourite quotation with the successful admirals St. Vincent and Nelson. Hawke's great and distinctive glory is this,—that he, more than any one man, was the source and origin of the new life, the new spirit, of his service. There were many brave men before him, as there were after; but it fell to him in a time of great professional prostration not only to lift up and hand on a fallen torch, but in himself to embody an ideal and an inspiration from which others drew, thus rekindling a light which it is scarcely an exaggeration to say had been momentarily extinguished.

Rodney: 1719-1792

CHAPTER 3

Rodney: 1719-1792

Unlike Hawke, Rodney drew his descent from the landed gentry of England, and had relatives among the aristocracy. The name was originally Rodeney. We are told by his son-in-law and biographer that the Duke of Chandos, a connection by marriage, obtained the command of the royal yacht for the admiral's father, Henry Rodney. In one of the trips which George I. frequently made between England and Hanover, he asked his captain if there were anything he could do for him. The reply was a request that he would stand sponsor for his son, who accordingly received the name of George; his second name Brydges coming from the family through which Chandos and the Rodneys were brought into relationship. The social position and surroundings resulting from such antecedents contributed of course to hasten the young officer's advancement, irrespective of the unquestionable professional merit shown by him, even in early years; but to them also, combined with narrow personal fortune, inadequate to the tastes thus engendered, was probably due the pecuniary embarrassment which dogged him through life, and was perhaps the moving incentive to doubtful procedures that cast a cloud upon his personal and official reputation.

Rodney was born in February, 1719, and went to sea at the age of thirteen; serving for seven years in the Channel Fleet. Thence he was transferred to the Mediterranean, where he was made lieutenant in 1739. In 1742 he went again to the Mediterranean with Admiral Mathews, who there gave him command of a "post" ship, with which he brought home the trade,—three hundred merchant vessels,—from Lisbon. Upon arriving in England his appointment by Mathews was "confirmed" by the Admiralty. Being then only twenty-four, he anticipated by five years the age at which Hawke reached the same rank of post-captain, the attainment of which fixed a man's standing in the navy. Beyond that, advancement went by seniority; a post-captain might be "yellowed,"—retired as a rear admiral,—but while in active service he kept the advantage of his early promotion.

When Rodney was in later years commander-in-chief in the West Indies, he made his son a post-captain at fifteen; an exercise of official powers which, though not singular to him, is too characteristic of the man and the times to be wholly unmentioned. His own promotion, though rapid, was not too much so for his professional good; but it is likely that neither that consideration, nor the good of the service, counted for much alongside of the influence he possessed. He appears, however, to have justified from the first the favour of his superiors. His employment was continuous, and in a military point of view he was more fortunate than Hawke was at the same period of his career. Within two years, when in command of a forty-gun ship, he fought and took a French privateer of the same nominal force, and with a crew larger by one hundred than his own. Thence he was advanced into the *Eagle*, sixty, in which, after some commerce-destroying more lucrative than glorious, he bore an extremely honourable part in Hawke's battle with L'Etenduère, already related. The *Eagle* was heavily engaged, and was one of the three small ships that on their own initiative pursued and fought, though unsuccessfully, the two escaping French vessels. Rodney shared Hawke's general encomium, that "as far as fell within my notice, the commanders, their officers, and ships' companies, behaved with the greatest spirit and resolution." Rodney came under his close observation, for, the *Eagle*'s "wheel being shot to pieces and all the men at it killed, and all her braces and bowlines gone," she drove twice on board the flag-ship. This was before her pursuit of the two fliers.

In the subsequent trial of Captain Fox,—the minutes of which the present writer has not seen,—it appears, according to the biographer of Lord Hawke,[6] that it was Captain Saunders's and Captain Rodney's—

> .... sense of being deserted by Fox, and of the two French ships having escaped through his failure of duty, which forms the chief feature of the Court-Martial. Rodney especially describes his being exposed to the fire of four of the enemy's ships, when, as he asserted, Fox's ship might well have taken off some of it.

The incident is very noteworthy, for it bears the impress of personal character. Intolerance of dereliction of duty, and uncompromising condemnation of the delinquent, were ever leading traits in Rodney's course as a commander-in-chief. He stood over his officers with a rod, dealt out criticism unsparingly, and avowed it as his purpose and principle of action so to rule. It is not meant that his censures were undeserved, or even excessive; but there entered into them no ingredient of pity. His despatches are full of complaints, both general and specific. When he spared, it was from a sense of expediency,—or of justice, a trait in which he was by no means deficient; but for human weakness he had no bowels. Hawke complains of but this one captain, Fox, and towards him he seems not to have evinced the strong feeling that animated his juniors. Each man has his special gift, and to succeed must needs act in accordance with it.

There are those who lead and those who drive; Hawke belonged to the one class, Rodney to the other.

In direct consequence of this difference of temperament, it will be found, in contrasting the schools of which Hawke and Rodney are the conspicuous illustrations, that the first represents the spirit, and the second the form, which were the two efficient elements of the progress made during the eighteenth century. The one introduces into a service arrested in development, petrified almost, by blindly accepted rules and unintelligent traditions, a new impulse, which transforms men from

---

6. *Life of Lord Hawke*, by Captain Montagu Burrows, Royal Navy, p. 194.

within, breaking through the letter of the law in order to realize its forgotten intent; the other gives to the spirit, thus freed from old limitations, a fresh and sagacious direction, but needs nevertheless to impose its own methods by constraint from without. It is the old struggle, ever renewed, between liberty and law; in the due, but difficult, combination of which consist both conservation and progress.

And so in the personality of the two great admirals who respectively represent these contrasting schools of practice; while we find in both these two elements, as they must exist in every efficient officer, yet it is to be said that the one inspires and leads, the other moulds and compels. The one, though seemingly reserved, is in character sympathetic, and influences by example chiefly; the other, austerely courteous, is towards associates distant and ungenial, working by fear rather than by love. For these broad reasons of distinction it is Mathews's battle that best measures the reaction of which Hawke is the type, for there was especially illustrated defect of spirit, to cover which the letter of the law was invoked; whereas in Byng's action, extremely bad form, in the attempt to conform to the letter of the Instructions, emphasizes the contrast with Rodney's methods, precise and formal unquestionably, but in which form ceases to be an end in itself and is reduced to its proper function as the means to carry into effect a sound military conception. Of these two factors in the century's progress, it needs hardly to be said that the one contributed by Hawke is the greater. In spirit and in achievement he, rather than Rodney, is the harbinger of Nelson.

A short time after the action with L'Etenduère the cruise of the *Eagle* came to an end. When she was paid off Rodney was presented at Court by Anson, the First Lord of the Admiralty; a merited and not unusual honour after distinguished service in battle. The King was struck by his youthful appearance, and said he had not known there was so young a captain in the Navy. As he was then nearly thirty, and had seen much and continuous service, it is singular that his face should not have borne clear traces of the facts. Anson replied that he had been a captain for six years, and it was to be wished that His Majesty had a hundred more as good as he. Making allowance for courtly manners and fair-speaking, the incident may be accepted as showing, not only that aptitude for the service which takes its hardships without undue wear and tear, but also an official reputation already well established and recognized.

Professional standing, therefore, as well as family influence, probably contributed to obtain for him in 1749 the appointment of Commodore and Commander-in-chief on the Newfoundland station; for he was still junior on the list of captains, and had ten years more to run before obtaining his admiral's flag. He remained in this post from 1749 to 1752. They were years of peace, but of peace charged full with the elements of discord which led to the following war. Canada was still French, and the territorial limits between the North American possessions of the two nations remained a subject of dispute and intrigue. The uncertain state of political relations around the Gulf of St. Lawrence added to the responsibility of Rodney's duty, and emphasized the confidence shown in assigning him a position involving cautious political action.

Explicit confirmation of this indirect testimony is found in a private letter to him from the Earl of Sandwich, who had succeeded Anson as First Lord in 1748.

> I think it necessary to inform you that, if the Governor of Nova Scotia should have occasion to apply to you for succour, and send to you for that purpose to Newfoundland, it would be approved by Government if you should comply with his request. It is judged improper, as yet, to send any public order upon a business of so delicate a nature, which is the reason of my writing to you in this manner; and I am satisfied that your prudence is such as will not suffer you to make any injudicious use of the information you now receive. There are some people that cannot be trusted with any but public orders, but I shall think this important affair entirely safe under your management and secrecy.

Language such as this undoubtedly often covers a hint, as well as expresses a compliment, and may have done so in this instance; nevertheless, in after life it is certain that Rodney gave proof of a very high order of professional discretion and of independent initiative. It is therefore perfectly reasonable to suppose that he had thus early convinced the Government that he was a man competent and trustworthy under critical conditions, such as then characterized the inter-colonial relations of the two states. The particular incident is farther noteworthy in connection with the backwardness, and even reluctance, of the Government to employ him in the War of the American Revolution, though Sandwich was again First Lord, and Rodney a strong political supporter of the party in power. The precise cause for this is probably not ascertainable; but it is a matter of perfectly reasonable inference that the early promise of the young officer had meanwhile become overclouded, that distrust had succeeded to confidence, for reasons professional, but not strictly military. Rodney's war record continued excellent from first to last; one not good only, but of exceptional and singular efficiency.

In October, 1752, Rodney returned to England, having been elected to Parliament. The Seven Years War, which, after two years of irregular hostilities, began formally in 1756, found him still a captain. With its most conspicuous opening incident, the attempted relief of Minorca, and the subsequent trial and execution of the unsuccessful commander, Admiral Byng, he had no connection, personal or official; nor was he a member of the Court-Martial, although he seems to have been in England at the time, and was senior to at least one of the sitting captains. The abortive naval engagement off Port Mahon, however, stands in a directly significant relation to his career, for it exemplifies to the most exaggerated degree, alike in the purpose of the admiral and the finding of the Court, the formal and pedantic conception of a correctly fought fleet action, according to the rules and regulations "in such cases prescribed" by the Fighting Instructions.[7] It was Rodney's lot to break with this tradition, and to be the first to illustrate juster ideas in a fairly ranged battle, where the enemy awaited attack, as he had done at Malaga in 1704, and at Minorca in 1756. Precisely such an opportunity never came to Hawke; for, although L'Etenduère waited, he did so under conditions and dispositions which gave the ensuing affair a nearer analogy to a general chase than to a pitched battle. Though the British approach then was in a general sense parallel to the enemy's line, it was from the rear, not from the beam; and through this circumstance of overtaking, and from the method adopted, their vessels came under fire in succession, not together. This was perfectly correct, the course pre-eminently suited to the emergency, and therefore tactically most sound; but the conditions were not those contemplated by the Fighting Instructions, as they were in the case of Byng, and also in the battle most thoroughly characteristic of Rodney—that of April 17, 1780. The contrast in conduct between the two commanders is strikingly significant of progress, because of the close approach to identity in circumstances.

Rodney accompanied the Rochefort expedition of 1757, under Hawke, some account of which is given in the life of that admiral; and he commanded also a ship-of-the-line in Boscawen's fleet in 1758, when the reduction of Louisburg and Cape Breton Island was effected by the combined British and colonial forces. After this important service, the necessary and effectual antecedent of the capture of Quebec and the fall of Canada in the following year, he returned to England, where on the 19th of May, 1759, he was promoted to Rear Admiral; being then forty. He was next, and without interval of rest, given command of a squadron to operate against Havre, where were gathering boats and munitions of war for the threatened invasion of England; with the charge also of suppressing the French coastwise sailings, upon which depended the assembling of the various bodies of transports, and the carriage of supplies to the fleet in Brest, that Hawke at the same time was holding in check. The service was important, but of secondary interest, and calls for no particular mention beyond that of its general efficiency as maintained by him.

In 1761, Rodney was again elected to Parliament, and, with a certain political inconsequence, was immediately afterwards sent out of the country, being appointed to the Leeward Islands

---

7. For account and analysis of Byng's action, see *ante*, pp. 47-67.

Station, which embraced the smaller Antilles, on the eastern side of the Caribbean Sea, with headquarters at Barbados; Jamaica, to the westward, forming a distinct command under an admiral of its own. He sailed for his new post October 21, 1761, taking with him instructions to begin operations against Martinique upon the arrival of troops ordered from New York. These reached Barbados December 24th, a month after himself, and on the 7th of January, 1762, the combined forces were before Martinique, which after a month of regular operations passed into the possession of the British on the 16th of February. Its fall was followed shortly by that of the other French Lesser Antilles,— Grenada, Santa Lucia, and St. Vincent. Guadeloupe had been taken in 1759, and Dominica in June, 1761.

Up to this time the contest on the seas had been between Great Britain and France only; but on March 5th a frigate reached Rodney with instructions, then already nine weeks old, to begin hostilities against Spain, whose clearly inimical purpose had induced the British Government to anticipate her action, by declaring war. The same day another vessel came in with like orders from the admiral at Gibraltar, while a third from before Brest brought word that a French squadron of seven ships-of-the-line, with frigates and two thousand troops, had escaped from that port at the end of the year. With these circumstances before him Rodney's conduct was like himself; prompt and officer-like. Lookout ships were stationed along the length of the Caribbees, to windward, to bring timely intelligence of the approach of the enemy's squadron; and as its first destination was probably Martinique, the fall of which was not yet known in Europe, he concentrated his fleet there, calling in outlying detachments.

So far there was nothing in his course markedly different from that of any capable officer, dealing with well ascertained conditions within the limits of his own command. Occasion soon arose, however, to require more exceptional action, and thus to illustrate at once the breadth of view, and the readiness to assume responsibility, which already raised Rodney conspicuously above the average level. On the 9th of March two lookout vessels came in with news that they had sighted a fleet, corresponding in numbers to the Brest division, fifteen miles to windward of Martinique and standing to the southward; the trade wind making it generally expedient to round the south point of the island in order to reach the principal port on the west side,—Fort Royal. The British squadron at once weighed anchor in pursuit; but the enemy, having ascertained that the surrender was accomplished, had turned back north, and were soon after reported from Guadeloupe as having passed there, standing to the westward.

Rodney at once inferred that they must be gone to Santo Domingo. To follow with the object of intercepting them was hopeless, in view of the start they had; but the direction taken threatened Jamaica, the exposed condition of which, owing to inadequate force, had been communicated to him by the military and naval authorities there. His measures to meet the case were thorough and deliberate, as well as rapid; no time was lost either by hesitancy or delay, nor by the yet more facile error of too precipitate movement. Orders for concentration were already out, but the point on which to effect it was shifted to Antigua, where, although inferior in natural resources to Martinique, the established British naval station with its accumulated equipment was fixed; and the work of provisioning and watering, so as to permit long continuance at sea unhampered by necessity of replenishing, there went on apace. It was the admiral's intention to leave his own command to look out for itself, while he took away the mass of his fleet to protect national interests elsewhere threatened.

Such a decision may seem superficially a commonplace matter of course; that it was much more is a commonplace historical certainty. The merit of Rodney's action appears not only in the details of execution, but in its being undertaken at all; and in this case, as in a later instance in his career, his resolution received the concrete emphasis that a sharp and immediate contrast best affords. Prior to the enemy's arrival he had laid the conditions before his colleague in service, General Moncton, commanding the forces on shore, and asked a reinforcement of troops for destitute Jamaica, if necessity arose. The result is best told in his own words; for they convey, simply and without egotistic enlargement, that settled personal characteristic, the want of which Jervis and Nelson in their day noted in many, and which Rodney markedly possessed. This was the capacity, which Sandwich eighteen years later styled "taking the great line of considering the King's whole dominions under your care;" an attribute far from common, as Moncton's reply showed.

> I acquainted him that I should certainly assist them with all the naval force that could possibly be spared from the immediate protection of His Majesty's Caribbee islands. I have again solicited the General for a body of troops, since the enemy left these seas, and must do him the justice to say, that he seems much concerned at the present distress of Jamaica, but does not think himself sufficiently *authorized* to detach a body of troops without orders from England. I flatter myself their Lordships will not be displeased with me if I take the liberty to construe my instructions in such a manner as to think myself *authorized and obliged* to succour any of His Majesty's colonies that may be in danger; and shall, therefore, without a moment's loss of time, hasten to the succour of Jamaica, with ten sail-of-the-line, three frigates and three bombs.[8]

It was not because, in so doing this, the obligation was absolute, and the authority indisputable, that Rodney's course was professionally meritorious. In such case his action would have risen little above that obedience to orders, in which, as Nelson said, the generality find "all perfection." The risk was real, not only to his station, but to the possible plans of his superiors at home; the authority was his own only, read by himself into his orders—at most their spirit, not their letter. Consequently, he took grave chance of the penalty—loss of reputation, if not positive punishment,—which, as military experience shows, almost invariably follows independent action, unless results are kind enough to justify it. It is, however, only the positive characters capable of rising to such measures that achieve reputations enduring beyond their own day. The incident needs to be cou-

---

8. The italics are the author's.

pled with Sandwich's compliment just quoted, as well as with the one paid him when on the Newfoundland command. Taken together, they avouch a personality that needs only opportunity to insure itself lasting fame.

As it happened, Rodney not only took the responsibility of stripping his own station to the verge of bareness in favour of the general interest, but in so doing he came very near traversing, unwittingly, the plans of the general government by his local action, laudable and proper as that certainly was. He was, however, professionally lucky to a proverb, and escaped this mischance by a hair's breadth. The purposed detachment had already started for Jamaica, and he was accompanying it in person, when there joined him on March 25th, off the island of St. Kitt's, not far from Antigua, a frigate bearing Admiralty despatches of February 5th. These required him to desist from any enterprises he might have in hand, in order to give his undivided attention to the local preparations for an expedition, as yet secret, which was shortly to arrive on his station, under the command of Admiral Pocock, with ultimate destination against Havana.

To be thus arrested at the very outset of a movement from which he naturally expected distinction was a bitter disappointment to Rodney. Several years later, in 1771, he wrote to Sandwich, who was not the First Lord when Pocock was sent out:

> I had the misfortune of being superseded in the command of a successful fleet, entrusted to my care in the West Indies, at the very time I had sailed on another expedition against the enemy's squadron at Santo Domingo, and was thereby deprived of pursuing those conquests which so honourably attended upon another, and which secured him such great emoluments.

Havana proved a wealthy prize. His steps, however, upon this unexpected reversal of his plans, were again characterized by an immediateness, most honourable to his professional character, which showed how thoroughly familiar he was with the whole subject and its possible contingencies, and the consequent readiness of his mind to meet each occasion as it arose; marks, all, of the thoroughly equipped general officer. The order as to his personal movements being not discretional, was of course absolutely accepted; but his other measures were apparently his own, and were instantaneous. A vessel was at once sent off to Barbados to notify Admiral Pocock that the best place in the West Indies for his rendezvous was Fort Royal Bay, in the newly acquired Martinique. The ten sail-of-the-line, accompanied by two large transports from St. Kitt's, were then sent on to Jamaica to move troops from there to join Pocock; the command of the detachment being now entrusted to Sir James Douglas, who received the further instruction to send back his fastest frigate, with all the intelligence he could gather, directing her to keep in the track Pocock would follow, in order to meet him betimes. The frigate thus sent, having first made a running survey of the unfrequented passage north of Cuba, by which the expedition was to proceed, joined Pocock, and, by the latter's report, acted as pilot for the fleet.

Having taken sketches of the land and kayos on both sides, Captain Elphinstone kept ahead of the fleet, and led us through very well.

This service is claimed to the credit of Rodney's foresight by his biographer. This may very well be, though more particular inquiry and demonstration by his letters would be necessary to establish specific orders beyond the general instructions given by him. It is, however, safe to say that such particularity and minuteness of detail would be entirely in keeping with the tenor of his course at this period. His correspondence bears the stamp of a mind comprehensive as well as exact; grasping all matters with breadth of view in their mutual relations, yet with the details at his fingers' ends. The certainty of his touch is as obvious as the activity of his thought.

In accordance with the spirit of his instructions, Rodney went in person to Martinique, the spot named by him as best for the rendezvous, there to superintend the preparations; to sow the seed for a harvest in which he was to have no share. Incidental mention reveals that the sending of the ships-of-the-line with Douglas had reduced him to three for his own command;

and also that Moncton, having now superior authority to do so, found himself able to spare troops for Jamaica, which were afloat in transports by the time Pocock came. In the same letter the admiral frankly admits his anxiety for his station, under the circumstances of the big detachment he had made; a significant avowal, which enhances the merit of his spontaneous action by all the credit due to one who endures a well-weighed danger for an adequate end.

The despatch of Pocock's expedition, which resulted in the fall of Havana, August 13, 1762, practically terminated Rodney's active service in the Seven Years War. In a career marked by unusual professional good fortune in many ways, the one singular mischance was that he reached a foremost position too late in life. When he returned to England in August, 1763, he was in his full prime, and his conduct of affairs entrusted to him had given clear assurance of capacity for great things. The same evidence is to be found in his letters, which, as studies of official character and competency, repay a close perusal. But now fifteen years of peace were to elapse before a maritime war again broke out, and the fifteen years between forty-five and sixty tell sorely upon the physical stamina which need to underlie the mental and moral forces of a great commander. St. Vincent himself staggered under the load, and Rodney was not a St. Vincent in the stern self-discipline that had braced the latter for old age. He had not borne the yoke in his youth, and from this time forward he fought a losing fight with money troubles, which his self-controlled contemporary, after one bitter experience, had shaken off his shoulders forever.

The externals of Rodney's career during the period now in question are sufficiently known; of his strictly private life we are left largely to infer from indications, not wholly happy. He returned to England a Vice-Admiral of the Blue, and had advanced by the successive grades of that rank to Vice-Admiral of the Red, when, in January, 1771, he was appointed Commander-in-chief at Jamaica. At this time he had been for five years Governor of Greenwich Hospital, and he took it hard that he was not allowed to retain the appointment in connection with his new command, alleging precedents for such a favour; the latest of which, however, was then twenty-five years old. The application was denied by Sandwich. From the earnest tone in which it was couched, as well as the comparatively weak grounds upon which Rodney bases his claims to such a recognition, it can scarcely be doubted that pecuniary embarrassment as well as mortification entered into his sense of disappointment. It is the first recorded of a series of jars between the two, in which, although the external forms of courtesy were diligently observed, an underlying estrangement is evident.

The Jamaica Station at that day required, in an even greater degree than Newfoundland before the conquest of Canada, a high order of political tact and circumspection on the part of the naval commander-in-chief. The island lies in the centre of what was then a vast semi-circular sweep of Spanish colonies—Porto Rico, Santo Domingo, Cuba, Mexico, Central America, and the mainland of South America from the Isthmus to the Orinoco. Over this subject empire the mother country maintained commercial regulations of the most medieval and exclusive type; outraging impartially the British spirit of commercial enterprise, and the daily needs of her own colonists, by the restrictions placed upon intercourse between these and foreigners. Smuggling on a large scale, consecrated in the practice of both parties by a century of tradition, was met by a coast-guard system, employing numerous small vessels called *guarda-costas*, which girt the Spanish coasts, but, being powerless to repress effectually over so extensive a shore line, served rather to increase causes of vexation. The British government, on the other hand, not satisfied to leave the illicit trade on which Jamaica throve to take care of itself, sought to increase the scope of transactions by the institution of three free ports on the island,—free in the sense of being open as depots, not for the entrance of goods, but where they could be freely brought, and transhipped to other parts of the world by vessels of all nations; broker ports, in short, for the facilitation of general external trade.

To this open and ingenuous bid for fuller advantage by Spanish resort, Spain replied by doubling her custom-house forces and introducing renewed stringency into her commercial orders. The two nations, with France in Haiti for a third, stood on ceaseless guard one against the other; all imbued with the spirit of exclusive trade, and differing only in the method of application, according to their respective day-today views of policy. The British by the free-port system, instituted in their central geographical position, hoped to make the profits of the middleman. Rodney reported that the effect had been notably to discourage the direct Spanish intercourse, and to destroy carriage by British colonial vessels in favour of those of France, which now flocked to Jamaica, smuggled goods into the island, and apparently cut under their rivals by the greater benevolence shown them in Spanish ports. "Commerce by British bottoms has totally ceased." Herewith, he added, disappeared the opportunities of British seamen to become familiar with the Spanish and French waters, while their rivals were invited to frequent those of Jamaica; so that in case of war—which in those days was periodical—the advantage of pilotage would be heavily on the side of Great Britain's enemies. He also stated that the diminution of employment to British merchant vessels had greatly impaired his means of obtaining information from within Spanish ports; for British ships of war were never allowed inside them, even when sent with a message from him. The French permitted them indeed to enter, but surrounded them throughout their visits with flattering attentions which wholly prevented the making of observations.

Under these conditions of mutual jealousy between the governments and officials, with the subjects on either side straining continually at the leashes which withheld them from traffic mutually beneficial, causes of offence were quick to arise. Rodney, like Sandwich, was a pronounced Tory, in full sympathy with traditional British policy, as well as an officer naturally of haughty temper and sharing all the prepossessions of his service; but he found himself almost at once involved in a difference with his superiors in his political party, which throws a good deal of side light on personal as well as political relations. The British man-of-war schooner *Hawke* was overhauled off the Venezuelan coast by two Spanish *guarda-costas* and compelled to enter the harbour of Cartagena, under alleged orders from the Governor of the colony. After a brief detention, she was let go with the admonition that, if any British ships of war were found again within twelve leagues of the coast, they would be taken and their crews imprisoned.

Rodney's course was unimpeachable, as far as appears. He wrote a civil letter to the Governor, and sent it by a ship of war, the captain of which was directed to deliver it in person. He was confident, he wrote, that the Governor would disavow the action by calling to strict account the officers concerned, and would also confirm his own belief that it was impossible such a menace could have proceeded from any adequate authority. A sufficient intimation of what would follow an attempt to carry out the threat was conveyed by the words:

> The British officer who has dishonoured his King's colours by a tame submission to this insult has been already dismissed the service.

It is difficult to see what less could have been done; but the British government was at the moment extremely reluctant to war, and sensitive to any step that seemed to make towards it. Spain was thought to be seeking a quarrel. She had entered the Seven Years War so near its termination as not to feel exhaustive effects; and the capture of Havana and Manila, with the pecuniary losses involved, had left her merely embittered by humiliation, prone rather to renew hostilities than to profit by experience. At the same time the foreign policy of Great Britain was enfeebled by a succession of short ministries, and by internal commotions; while the discontent of the American continental colonies over the Stamp Act emphasized the weakness of her general position. Barely a year before the *Hawke* incident the insult by Spain at the Falkland Islands had brought the two nations to the verge of rupture, which was believed to have been averted only by the refusal of Louis XV., then advanced in years, to support the Spanish Bourbons at the cost of another war.

Under these circumstances Rodney's report of the occurrences at Cartagena filled the ministry with apprehensions, and brought him from Sandwich an expression of dissatisfaction little removed from a reprimand. The communication is remarkable rather for what it intimates, and from the inferences naturally deducible, than for its direct utterances.

> I cannot help cautioning you, as a friend, to be upon your guard, to avoid by every justifiable means the drawing this country into a war, which, if it comes on too speedily, I fear we shall have cause to lament.

The warning is renewed in a later part of the letter, but in itself has little significance compared with other hints, rather personal than official.

> I cannot conceal from you, that many people have industriously spread stories here, that, among the foreign ministers and others, you have expressed your wishes for a Spanish war.

Such expressions—if used—were asserted of the time succeeding his appointment to Jamaica, and near his departure for it; for Sandwich adds:

> This sort of declaration is too little founded on your instructions, and too indiscreet, to allow me to give them the least credit.

It is clear, however, that he thought them not improbable,—a Spanish war was popular with seamen for the prize-money it brought, and Rodney was poor,—for he adds, "I shall discredit the idea till I have received your answer to this letter." He concludes with a warning, not to be misunderstood, that a war, so far from helping Rodney, would probably cause his supersession.

> I will add one word more: Upon a declaration of war larger squadrons must be sent out, and, very probably, senior officers to most of our stations in foreign parts.

In face of an intimation thus thinly veiled, one scarcely needs to be told what was being said round the table of the Cabinet.

That Rodney would have welcomed war for reasons personal as well as professional, for money and for glory, can readily be believed; but his measures in this case give no ground for such an innuendo as Sandwich conveyed. Therefore, after making full allowance for the panic of ministers ready to fear the worst, and to throw blame on anybody, it is the more significant that he should have been suspected of an unworthy personal motive underlying a worthy official act. It is an indication of reputation already compromised by damaging association with pecuniary embarrassments; an evidence of latent distrust easily quickened into active suspicion. An officer of his rank and service, so far from home, and with the precedents of his day, could scarcely be faulted for what he had done to uphold the honour of the country; and his manner of doing it was dignified and self-restrained, as well as forcible. There was no violence like that of Hawke at Gibraltar, less than twenty years before, which that admiral had boldly vindicated to Pitt himself; but there were no weak joints in Hawke's armour. In the particular instance, time and cooler judgment set Rodney right in men's opinion; but subsequent events showed that his general reputation did not recover, either then, or through his Jamaica career.

After immediate apprehension had subsided, Rodney's action was justified by the government. Sandwich wrote him, a little later, that no commander-in-chief stood upon a better footing, and assured him that his private interests were safe in his hands. Sandwich, however, was an extremely practical politician, who had much personal use for his own patronage; and Rodney's necessities were great. Fulfilment therefore fell far short of promise. Employment was necessary to the admiral, and his hopes fixed upon a colonial governorship when his present appointment should expire; Jamaica being his first choice. Sandwich renewed assurances, but advised a personal application also to the Prime Minister and other Cabinet officers. New York was mentioned, but nothing came of it all. After three years Rodney was superseded, with permission to remain in the island instead of returning to England. This he declined.

I cannot bear to think of remaining here in a private station, after commanding in chief with the approbation of the whole island.

How far this approbation was universal, or unqualified, is perhaps doubtful; but the letters quoted by his biographer from his correspondence bear continuous evidence, in this peace employment, of the activity and perspicacity of mind characteristic of his more strictly military proceedings.

In September, 1774, Rodney landed again in England, a disappointed man and in embarrassed circumstances. Professional occupation was almost hopeless, for in peace times there were few positions for an officer of his rank; and, although recognized for able, he had not then the distinction by which he is known to us. It is also evident, from subsequent events, that he just now lacked the influence necessary to obtain a preference over rivals in quest of employment. Under the circumstances, his debts determined his action, and to escape harassments he before long passed over into France and settled in Paris. In that capital, as in London, he mixed with the best society; and there, as before, the mode of life among his associates led him beyond his means and involved him in further distresses. Consequently, when war between France and Great Britain became imminent, in 1778, the vigilance of his creditors prevented his going home in person to offer his services. In February of that year, however, he made formal application to the Admiralty to be sent at a moment's warning on any enterprise. To this Sandwich, who was still First Lord, despite his previous assurances of friendship, paid no attention beyond the formal customary acknowledgment given to all such letters when they came from officers of Rodney's standing. No indication was shown of intention, or even of wish, to employ him.

Rodney was therefore compelled to look on idly while others, of well-earned reputation indeed but as yet of less experience than himself in high command, were preferred before him. Howe had already been sent to North America in 1776, on a mission at once diplomatic and military; and there he still was when war began. As it became imminent, Keppel was appointed to the Channel Fleet, and Byron to the North American command, from which Howe had asked to be relieved. All these were junior to Rodney; and, as though to emphasize the neglect of him, rear-admirals were sent to the two West India stations, Jamaica and the Leeward Islands, which he had formerly commanded, and to which it would seem, from one of his letters, that he desired to return. He had, too, now reached the rank, the want of which had formed the burden of Sandwich's warning that he was in danger of supersession at Jamaica; for in a general flag promotion in January, 1778, he had become Admiral of the White Squadron, than which no higher then obtained, commissions as Admirals of the Red not being issued. For this persistent ignoring of an officer of his unquestionable ability there were necessarily reasons more controlling than appears on the surface; for the naval conditions and the national emergency called for men of demonstrated high capacity. Such Rodney was professionally; and although his age—he was now in his sixtieth year—was against him, this consideration did not in those days weigh; nor should it, unless accompanied by probable indication of powers sapped.

The conclusion is inevitable that the objection lay in personal record as bearing upon military efficiency. The Administration, responsible for results, knew Rodney's capacity, though its full extent was yet to be revealed; the question in their minds clearly must have been, "Can we depend upon its exertion, full, sustained, and disinterested?" Sandwich, despite the coldness with which he had received Rodney's application,—going so far as to refuse to support it actively,—was apparently in a minority among his colleagues in believing that they could. He declared in the House of Lords that, "When it was first proposed in the Council to employ Sir George, I, who knew him from a very young man, declared that Rodney *once afloat* would do his duty." Naval officers will recognize a familiar ring in these words, and will recall instances where high professional ability has been betrayed by personal foible. Nor does Sandwich stand alone in offering a clue to the hesitation of the Government. Rodney's biographer and son-in-law quotes without reprobation the account of Mr. Richard Cumberland, who professed to have interested himself warmly for Rodney's employment and to have secured the support of the Secretary for War, Lord George Germaine.

> The West India merchants had been alarmed, and clamoured against the appointment so generally and so decidedly as to occasion no small uneasiness in my friend and patron, Lord George, and drew from him something that resembled a remonstrance for the risk I had exposed him to. But in the brilliancy of the capture of Langara's squadron all was done away, and past alarms were only recollected to contrast the joy which this success diffused.

The opposition of the commercial class in the West Indies might arise from an officer's over-faithfulness to duty, as Nelson found to his cost; but it seems clear that in this case distrust rested upon personal observation, which raised doubts as to the single-mindedness of Rodney's administration of a command. Of the particulars of observation or experience from which the feeling sprang, we have no information; but St. Eustatius was destined to show that apprehension was not wholly unfounded.

A summons to active employment would at once have silenced Rodney's creditors by the assurance of increase of means, both through regular income and probable prize-money; Admiralty neglect left him in fetters. Lady Rodney returned to England to negotiate the means for his liberation; but the matter dragged, and in the end he owed his release to the friendly intervention of a French nobleman, the Maréchal Biron, who volunteered in warm terms to make him an advance to the amount of £2,000. This chivalrous offer was for some time declined; but finally conditions became so threatening, and his position so intolerable, that he accepted a loan of about a thousand louis. He wrote to his wife:

> Nothing but a total inattention to the distressed state I was in could have prevailed upon me to have availed myself of his voluntary proposal; but not having had, for a month past, a letter from any person but Mr. Hotham and

yourself, and my passport being expired, it was impossible for me to remain in this city at the risk of being sued by my creditors, who grew so clamorous it was impossible to bear it; and had they not been overawed by the Lieutenant of police, would have carried their prosecutions to the greatest length. Their demands were all satisfied this day.—May 6th, 1778.

Friends in England enabled him to repay Biron immediately after his return.

This benevolent interference on behalf of a national enemy, although in its spirit quite characteristic, at once of the country and of the class to which the individual extending it belonged, has retained a certain unique flavour of its own among military anecdotes; due undoubtedly to the distinction subsequently acquired by Rodney at the expense of the people to which his liberator belonged, rather than to anything exceptional in its nature. As it is, it has acquired a clear pre-eminence among the recorded courtesies of warfare. It is pleasant to add that Great Britain had the opportunity in after times to requite Biron's daughters an act from which she had so greatly benefited. They having sought refuge, though with loss of fortune, from the early excesses of the French Revolution, received for some time pensions from the British Government.

Rodney came back to England feeling anything but cordial towards Sandwich, whose decided support he had found wanting throughout a very critical period of his career. More than any one else the First Lord had had both the opportunity and the insight to see his professional value. Tory though Rodney was, he hoped that "Lord Chatham (Pitt) would be minister, and another First Lord of the Admiralty be appointed."

"We hear of a change of Administration. I hope it is true, and that I may have a chance of being employed, should another be at the Admiralty."

"The refusal of Lord Sandwich does not surprise me. He cannot say but I have offered my services, and some friend will let the King know I have so done." Apparently he was to be ignored as well as overlooked.

Circumstances, however, soon compelled his employment. Sandwich was an able man, but his personal character inspired mistrust. Not only was he controlled by political considerations in administration; he was suspected of corruptly using the Navy for party advantage. Whatever might be thought of Byng's conduct, his execution, but twenty years before, was commonly ascribed to political exigency, making him a vicarious sacrifice to cover the neglects of a Government. As in Byng's case, the material of the service was believed to be now inadequate to the emergency come upon it; and it was known to have deteriorated gravely during the seven years of Sandwich's tenure of office. He was a Tory, as were his colleagues of the Cabinet; the leaders of the Navy in professional estimation, Hawke and Keppel, with other distinguished officers, were pronounced Whigs, whom it was thought the Administration would be willing to destroy. Keppel evidently feared an intention to ruin him by the command of the Channel Fleet, and the public discussion of the Courts-Martial which followed his indecisive action with D'Orvilliers, in July, 1778, assumed a decided and rancorous party tone. His accuser then was his third-in-command, Vice-Admiral Palliser, who had left his place on the Admiralty Board to take this position in the fleet; and popular outcry charged him with having betrayed his chief in the battle. So far was professional feeling moved that twelve prominent admirals,—not all of whom were Whigs,—with Hawke at their head, presented to the King a memorial, deprecating "particularly the mischief and scandal of permitting men, *who are at once in high office and subordinate military command*, previous to their making recriminating accusations against their commander-in-chief, to attempt to corrupt the public judgment by the publication of libels on their officers in a common newspaper, thereby exciting mutiny in your Majesty's Navy," etc. The words italicized show that this was aimed at Palliser; and at Sandwich, who inferentially had "permitted" his action, and ultimately rewarded him with the Governorship of Greenwich Hospital.

In this demoralized condition of professional sentiment the Admiralty could no longer command the services of the best men. Howe came home in disgust from America. Keppel threw up the command of the Channel Fleet, and Barrington subsequently refused it on the expressed ground of self-distrust, underlying which was real distrust of the ministry. He would serve as second, but not as first. Byron, after relieving Howe in New York, went to the West Indies, there made a failure, and so came home in the summer of 1779. The Channel squadron fell into the hands of men respectable, indeed, but in no way eminent, and advanced in years, whose tenures of office were comparatively short. Hardy was sixty-three, Geary seventy; and on both Hawke, who was friendly to them, passed the comment that they were "too easy." The first had allowed "the discipline of the fleet to come to nothing," and he feared the same for the other. Not until the fall of the ministry, consequent upon Cornwallis's surrender, was the post filled by a distinguished name, when Howe took the command in 1782.

The Administration was thus forced back upon Rodney; fortunately for itself, for, as far as history has since revealed, there was no other man then in the service, and of suitable rank, exactly fitted to do the work he did. Samuel Hood alone, then an unproved captain, and practically in voluntary retirement, could have equalled and surpassed him. Howe, like Rodney, was an accomplished tactician, and in conception far in advance of the standards of the day. In his place he did admirable service, which has been too little appreciated, and he was fortunate in that the work which fell to him, at the first, and again at the last of this war, was peculiarly suited to his professional characteristics; but he was not interchangeable with Rodney. In the latter there was a briskness of temper, a vivacity, very distinguishable from Howe's solidity of persistence; and he was in no sense one to permit "discipline to come to nought," the direction in which Howe's easy though reserved disposition tended. The West Indies were to be the great scene of battles, and, while the tactical ideas of the two appear to have been essentially alike, in the common recognition of combination as imperative to success, the severity of Rodney was needed to jerk the West India fleet sharply out of sleepy tradition; to compel promptness of manoeuvre and intelligent attention to the underlying ideas which signals communicate. Flexibility of movement, earnestness and rapidity of attack, mutual support by the essential coherence of the battle order without too formal precision,—these were the qualities which Rodney was to illustrate in practice, and to enforce by personal impression upon his officers. The official staff of the fleet had to pass under the rod of the schoolmaster, to receive new ideas, and to learn novel principles of obedience,—to a living chief, not to a dead letter crusted over by an unintelligent tradition. Not till this step had been made, till discipline had full hold of men's affections and understanding, was there room for the glorious liberty of action which Nelson extended to his officers; preaching it in word, and practising it in act. Hawke rebegat the British Navy in the spirit he imparted to it; Rodney, first of several, trained its approaching maturity in habits which, once acquired, stand by men as principles; Nelson reaped the fullness of the harvest.

On October 1, 1779, Rodney was again appointed to the command of the Leeward Islands Station. The year had been one of maritime misfortune and discouragement. The French declaration of war in 1778 had been followed by that of Spain in June, 1779; and a huge allied fleet—sixty-six ships-of-the-line, to which the British could oppose only thirty-five—had that summer entered and dominated the English Channel. Nothing was effected by it, true; but the impression produced was profound. In the West Indies Grenada had been lost, and Byron badly worsted in an attempt to relieve it. On assuming his command, Rodney could not but feel that he had more to do than to establish a reputation; he had a reputation to redeem, and that under a burden of national depression which doubly endangered the reputation of every officer in responsible position. He must have known that, however undeservedly, he had not the full confidence of the government, although party and personal ties would naturally have predisposed it in his favour. He therefore entered upon his career under the necessity to do and to dare greatly; he had not a strong hand, and needed the more to play a game not only strong, but to some extent adventurous.

To the radical difference between his personal standing at this opening of his command, and that which he had at its close, in 1782, may reasonably be attributed the clear difference in his action at the two periods. The first was audacious and brilliant, exhibiting qualities of which he was capable on occasion, but which did not form the groundwork of his professional character. The display was therefore exceptional, elicited by exceptional personal emergency. It was vitally necessary at the outset, if opportunity offered, to vindicate his selection by the government; to strike the imagination of the country, and obtain a hold upon its confidence which could not easily be shaken. This prestige once established, he could safely rest upon it to bear him through doubtful periods of suspense and protracted issues. It would have been well had he felt the same spur after his great battle in 1782. A necessity like this doubtless lies upon every opening career, and comparatively few there be that rise to it; but there is an evident distinction to be drawn between one in the early prime of life, who may afford to wait, who has at least no errors to atone, and him who is about to make his last cast, when upon the turning of a die depends a fair opportunity to show what is in him. Rodney was near sixty-one, when he took up the command which has given him his well earned place in history.

He experienced at once indications of the attitude towards him; and in two directions, from the Admiralty and from his subordinates. A month before he was ready, Sandwich urges him, with evident impatience, to get off.

> For God's sake, go to sea without delay. You cannot conceive of what importance it is to yourself, to me, and to the public (this very order of importance is suggestive), that you should not lose this fair wind; if you do, I shall not only hear of it in Parliament, but in places to which I pay more attention.... I must once more repeat to you that any delay in your sailing will have the most disagreeable consequences.

On the other hand, he had to complain not only of inattention on the part of the dockyard officials, but of want of zeal and activity in the officers of the fleet, many of whom behaved with a disrespect and want of cordiality which are too often the precursor of worse faults. Rodney was not the man to put up with such treatment. That it was offered, and that he for the moment bore with it, are both significant; and are to be remembered in connection with the fast approaching future.

Gibraltar was then at the beginning of the three years siege, and his intended departure was utilized to give him command of the first of the three great expeditions for its relief, which were among the characteristic operations of this war. He sailed from Plymouth on the 29th of December, 1779, having under him twenty-two sail-of-the-line, of which only four were to continue with him to the West Indies. With this great fleet, and its attendant frigates, went also a huge collection of store ships, victuallers, ordnance vessels, troop ships, and merchantmen; the last comprising the "trade" for Portugal and the West Indies, as the other classes carried the reinforcements for the Rock.

On January 7th, the West India trade parted company off Cape Finisterre, and the next day began the wonderful good fortune for which Rodney's last command was distinguished. It is no disparagement to his merit to say that in this he was, to use Ball's phrase about Nelson, "a heaven-born admiral." A Spanish convoy of twenty-two sail, seven of which were ships of war, the rest laden with supplies for Cadiz, were sighted at daylight of the 8th, and all taken; not one escaped. Twelve loaded with provisions were turned into the British convoy, and went on with it to feed the Gibraltar garrison. A prince of the blood-royal, afterwards King William IV., was with the fleet as a midshipman. One of the prizes being a line-of-battle ship, Rodney had an opportunity to show appositely his courtliness of breeding. "I have named her the *Prince William*, in respect to His Royal Highness, in whose presence *she had the honour to be taken*."

Repeated intelligence had reached the admiral that a Spanish division was cruising off Cape St. Vincent. Therefore, when it was sighted at 1 p.m. of January 16th, a week after the capture of the convoy, he was prepared for the event. A brief attempt to form line was quickly succeeded by the signal for a general chase, the ships to engage to leeward as they came up with the enemy, who, by taking flight to the southeast, showed the intention to escape into Cadiz. The wind was blowing strong from the westward, giving a lee shore and shoals to the British fleet in the approaching long hours of a wintry night; but opportunity was winging by, with which neither Rodney nor the Navy could afford to trifle. He was already laid up with an attack of the gout that continued to harass him throughout this command, and the decision to continue the chase was only reached after a discussion between him and his captain, the mention of which is transmitted by Sir Gilbert Blane, the surgeon of the ship, who was present professionally. The merit of the resolution must remain with the man who bore the responsibility of the event; but that he reached it at such a moment only after consultation with another, to whom current gossip attributed the chief desert, must be coupled with the plausible claim afterwards advanced for Sir Charles Douglas, that he suggested the breaking of the enemy's line on April 12th. Taken together, they indicate at least a common contemporary professional estimate of Rodney's temperament. No such anecdote is transmitted of Hawke. The battle of Cape St. Vincent, therefore, is not that most characteristic of Rodney's genius. Judged by his career at large, it is exceptional; yet of all his actions it is the one in which merit and success most conspicuously met. Nor does it at all detract from his credit that the enemy was much inferior in numbers; eleven to twenty-one. As in Hawke's pursuit of Conflans, with which this engagement is worthy to be classed, what was that night dared, rightly and brilliantly dared, was the dangers of the deep, not of the foe. The prey was seized out of the jaws of disaster.

The results were commensurate to the risk. The action, which began at 4 p.m., lasted till two the following morning, the weather becoming tempestuous with a great sea, so that it was difficult to take possession of the captured vessels. Many of the heavy British ships continued also in danger during the 17th, and had to carry a press of sail to clear the shoals, on which two of their prizes were actually wrecked. One Spanish ship-of-the-line was blown up and six struck, among them the flag-ship of Admiral Langara, who was taken into Gibraltar. Only four escaped.

Two such strokes of mingled good fortune and good management, within ten days, formed a rare concurrence, and the aggregate results were as exceptional as the combination of events. Sandwich congratulated Rodney that he had already "taken more line-of-battle ships than had been captured in any one action in either of the two last preceding wars." Militarily regarded, it had a further high element of praise, for the enemy's detachment, though in itself inferior, was part of a much superior force; twenty-four allied ships-of-the-line besides it being at the moment in Cadiz Bay. It is the essence of military art thus to overwhelm in detail. A technical circumstance like this was doubtless overlooked in the general satisfaction with the event, the most evident feature in which was the relief of the Government, who just then stood badly in need of credit. "The ministerial people feel it very sensibly," Lady Rodney wrote him. "It is a lucky stroke for them at this juncture." Salutes were fired, and the city illuminated; the press teemed with poetical effusion. Sandwich, somewhat impudently when the past is considered, but not uncharacteristically regarded as an officeholder, took to himself a large slice of the credit. "The worst of my enemies now allow that I have pitched upon a man who knows his duty, and is a brave, honest, and able officer.... I have obtained you the thanks of both houses of Parliament." The letter does not end without a further caution against indiscreet talking about the condition of his ships. It all comes back on the Government, he laments. What Rodney may have said to others may be uncertain; to his wife, soon after reaching his station, he wrote:

> What are the ministers about? Are they determined to undo their country? Is it fair that the British fleet should be so inferior to the French, and that the British officers and men are always to be exposed to superior numbers? What right had the administration to expect anything but defeat?

Then he passes on to remark himself, what has been alluded to above, the change in his personal position effected by his successes.

> Thank God, I now fear no frowns of ministers, and hope never again to stand in need of their assistance. I know them well. All are alike, and no dependence is to be placed on their promises.

It is to be feared his sense of obligation to Sandwich did not coincide with the latter's estimate.

In his official report Rodney gave much credit to his officers for the St. Vincent affair.

> The gallant behaviour of the admirals, captains, officers and men, I had the honour to command, was conspicuous; they seemed animated with the same spirit, and were eager to exert themselves with the utmost zeal.

Here also, however, he was biding his time for obvious reasons; for to his wife he writes:

> I have done them all like honour, but it is because I would not have the world believe that there were officers slack in their duty. Without a thorough change in naval affairs, the discipline of our navy will be lost. I could say much, but will not. You will hear of it from *themselves*.

That is, probably, by their mutual recriminations. Such indulgent envelopment of good and bad alike in a common mantle of commendation is far from unexampled; but it rarely fails to return to plague its authors, as has been seen in instances more recent than that of Rodney. He clearly had told Sandwich the same in private letters, for the First Lord writes him:

> I fear the picture you give of the faction in your fleet is too well drawn. Time and moderation will by degrees get the better of this bane of discipline. I exceedingly applaud your resolution to shut your ears against the illiberal language of your officers, who are inclined to arraign each other's conduct.

In this two things are to be remarked: first, the evident and undeniable existence of serious cause of complaint, which was preparing Rodney for the stern self-assertion soon to be shown; and, second, that such imputations are frequent with him, while he seems in turn to have had a capacity for eliciting insubordination of feeling, though he can repress the act. It is a question of personal temperament, which explains more than his relations with other men. Hawke and Nelson find rare fault with those beneath them; for their own spirit takes possession of their subordinates. Such difference of spirit reveals itself in more ways than one in the active life of a military community.

If there was joy in England over Rodney's achievement, still more and more sympathetic was the exultation of those who in the isolation of Gibraltar's Rock, rarely seeing their country's flag save on their own flagstaff, witnessed and shared the triumph of his entrance there with his train of prizes. The ships of war and transports forming the convoy did not indeed appear in one body, but in groups, being dispersed by the light airs, and swept eastward by the in-drag of the current from the Atlantic to the Mediterranean; but the presence of the great fleet, and the prestige of its recent victory, secured the practical immunity of merchant vessels during its stay. Of the first to come in, on January 15th, an eye-witness wrote:

> A ship with the British flag entering the Bay was so uncommon a sight that almost the whole garrison were assembled at the southward to welcome her in; but words are insufficient to describe their transports on being informed that she was one of a large convoy which had sailed the latter end of the preceding month for our relief.

The admiral himself had been carried beyond and gone into Tetuan, in Morocco, whence he finally arrived on January 26th, having sent on a supply fleet to Minorca, the garrison of which was undergoing a severance from the outer world more extreme even than that of Gibraltar. Upon the return thence of the convoying ships he again put to sea, February 13th, with the entire fleet, which accompanied him three days sail to the westward, when it parted company for England; he with only four ships-of-the-line pursuing his way to his station. On March 27th he reached Santa Lucia, where he found seventeen of-the-line, composing his command. Three weeks later he met the enemy; barely three months, almost to a day, after the affair at St. Vincent.

The antecedent circumstances of the war, and the recent history of the French navy, gave a singular opportuneness of occasion, and of personal fitness, to Rodney's arrival at this moment. The humiliations of the Seven Years War, with the loss of so much of the French colonial empire, traceable in chief measure to naval decadence, had impressed the French government with the need of reviving their navy, which had consequently received a material development in quality, as well as in quantity, unparalleled since the days of Colbert and Seignelay, near a century before. Concomitant with this had been a singular progress in the theory of naval evolutions, and of their handmaid, naval signalling, among French officers; an advance to which the lucid, speculative, character of the national genius greatly contributed. Although they as yet lacked practice, and were numerically too few, the French officers were well equipped by mental resources, by instruction and reflection, to handle large fleets; and they now had large fleets to handle. No such conjunction had occurred since Tourville; none such recurred during the Revolution.

The condition was unique in naval history of the sail period. To meet it, assuming an approach to equality in contending fleets, was required, first, a commander-in-chief, and then a competent body of officers. The latter the British had only in the sense of fine seamen and gallant men. In courage there is no occasion to institute comparisons between the two nations; in kind there may have been a difference, but certainly not in degree. The practical superiority of seamanship in the British may be taken as a set-off to the more highly trained understanding of military principles and methods on the part of their enemy. For commander-in-chief, there were at this time but two, Howe and Rodney, whose professional equipment, as shown in practice, fitted them to oppose the French methods. Of these Rodney was the better, because possessed of a quicker power of initiative, and also of that personal severity required to enforce strict conformity of action among indifferent or sullen subordinates.

Rodney has therefore a singularly well defined place among British naval chiefs. He was to oppose form to form, theory to theory, evolution to evolution, upon the battle ground of the sea; with purpose throughout tactically offensive, not defensive, and facing an adversary his equal in professional equipment. Had he arrived a year before he would have met no fair match in D'Estaing, a soldier, not a sailor, whose deficiencies as a seaman would have caused a very different result from that which actually followed his encounter with Byron, who in conduct showed an utter absence of ideas and of method inconceivable in Rodney. The French were now commanded by De Guichen, considered the most capable of their officers by Rodney, whose recent abode in Paris had probably familiarized him with professional reputations among the enemy. Everything therefore conspired to make the occasion one eminently fitted to his capacities. Such are the conditions—the man *and* the hour—that make reputations; though they do not form characters, which are growths of radically different origin.

De Guichen put to sea from Martinique on April 15th, with a convoy for Santo Domingo which he intended to see clear of British interference. Rodney, whose anchorage was but thirty miles away, learned instantly the French sailing and followed without delay. On the evening of April 16th, the two fleets were in sight of each other to leeward of Martinique, the British to windward; an advantage that was diligently maintained during the night. At daylight of the 17th the two enemies were twelve to fifteen miles apart, ranged on nearly parallel lines, the British twenty heading northwest, the French twenty-three southeast. The numerical difference represents sufficiently nearly the actual difference of force, although French vessels averaged more powerful than British of the same rates.

At 6.45 a.m. Rodney signalled that it was his intention to attack the enemy's rear with his whole force. This was never annulled, and the purpose governed his action throughout the day. This combination—on the rear—is the one generally preferable to be attempted when underway, and the relative situations of the fleets at this moment made it particularly opportune; for the British, in good order, two cables interval between the ships, were abreast the rear centre and rear of the enemy, whose line was in comparison greatly extended,—the result probably of inferior practical seamanship. To increase his advantage, Rodney at 7 ordered his vessels to close to one cable, and at 8.30, when the antagonists were still heading as at daybreak, undertook to lead the fleet down by a series of signals directive of its successive movements. In this he was foiled by De Guichen, who by wearing brought what was previously his van into position to support the extreme threatened. "The different movements of the enemy," wrote Rodney, "obliged me to be very attentive and watch every opportunity of attacking them at advantage;" a sentence that concisely sums up his special excellencies, of which the present occasion offers the most complete illustration. It may be fully conceded also that it would have vindicated his high title to fame by conspicuous results, had the intelligence of his officers seconded his dispositions.

The forenoon passed in manoeuvres, skilfully timed, to insure a definite issue. At 11.50 Rodney considered that his opportunity had arrived. Both fleets were then heading in the same direction, on the starboard tack, and he had again succeeded in so placing his own that, by the words of his report, he expected to bring—

> . . . . the whole force of His Majesty's fleet against the enemy's rear, and of course part of their centre, by which means the twenty sail of British ships would have been opposed to only fifteen sail of the enemy's, and must in all probability have totally disabled them before their van could have given them any assistance.

It would be difficult to cite a clearer renouncement of the outworn "van to van," ship to ship, dogma; but Rodney is said to have expressed himself in more emphatic terms subsequently, as follows:

During all the commands Lord Rodney has been entrusted with, he made it a rule to bring his whole force against a part of the enemy's, and never was so absurd as to bring ship against ship, when the enemy gave him an opportunity of acting otherwise.

Though not distinctly so stated, it would seem that his first movement on the present occasion had failed because of the long distance between the fleets permitting the enemy to succour the part threatened, before he could close. He was now nearer, for at this second attempt only an hour proved to be needed for the first British ship to open fire at long range. It may be for this reason, also, that he at this stage threw himself upon his captains, no longer prescribing the successive movements, but issuing the general signal to bear down, each vessel to "steer," according to the 21st Article of the *Additional* Fighting Instructions—

. . . . for the ship of the enemy which from the disposition of the two squadrons it must be her lot to engage, notwithstanding the signal for the line ahead will be kept flying: making or shortening sail in such proportion as *to preserve the distance assigned by the signal for the line*, in order that the whole squadron may, as near as possible, come into action at the same time.

Unfortunately for his manoeuvre, the Admiral here ran up against the stolid idea of the old—and still existing—Fighting Instructions concerning the line-of-battle in action, embodied in a typical representative in the senior captain of his fleet. This gentleman, Robert Carkett, had risen from before the mast, and after a lieutenancy of thirteen years had become post in 1758, by succeeding to the command when his captain was killed, in one of the most heroic single-ship fights of the British navy. Unluckily, his seniority gave him the lead of the fleet as it was now formed on the starboard tack, and he considered that the signal for attacking the enemy's rear was annulled by the present situation. He stated in a letter to the Admiralty:

Both fleets were at 11.15 parallel to and abreast of each other. As I was then the leading ship, it became my duty to engage the leading ship of the French fleet, as this signal disannulled all former ones relative to the mode of attack.

The word "abreast," critically used, would imply that the fleets were abreast, ship to ship, van to van; but there appears no reason to question Rodney's statement of the facts made to Carkett himself:

> Forgetting that the signal for the line was only at two cables length distance from each other, the van division was by you led to more than two leagues distance from the centre division, which was thereby exposed to the greatest strength of the enemy, and not properly supported.

Rodney, in short, meant by opposite the enemy's ship opposite at the moment the signal was made; and he also expected that the movements of his ships would be further controlled by the words of the 21st Article, "preserve the distance assigned by the signal for the line," which distance was to be taken from the centre; or, as sometimes worded in the Instructions, "the distance shall be that between the admiral and the ships next ahead and astern of him." Carkett conceived that he was to attack the ship opposite him in numerical order, that is, the leader of the enemy, and that the remaining British would take distance from him.

Why the rest of the van should also have been led thus astray can be explained only on the ground that Carkett's general views were shared by the divisional commander, a rear-admiral, who, as was proved a year later, possessed high courage of the pure game-cock order, but was wholly thoughtless of gaining an unfair advantage, two against one, by tactical ingenuity. The result was that the van as a body left the centre to itself, and thereby not only wrecked the concentration at which Rodney aimed, but was out of hand to support his flag and his division, when badly battered by the enemy's fire. This was the great tactical blunder which brought to nought Rodney's patient, wary manoeuvres of the past six hours. To it especially, but not to it alone, he referred in the stinging words of his despatch:

'Tis with concern inexpressible, mixt with indignation, that the duty I owe my sovereign and country obliges me to acquaint their Lordships that, during the action with the French fleet on the 17th instant His Majesty's, the British flag was not properly supported.

To the specific error of the van was added a widespread disregard of the order for close action, despite the example of the commander-in-chief, who pressed the enemy so hard that towards the end his flag-ship was to leeward of De Guichen's wake.

Perceiving several of our ships engaging at a distance, I repeated the signal for close action. With truth, but sorrow, I must say it was little attended to.

It is noticeable that one of the ships thus censured, the *Cornwall*, next ahead of Rodney, lost as heavily in killed and wounded as did the flag-ship herself; one of many instances showing that distance lessened efficiency without increasing safety. The forwardness of Rodney's flag on this occasion proves clearly enough his consciousness that tactics, to succeed, must be more than a veil for timidity; that hard hitting is as essential as skilful leading.

This combination of steady, patient, wary, skilful guidance, with resolute and tenacious personal leadership, constituted the firm tissue of Rodney's professional character, and at no time received such clear illustration as in the case before us; for no like opportunity recurred. One experience was enough for De Guichen; he did not choose again to yield the advantage of the weather gage, and he had the tactical skill necessary to retain it in his future contacts with this adversary. The battle of April 12, 1782, upon which Rodney's fame has rested, was rather an accident than an achievement, and as a revelation of character its most conspicuous feature is wariness exaggerated into professional timidity. He himself has weighed the relative professional value of the two affairs. A letter published in 1809, anonymous, but bearing strong internal evidence of being written by Sir Gilbert Blane, long on a trusted physician's terms of intimacy with Rodney, states that he "thought little of his victory on the 12th of April." He would have preferred to rest his reputation upon this action with De Guichen, and—

> .... looked upon that opportunity of beating, with an inferior fleet, such an officer, whom he considered the best in the French service, as one by which, but for the disobedience of his captains, he might have gained an immortal renown.

The misconduct of his officers brought out in full vigour the severity which was a salient feature of Rodney's professional character. In the St. Vincent business he may have been partly actuated to spare, by the reflection that the offenders were not his own captains; that they were about to quit him finally. Moreover, there had been then a very considerable tangible success; results cover a multitude of sins. No such extenuations applied here. The wreck of his reasonable hopes of personal distinction coincided with failure towards the nation itself. Rodney's hand came down heavy upon the offenders; but so far as seen it was the hand always of a gentleman. In private letters his full feelings betrayed themselves in vehemence; but in public they were measured to austerity. To Carkett, when questioned concerning the rumoured expressions in his despatch, he is withering in the pointed enumeration of varied shortcomings; but he never lapses into a breach of professional decorum of utterance. The unfortunate man represented to the Admiralty his view of the matter,—already cited; but it bears no endorsement to show that it had passed under Rodney's eye. Captain, ship, and ship's company, were swept away a few months later in the memorable hurricane of October, 1780.

The despatch specified no other delinquent by name; but the selection of five captains to receive personal commendation, and the persistent refusal of the same to all other subordinates, including the junior flag-officers, made censure sufficiently individual; and the admiral's subsequent line of conduct emphasized rebuke bitterly. The cruise was not yet finished; for the French having taken refuge at Guadeloupe, it was important to prevent them from regaining Martinique, their chief depot and place of repairs.

To intercept them there, Rodney at first took station off Fort Royal, and when compelled for a moment to return to Santa Lucia, kept lookouts to warn him betimes of the enemy's appearance. So, when De Guichen approached from the windward side of the islands, on May 9th, he found the British getting underway to meet him. From that time until the 20th—eleven days—the fleets were manoeuvring in sight of one another, beating to windward; the British endeavouring to force action, the French to avoid it. De Guichen's orders from home were "to keep the sea, so far as the force maintained by England in the Windward Islands would permit, *without too far compromising* the fleet entrusted to him." Such instructions compelled him to defensive tactics; as Rodney's views, and those traditional in his service, impelled him to attack. Hence ensued a struggle of sustained vigilance, activity, and skill, profoundly interesting professionally, but which does not lend itself to other than technical narrative. Rodney wrote:

> For fourteen days and nights the fleets were so near each other that neither officers nor men could be said to sleep. Nothing but the goodness of the weather and climate could have enabled us to endure so continual a fatigue. Had it been in Europe, half the people must have sunk under it. For my part, it did me good.

No evidence of professional aptness could be given clearer than the last words. A man is easy under such circumstances only when they fit him. De Guichen asked to be superseded; "my health cannot endure such continual fatigue and anxiety." Twice the wary Frenchman was nearly caught, but the wind did not favour Rodney long enough to give him the weather position, the only sure one for offence. But, while thus unable to compass results, he gave conclusive evidence of the quickness of his eye, the alertness of his action, and the flexibility which he was enabled to impress upon his fleet by sheer force of personal character. The contest resembled that of two expert swordsmen; more intermittent doubtless, but also much more prolonged.

There can be no trifling with such conditions. A moment's relaxation, or inaptness, may forfeit opportunity, offered only by chance and not to be regained by effort. Rodney was fixed that no such slip should occur through the neglect of others, and his stern supervision, as represented by himself to his wife, was that of a slave driver, lash in hand.

> As I had given public notice to all my captains, etc. that I should hoist my flag on board one of my frigates, and that I expected implicit obedience to every signal made, under the certain penalty of being instantly superseded, it had an admirable effect, as they were all convinced, after their late gross behaviour, that they had nothing to expect at my hands but instant punishment to those who neglected their duty. My eye on them had more dread than the enemy's fire, and they knew it would be fatal. No regard was paid to rank,—admirals as well as captains, if out of their station, were instantly reprimanded by signals, or messages sent by frigates: and, in spite of themselves, I taught them to be what they had never been before—*officers*: and showed them that an inferior fleet, properly conducted, was more than a match for one far superior.

Making allowance for exaggeration in the irresponsible utterances of family life, the above is eminently characteristic of temperament. It must be added, as equally characteristic of an underlying justice which Rodney possessed, that in his official account of these last manoeuvres he gave credit to his subordinates as a whole.

> I must inform their Lordships, in justice to the commanders and officers of the fleet under my command, that since the action of the 17th of April, and during the pursuit of the enemy's fleet, and in the two rencontres with them, all my officers, of every rank and denomination, were obedient and attentive to orders and signals, and, I am convinced, if the enemy had given them an opportunity, they would have done their duty to their King and Country.

The claims of justice against its own strict requirements he also recognized to Carkett.

Nothing but the former service you had done your King and Country, and my firm belief of your being a brave man, could have induced me, as commander of a great fleet, to overlook.

It will not escape attention that this exact observance of credit, where due, lends increased weight to censure, when inflicted.

To the pursuit of the French fleet, relinquished forty leagues eastward of Martinique after the brush of May 19th, succeeded a period marked only by the routine administrative cares attendant upon an admiral charged with the defence of a lengthy, exposed chain of islands, and an extensive trade, against enemies numerically much superior. The details serve to show the breadth of intelligence, the sound judgment, and clear professional conceptions that characterized Rodney in small things as well as great; but it would be wearisome to elaborate demonstration of this, and these qualities he had in common with many men otherwise inferior to himself. Reaction from the opening strain of the campaign, with the relaxation of vigour from the approach of the hot rainy season, now began to tell on his health; and to this contributed the harassment of mind due to the arrival of a large Spanish fleet, while reinforcements promised him unaccountably failed to appear. Nevertheless, his personal efficiency was not impaired, and towards the end of July he resolved to execute a project which he had long entertained, of carrying the mass of his fleet from the islands to the Continental waters of North America.

During the year between his return from Paris and his present appointment, he had laid before the Admiralty two papers, containing an admirable summary of the leading strategic conditions of the whole scene of war in the western hemisphere, with suggestions for action amounting to a plan of campaign. One feature of this was based upon the weather differences, which rendered cruising dangerous in the West Indies when most favourable to the northward, and unsure in North America when most certain among the islands. He proposed to utilize this alternation of seasons, by shifting a mobile reinforcement suddenly and secretly from one end to the other of the long front of operations. This is a common enough expedient in military art, but had rarely received the convincing formulation which he gave it; while that such a conception was a novelty to the average naval mind of the day, may be inferred from the startled wrath of the admiral in North America at Rodney's unexpected intrusion upon his bailiwick.

Sandwich, however, had entertained the project, and in October, 1779, just as Rodney's appointment issued, a vessel sailed from England with letters to Admiral Arbuthnot in New York, directing him to send several ships-of-the-line to the West Indies for the winter campaign. The vessel lost a mast, kept off to Nassau in the Bahamas, and after arrival there her captain, while spending some months in repairs, did not think to send on the despatches. Arbuthnot, therefore, received them only on March 16, 1780; too late, doubtless, to collect and equip a force in time to reach Rodney before the affair of April 17th.

At the end of July, 1780, the conditions in the West Indies were that the allied French and Spanish fleets had gone to leeward from Martinique; to Havana, and to Cap François, in Haiti. At the latter port was assembling a large trade convoy—three hundred ships, according to Rodney's information. He reasoned that this must go to Europe, but would not require the full strength of the French fleet; therefore, transferring his own insight to the enemy's mind, he convinced himself that a part of their vessels would seek Narragansett Bay, to reinforce the seven ships-of-the-line that had reached there on July 12th, under De Ternay, of whose arrival Rodney now knew. Great possibilities might be open to such a combination, skilfully handled against the inferior numbers of Arbuthnot.

> As it plainly appeared to me that His Majesty's territory, fleet, and army, in America were in imminent danger of being overpowered by the superior force of the public enemy, I deemed it a duty incumbent upon me to forego any emoluments that might have accrued by the enterprise intended by General Vaughan and myself during the hurricane months, and without a moment's hesitation flew with all despatch possible to prevent the enemy's making any impression upon the continent before my arrival there.

The protestation of disinterestedness here is somewhat intrusive, and being wholly unnecessary excites rather criticism than confidence.

Although reasonable precautions had been taken for the security of his own station, and all circumstances carefully weighed, there was in this step of Rodney's an assumption of responsibility,—of risk,—as in his similar action of 1762, before noted. This, as well as the military correctness of the general conception, deserves to be noted to the credit of his professional capacity. Making the land about Charleston, South Carolina, he swept along the coast to the northward, until he anchored off Sandy Hook, September 14th. The following day he issued an order to Admiral Arbuthnot, directing him to put himself under his command and to obey his instructions.

Rodney's coming was a grievous blow to Washington, who instead had hoped, as Rodney had feared, the arrival of De Guichen, or at the least of a strong French naval division. The enemy's disappointment is perhaps the best proof of sagacity in a military movement, but Sandwich's clear approval was also forthcoming.

> It is impossible for us to have a superior fleet in every part; and unless our commanders-in-chief will take the great line, as you do, and consider the King's whole dominions as under their care, our enemies must find us unprepared somewhere, and carry their point against us.

Arbuthnot, nevertheless, saw only personal injury to himself; a natural feeling, but one which should not be allowed display. Rodney had given various particular orders, and had suggested that it would be better that the commander-in-chief on the station should keep headquarters at New York, leaving the blockade of Ternay, a hundred and thirty miles distant, to a junior admiral; also, he intimated the opinion that such a blockade would be better conducted underway than anchored in Gardiner's Bay, fifty miles from the enemy's port. Though suggestion did not override discretion, Arbuthnot resented it in all its forms. After explaining his reasons, he added:

> How far, Sir, your conduct (similarly circumstanced as you are) is praiseworthy and proper, consequences must determine. Your partial interference in the conduct of the American War is certainly incompatible with principles of reason, and precedents of service. The frigates attending on a cruising squadron you have taken upon you to counter-order, (a due representation of which and other circumstances I shall make where it will have every possible effect), and thus I have been for some time without even a repeater of signals.

Though Rodney's step was unusual, his position as Arbuthnot's superior officer, locally present, was impregnable. He nevertheless kept his temper under provocation, and the dignified restraint of his reply is notable; indeed, the only significant feature of this incident, from the biographical point of view.

> No offence to you was intended on my part. Every respect due to you, as an officer and a gentleman, my inclination as well as my duty led me to pay you in the strictest sense.

He leaves no doubt, however, that he does not intend to allow his functions to lapse into a mere official primacy,—that he will rule, as well as reign.

> Duty, not inclination, brought me to North America. I came to interfere in the American War, to command by sea in it, and to do my best endeavours towards the putting an end thereto. I knew the dignity of my own rank entitled me to take the supreme command, which I ever shall do on every station where His Majesty's and the public service may make it necessary for me to go, unless I meet a superior officer, in which case it will be my duty to obey his orders.

He then proceeds to exercise his authority, by explicit directions and some criticism of existing arrangements. Afterwards, in submitting the papers to the Admiralty, Rodney wrote:

> I am ashamed to mention what appears to me the real cause, and from whence Mr. Arbuthnot's chagrin proceeds, but the proofs are so plain that prize-money is the occa-

sion that I am under the necessity of transmitting them. I can solemnly assure their Lordships that I had not the least conception of any other prize-money on the coast of America but that which would be most honourably obtained by the destruction of the enemy's ships of war and privateers—but when prize-money appeared predominant in the mind of my brother officer, I was determined to have my share of that bounty so graciously bestowed by His Majesty and the public.

Nelson's retort to Arbuthnot's successor, two years later, may be recalled. "You have come to a good station for prize-money."

"Yes, but the West Indies is the station for honour."

The visit to continental waters was on this occasion productive of little result. Contrary alike to Rodney's anticipations and those of Washington, De Guichen's whole fleet had returned to Europe. Some slight redistribution of cruisers, the more frequent capture of privateers, with increased security to the trade of New York and incidental support to some rather predatory land operations, were all that Rodney could show of tangible consequence from his presence. Arbuthnot alone was superior to Ternay if neither received reinforcements. Rodney's health felt the keener atmosphere, so that he had to go ashore in New York, and he accepted the views of Arbuthnot as to the strength of the French fleet's position in Newport, without examining it himself. Had he done so, however, it is unlikely that he would have formed more strenuous purposes. The disposition of the enemy's squadron there was so imposing that only the genius of a Nelson, mindful as at Revel of the moral influence of a great blow at a critical period of the war, could have risen to the necessity of daring such a hazard. His phrase was there applicable, "Desperate affairs require desperate remedies." There is no indication of this supreme element in Rodney's composition. It is interesting to note, however, that personal observation had given conviction of success at Newport to the officer who was afterwards Nelson's gallant second at Copenhagen,—Sir Thomas Graves.

This paucity of results in no way lessens the merit of the movement from the West Indies to the continent. It was indubitably correct in idea, and, as has been pointed out, the conception was Rodney's own, the possibilities were great, the risk in many ways undeniable; when these can be affirmed of a military action, failure to obtain results, because conditions take an improbable direction, does not detract from credit. Nor should the obviousness of this measure hide the fact that the suggestion appears to have been original with him, occurring fully developed in his memorandum of May, 1778, to the Admiralty; whether written in Paris or England does not appear. The transfer of Hotham's squadron to the southward in the following December, 1779, enabling Barrington to conquer Santa Lucia,—a place insisted upon in the same memorandum as of the first importance,—may not improbably be attributed to this fruitful paper. In the next year, 1781, a detachment was again sent to New York, and had Rodney been able to accompany it in person there is no room to doubt that he would have saved Cornwallis; reversing issues, at least momentarily, certainly prolonging the war, possibly deciding the contest otherwise than as befell.

Rodney's return to the West Indies in December, 1780, concluded the most eventful and illustriously characteristic year of his life. The destruction of Langara's fleet in January, the brilliant tactical displays of April 17th, and of the chase manoeuvres in May, the strategic transference in August of a large division, unawares to the enemy, from one point of the field of action to another, are all feats that testify to his great ability as a general officer. Nor should there be left out of the account the stern dignity of conduct which assured his personal control of the fleet, his certainty of touch in the face of an enemy. Thus considered, it was a year full of events, successful throughout as regards personal desert, and singularly significant of ability and temperament.

The year 1781 was far less happy, nor does the great victory, which in 1782 crowned his career with glory, contribute to the enhancement of his professional distinction; rather the contrary. Upon reaching Barbados, December 5th, he found the island shorn to the ground by the noted hurricane, which in the previous October had swept the Caribbean, from the Lesser Antilles to Jamaica. Eight of the division left by him in the West Indies had been wrecked,—two being ships-of-the-line; and the efficiency of the whole fleet was grievously impaired by the widespread injury to vessels.

An event charged with more serious consequences to himself soon followed. On the 27th of January, 1781, at Barbados, despatches from the Admiralty notified him that Great Britain had declared war against Holland, and directed him to proceed at once against the Dutch shipping and West Indies. First among the enumerated objects of attack was the small island of St. Eustatius. This, having enjoyed the advantages of neutrality at a time when almost the whole Caribbean was in hostilities, had become a depot for the accumulation and distribution of stores, commercial and warlike. Ostensibly, it served all parties, giving to and receiving from Europe, America, and the Caribbean alike. The political sympathies of Holland, however, and it may be added those of the West Indies in general, even of the British islands themselves, were rather adverse to Great Britain in the current struggle; and this, combined with the greater self-sufficingness of the British naval and commercial administration, had made the neutral support of St. Eustatius more benevolent, and much more useful, to the enemies of Great Britain, including the revolted colonists, than it was to the mother country. Rodney asserted that help from there was readily forthcoming to supply French and Spanish requirements, while professions of inability abounded whenever his fleet made a demand in occasional emergencies.

He was therefore full of gall against the island and its merchants, the more so because he suspected that British subjects, unpatriotically ardent for gain, were largely concerned in maintaining conditions thus hurtful to their country; and, when the orders to act came, it needed but three days for himself and General Vaughan to sail on an errand of which they probably had previous intimations. On the 3rd of February they arrived off St. Eustatius, which in the face of their imposing force submitted at once. They took possession of the island, with goods stored to the estimated value of £3,000,000,—an immense spoil in those days. A Dutch ship-of-war, with a hundred and fifty sail of traders of various nationalities, were also seized; while a convoy of thirty merchant ships, which had sailed thirty-six hours before, was pursued and captured by a British detachment,—the Dutch admiral commanding the ships-of-war being killed in the attendant action.

From one point of view this was an enormous success, though unproductive of glory. It destroyed at a blow a centre of commerce and supply powerfully contributive to the maintenance of the enemies of Great Britain; both to their hostile operations, and to the indirect but no less vital financial support that trade gives to national endurance,—to the sinews of war. Besides this, however, there was the unprecedented immediate booty, transferable as so much asset to the conquerors. It was upon this present tangible result that Rodney's imagination fastened, with an engrossment and tenacity that constitute a revelation of character. It perverted his understanding of conditions, and paralyzed his proper action as commander-in-chief. It is needless in this connection to consider whether it was the matter of personal profit, through legitimate prize-money, that thus influenced him,—an effect to some extent pardonable in a man who had long suffered, and still was suffering, from pecuniary straightness,—or whether, as he loudly protested, it was the interest to the nation that made his personal superintendence of the proceeds imperative. In either case the point to be noted is not a palpable trait of covetousness,—if such it were,—but the limitation to activity occasioned by preoccupation with a realized, but imperfect, success. The comparatively crude impression of greediness, produced by apparent absorption in a mere money gain, has prevented the perception of this more important and decisive element in Rodney's official character, revealed at St. Eustatius and confirmed on the evening of the 12th of April. What he had won, he had won; what more he might and should do, he would not see, nor would he risk.

His discontent with his junior flag-officers in the West Indies, and the peculiar demoralization of professional tone at the moment, had made it difficult for the Admiralty to provide him a satisfactory second in command. In order to do this, they had "to make a promotion," as the phrase went; that is, in order to get the man wanted, the seniors on the captains' list were promoted down to and including him. The choice had fallen on Sir Samuel Hood,—in later days Nelson's honoured Lord Hood,—than which none could have been happier in respect of capacity. It has been truly said that he was as able as Rodney, and more energetic; but even this falls short of his merit. He had an element of professional—as distinguished from personal—daring, and an imaginative faculty that penetrated the extreme possibilities of a situation, quickened by the resolve, in which Rodney was deficient, to have all or nothing; and these invaluable traits were balanced by the sound and accurate judgment of a thorough seaman, without which imagination lures to disaster. The man who as a junior formed the idea of seizing De Grasse's anchorage in the Chesapeake in 1781, to effect the relief of Cornwallis, and who in 1782, when momentarily in chief command, illustrated the idea by actual performance under similar conditions in the West Indies, rose to heights of conception and of achievement for which we have no equivalent in Rodney's career. Unfortunately for him, though thus mighty in act, opportunity for great results never came to him. The hour never met the man.

Hood with eight ships-of-the-line and a large convoy arrived on the station in January, 1781, and was at St. Eustatius with the commander-in-chief when Rodney received a report, which proved to be false, that eight to ten French ships-of-the-line, with a numerous supply-fleet, had been sighted in European waters evidently bound for the West Indies. He thereupon detached Hood, on February 12th, and directed him with seventeen of-the-line to await the enemy to windward of Martinique, their probable destination. A month later he ordered the position to be shifted to leeward of the island, in front of the French arsenal port, Fort Royal. Hood dissented from this, remonstrating vigorously, and the event proved him right; but Rodney insisted, the more injudiciously in that he was throwing the tactical burden upon his junior while fettering thus his tactical discretion. Meantime, twenty French ships-of-the-line did sail on March 22nd for Martinique, under Count De Grasse: beginning then the campaign which ended in the great disaster of April 12, 1782, but not until it had been signalized by the surrender of Cornwallis, due to this fleet, as Washington said. On the 28th of April it came in sight of Hood; but, owing to the leewardly position insisted upon by Rodney, the English commander could not prevent the junction to it of four French ships then in the port. A battle followed next day, of eighteen British—one having just joined—against twenty-four enemies; odds which, combined with the weather gage held by the French, should have insured them a decisive victory. This result was prevented by the tentative action of De Grasse, encountering the tactical capacity and imperturbable self-possession of Hood.

Rodney could not have bettered Hood's management, though he of course attributed to him the blame for results. It is evident, however, that for various reasons the commander-in-chief should have been with the body of his fleet. Even barring certain and timely information of the French coming, which Hood at least did not have, there was every reasonable probability that such an expedition would arrive at about the season it did. Hood's insight, which was adequate to divining possibilities as well as to dealing with ascertained conditions, had taught him that the latter half of April—and not sooner—was the time by which the British should be refitted, provisioned and watered full, and in all respects ready for prolonged operations against a powerful enemy; as well as concentrated to windward. He reasoned thus from the fact that the French navy, to the number of forty odd,—being the combined fleets of D'Estaing from Brest and De Guichen from the West Indies,—had been assembled in Cadiz towards the end of 1780, and did not return to Brest until January, 1781. To refit, sail, and reach Martinique again, would in his judgment postpone arrival to the middle of April, and this respite should be improved by getting the British ships into the best campaigning condition, so as not to be hampered in subsequent movements by necessities of repair and supply. With this persuasion he became eager, by the first of the month, for the admiral's presence; the more so because confident that, if he were on the spot, he would see the necessity of changing position from leeward to windward. "I begin to be extremely impatient for the honour of being and acting immediately under your flag, as I do not find myself pleasant in being to leeward; for should an enemy's fleet attempt to get into Martinique, and the commander of it inclines to avoid battle, nothing but a skirmish will probably happen, which in its consequences may operate as a defeat to the British squadron, though not a ship is lost and the enemy suffer most."

This is a clear case in which events that actually befell were foreseen; not by supernatural illumination, but by the clear light of unbiased reason acting upon evident considerations. There *was* but a skirmish, the British *did* suffer badly, and the consequences *were* equivalent to defeat; for, had the whole British force of the line been present to windward, it would have prevented the junction of the French, and therefore have been so nearly equal to the main body as to have assured an action inflicting very serious injury, incapacitating the enemy for the attacks upon Santa Lucia and Tobago, before which the latter fell, and not improbably deterring De Grasse from the expedition to the Chesapeake which forced the capitulation of Cornwallis. Such deductions are of course dependent upon the contingencies inseparable from warfare. They are not certainties, indeed; but they are inferences of very great probability. So much hinged upon the presence of an officer with the full discretion denied to Hood; of the officer primarily responsible for the fleet, which was entrusted to him and not to another.

Probable also is Hood's solution of Rodney's persistence in remaining at St. Eustatius, and keeping the squadron under the command of his second to leeward of Martinique. He was possessed with the fancied paramount necessity of protecting St. Eustatius against a sudden attack by the enemy, which he imagined might be supported by the small division in Fort Royal; and the value of the booty shut his eyes to every other consideration. As on the evening of the 12th of April, the great day of glory in his career, the captures already made assumed sufficiency in his eyes, and co-operating with surmisings as to what the beaten and scattered French might do deterred him from further action; so now the prize already secured at St. Eustatius combined with the imaginative "picture he made for himself"—to use Napoleon's phrase—of its possible dangers, to blind him to the really decisive needs of the situation. It is clear, however, that local naval provision for the safety of a petty island was in point of difficulty, as of consequence, a secondary matter, within the competence of many of his captains; and that the primary factor, on which all depended, was the control of the sea, by the British fleet predominating over the enemy's. Consequently the commander-in-chief should have been where his second was, at the centre of decisive action, where an enemy's fleet was to be expected.

This was the more incumbent because Rodney himself, writing to Admiral Parker in Jamaica on April 16th, said, "As the enemy hourly expect a great fleet in these seas, I have scarcely a sufficient number of line-of-battle-ships to blockade the island of Martinique, or to engage the enemy's fleet should they appear, if their number should be so large as reported,"—twenty-four. This report came from French sources, and it will be noted, from the date of his letter, was in his possession twelve days before the enemy arrived. It was both specific and antecedently probable, and should have determined the admiral's action. Whether he had similar news from home does not appear. Sandwich writing him on March 21st, the day before the French left Brest, professed ignorance of their destination, but added, "the most prevailing and most probable opinion is that they are to go to the West India Islands, and afterwards to North America." Their number he estimated at twenty-five, which tallied with Rodney's intelligence of twenty-four. The latter was exact, save that four were armed *en flûte*; that is, as transports, with their guns below, to be subsequently mounted. Despite everything, the admiral remained at St. Eustatius until May 4th, when the arrival of a crippled ship from Hood brought him the news of the skirmish. He was attending, doubtless, to details pertaining to his command, but he was chiefly occupied with the disposition of the property seized on the island; a matter which he afterwards found to his cost would have been much better committed to administrators skilled in the law. Hood wrote:

> Had they abided by the first plan settled before I left them, and not have interfered, but have left the management to the land and sea folk appointed for that purpose, all would have gone smooth and easy.

However this might have proved, the immediate supervision of the island and its spoils was no business for a commander-in-chief in active war time; particularly when it entailed leaving the charge of his main fleet, at a critical moment, to a junior admiral of very recent appointment, and still unproved. It was not the separate importance of the position entrusted to Hood that made it peculiarly the station for the commander-in-chief. It might have been intrinsically as important, yet relatively secondary; but actually it was the centre and key upon which, and upon which alone, the campaign could turn and did turn. Neither was the question one of the relative merits, as yet unknown, of Rodney and Hood. A commander-in-chief cannot devolve his own proper functions upon a subordinate, however able, without graver cause than can be shown in this instance. The infatuation which detained Rodney at a side issue can only be excused—not justified—by a temporary inability to see things in their true proportion, induced on more than one occasion by a temperamental defect,—the lack of the single eye to military considerations,—which could find contentment in partial success, and be indifferent to further results to be secured by sustained action.

There is a saying, apt to prove true, that war does not forgive. For his initial error Rodney himself, and the British campaign in general, paid heavily throughout the year 1781. The French fleet in undiminished vigour lay a dead weight upon all his subsequent action, which, like the dispositions prior to its arrival, underwent the continued censure of Hood; acrid, yet not undiscriminating nor misplaced. As already observed, the surrender of Cornwallis can with probability be ascribed to this loss of an opportunity afforded to strike a blow at the outset, when the enemy was as yet divided, embarrassed with convoy, raw in organization and drill, in all which it could not but improve as the months passed. The results began at once to be apparent, and embarrassments accumulated with time. Hood's ships, though no one was wholly disabled, had suffered very considerably; and, while indispensable repairs could temporarily be made, efficiency was affected. They needed, besides, immediate water and supplies, as Rodney himself stated—a want which Hood would have anticipated. To increase difficulty, the French mounted the batteries of the vessels *en flûte*, and so raised their total nominal force to twenty-eight. Hood was unable to regain Santa Lucia, because his crippled ships could not beat against the current. He therefore left it to itself, and bore away to the northward, where he joined Rodney on May 11th, between St. Kitts and Antigua. The campaign of 1781, destined to be wholly defensive for the British, opened under these odds, the responsibility for which lies in considerable measure on Rodney.

After the junction, the British fleet went to Barbados, where it arrived May 18th. Meantime, the French had proceeded in force against Santa Lucia, landing a considerable body of troops, and investing the island with twenty-five sail-of-the-line, two of which with 1300 soldiers went on to attempt the British Tobago. The attack on Santa Lucia failed, and the French returned to Martinique; but learning there that Rodney was at sea, heading southward, De Grasse became alarmed for his detachment at Tobago, and moved to its support with his entire fleet. Rodney, knowing of the detachment only, sent against it six ships under Rear Admiral Drake; a half-measure severely censured by Hood, whose comments throughout indicate either a much superior natural sagacity, or else the clearer insight of a man whose eye dwells steadfastly on the military situation, untroubled by conflicting claims.

> What a wonderful happy turn would have been given to the King's affairs in this country had Sir George Rodney gone with his whole force to Tobago as soon as he might, and in my humble opinion ought to have done. Nay, had

he even gone when Mr. Drake did, the island would have been saved. I laboured much to effect it, but all in vain, and fully stated my reasons in writing as soon as the intelligence came. Every ship there with all the troops must have fallen into our hands two days before De Grasse got there with his twenty-one sail.

To which Rodney, in full strength, would again have opposed twenty. "*Now* the enemy may do as they will;" for they were united in Martinique, twenty-eight to twenty. In short, Rodney saw at Tobago only the one French detachment; Hood saw therein the definition of the enemy's purpose, the necessity laid on them to fly to the aid of their exposed division, and the chance to anticipate them,—to gain an advantage first, and to beat them afterwards.

Rodney's tentative and inadequate action was not improbably induced partly by the "extreme want of water," which he reported in his despatches; and this again was due to failure to prepare adequately during the period of respite foreseen by Hood, but un-noted by his own preoccupied mind. The result is instructive. Drake fell in with the main body of the French, and of course had to retire,—fortunate in regaining his commander-in-chief unmolested. De Grasse's movement had become known in Barbados, and as soon as Drake appeared Rodney sailed with the fleet, but upon arriving off Tobago, on June 5th, learned that it had surrendered on the 2nd. Its fall he duly attributed to local neglect and cowardice; but evidently the presence of the British fleet might have had some effect. He then returned to Barbados, and during the passage the hostile fleets sighted each other on the 9th,—twenty British to twenty-three French; but Rodney was unwilling to engage lest he might be entangled with the foul ground about Grenada. As that island was then in the enemy's hands, he could get no anchorage there, and so might be driven to leeward of his opponent, exposing Barbados. It is perhaps needless to point out that had he been to windward of Martinique when De Grasse first arrived, as Hood wished, he would have been twenty to twenty, with clear ground, and the antagonist embarrassed with convoy. His present perplexities, in their successive phases, can be seen throughout to be the result of sticking to St. Eustatius, not only physically, but mentally.

And so it was with what followed. On reaching Barbados again, he had to report that the French were back in Martinique, and now twenty-eight through the arming of the ships *en flûte*. Despite their superiority, "they do not venture to move," he said somewhat sneeringly, and doubtless his "fleet in being" had an effect on them; but they were also intent on a really great operation. On July 5th, De Grasse sailed for Cap François in Haiti, there to organize a visit to the continent in support of Washington's operations. Rodney, pursuant to his sagacious plan of the previous years, sent also a detachment of fourteen ships under Hood, which he endeavoured, but unsuccessfully, to have increased by some from Jamaica. That De Grasse would take his whole fleet to North America, leaving none in the West Indies, nor sending any to Europe, was a step that neither Rodney nor Hood foresaw. The miscalculation cannot be imputed to either as an error at this time. It was simply one of the deceptions to which the defensive is ever liable; but it is fairly chargeable to the original fault whereby the French admiral was enabled to enter Fort Royal uninjured in the previous April. From the time his fleet was concentrated, the British had to accept the defensive with its embarrassments.

Rodney had contemplated going in person with his ships, which Sandwich also had urged upon him; but his health was seriously impaired, and the necessity for a surgical operation combined to induce his return to England. The final decision on this point he postponed to the last moment of the homeward voyage, keeping a frigate in company in which to go to New York, if able; but ultimately he felt compelled to give up. This conclusion settled Cornwallis's fate, antecedently but finally. That year Great Britain fell between two stools. In view of De Grasse's known expressions, it may be affirmed with great confidence that he would have seen reason to abandon the Chesapeake, leaving open the sea road for Cornwallis to escape, had either Rodney or Hood commanded the British fleet there in the battle of September 5th; but Rodney was away, and Hood second only to an incompetent superior.

Rodney landed in England, September 19th, and was again afloat by December 12th, although he did not finally sail for his station until the middle of January, 1782. This brief period was one of the deepest military depression; for during it occurred Cornwallis's surrender, October 19th, under conditions of evident British inferiority, on sea and shore alike, which enforced the conviction that the colonies must be granted their independence. Not only so, but the known extensive preparations of the Bourbon courts pointed to grave danger also for the Caribbean colonies, the sugar and import trade of which counted largely in the financial resources of the empire. Amid the general gloom Rodney had his own special vexation; for, before he left, news was received of the recapture of St. Eustatius by a small French expedition, prior to the return of Hood to the West Indies from the unfortunate operations on the continent. As in the case of Tobago, Rodney severely blamed the local defence, and very possibly justly; but attention should not wander from the effect that must have been produced upon all subsequent conditions by preparation and action on the part of the British fleet, in the spring of 1781, on the lines then favoured by Hood.

Shortly before he had sailed for home, Rodney had written his wife, "In all probability, the enemy, when they leave these seas, will go to America. Wherever they go, I will watch their motions, and certainly attack them if they give me a proper opportunity. The fate of England may depend upon the event." The last sentence was in measure a prophecy, so far, that is, as decisive of the original issue at stake,—the subjugation or independence of the United Colonies; but, without further labouring the point unduly, it may be permitted here to sum up what has been said, with the remark that in the summer of 1781 control of events had passed out of Rodney's hands. From the time of the original fault, in suffering the French to meet Hood to leeward of Martinique, with an inferior force, more and more did it become impossible to him to assure conditions sufficiently favourable. With the highest personal courage, he did not have eminent professional daring; nor, with considerable tactical acquirement, was he gifted with that illuminative originality which characterized Hood and Nelson. He therefore needed either a reasonable probability of success, or the spur of imminent emergency, to elicit the kind of action needed to save the British cause. The chances to windward of Martinique would have been ninety out of a hundred; from that time forward they diminished with continually increasing rapidity. With such a situation he was not the man to cope.

On reaching Barbados, February 19, 1782, Rodney learned that the garrison of St. Kitts was besieged in Brimstone Hill, and the island itself beleaguered by the French fleet, thirty-three of-the-line, which Sir Samuel Hood, with two thirds their number, had so far held in check by a series of manoeuvres unusually acute in conception and brilliant in execution. Proceeding immediately to Antigua, he there heard on the 23rd that St. Kitts had capitulated on the 13th. Two days later he was joined by Hood, and then took the united fleet to Santa Lucia, where he was on March 5th. The knowledge of a large supply fleet expected for the French, and essential to the known project of the allies against Jamaica, carried the British fleet again to sea; but it failed to intercept the convoy, and returned once more to Santa Lucia, where it anchored in Gros Ilet Bay, thirty miles from Fort Royal, where the French were lying. Various changes made the respective numbers, when operations opened, British thirty-six of-the-line, French thirty-five, with two fifty-gun ships; a near approach to equality.

Rodney's faculties were now all alert. He had had some needed repose, and he was again under the stimulus of reputation to restore; for it would have been vain to assert, even to himself, that he was entirely clear, not merely of error, to which the most careful is liable, but of serious fault in the previous year. Moreover, he had been sharply assailed in Parliament for the transactions at St. Eustatius on the civil side, distinct from his military conduct. To such ills there is no plaster so healing as a victory; and the occasion about to arise proved, in its successive stages,—until the last,—admirably adapted to his natural and acquired qualifications. First, a series of manoeuvres protracted over three or four days; and afterwards a hard fought battle, converted by a happy yet by no means unusual accident into a decided and showy success. Decided, but not decisive; for, like the soldier desperate in deed before rewarded, but who, when summoned again, advised that the chance be given to a man who had not a purse of gold, Rodney preferred to pause on that personally safe side of moderation in achievement which is rarely conducive to finality, and is nowhere so ill-placed as in the aims of a commander-in-chief. The true prudence of war,—as it is also its mercy, to friend and to foe,—is to strike without cessation or slackness till power of future action is crushed.

De Grasse's immediate task was to protect a large convoy from Martinique to Cap François (now Cap Haytien), in Haiti, a distance of about a thousand miles. Cumbered with merchant vessels, and aware that Rodney would be at once on his track, he could not go straight across the Caribbean; the British fleet, not so hampered, would be sure to overtake and destroy. He purposed, therefore, to skirt the Antilles, keeping continually in reach of a port of refuge. Rodney, knowing the aim to be Jamaica, had little doubt of overtaking in any case, if started promptly. He therefore kept himself in signal touch of Fort Royal by a chain of frigates, extending from its offing to his own anchorage.

On the 8th of April the French sailed. The British followed instantly, and before sundown had them in sight, not only by lookout vessels, but from the mastheads of the main fleet. At daybreak next morning they were visible from the decks of the British van; a very marked gain. De Grasse saw that at that rate, unless he got rid of the convoy, he would certainly be overtaken, which it was his aim to elude in pursuance of the usual French policy of ulterior purposes; so, being then north of Dominica, he sent the merchant vessels into Guadeloupe, and undertook to carry the ships-of-war through the passage between the two islands, beating to windward. This would draw the British away from the convoy, unless they were content to let the fleet go, which was not to be expected.

Between 8 a.m. and 2 p.m. of April 9th, several sharp skirmishes took place between the French and the British van, under Hood.[9] De Grasse had here an opportunity of crushing a fraction of the enemy, but failed to use it, thus insuring his own final discomfiture. Rodney, who was becalmed with the centre and rear of his command, could do nothing but push forward reinforcements to Hood as the wind served; and this he did. Pursuit was maintained tenaciously during the following night and the next two days,—April 10th and 11th; but in sustained chases of bodies of ships, the chased continually drops units, which must be forsaken or else the retreat of the whole must be retarded. So in this case, certain of De Grasse's ships were either so leewardly or so ill handled that the bulk of the fleet, which had gained considerably to windward, had to bear down to them, thus losing the ground won. Under such circumstances the chapter of accidents—or of incidents—frequently introduces great results; and so it proved here.

At 2 a.m. of April 12th, De Grasse's flag-ship, the *Ville de Paris*, and the seventy-four-gun ship *Zélé*, crossing on opposite tacks, came into collision. The former received little damage, but the *Zélé* lost her foremast and bowsprit. De Grasse then ordered her into Guadeloupe, in tow of a frigate. When day broke, about five o'clock, these two were only about six miles from the British rear, under Hood, whose division had been shifted from the van in consequence of injuries received on the 9th. The British column was then standing east-northeast, closehauled on the starboard tack, the crippled vessel under its lee, but the French of the main body well to windward. To draw them within reach, Rodney signalled Hood to send chasers after the *Zélé*. De Grasse took the bait and ran down to her support, ordering his ships to form line-of-battle on the port tack, which was done hastily and tumultuously. The two lines on which the antagonists were respectively advancing now pointed to a common and not distant point of intersection, which the French, despite the loss of ground already undergone, reached first, passing in front and to

---

9. The writer does not purpose to give an account of these actions, except so far as Rodney himself is concerned. They can be found in Mahan's *Influence of Sea Power upon History*," pp. 480-495, or in the *History of the Royal Navy*, (Sampson Low, Marston & Co.), edited by Mr. W. Laird Clowes, vol. iii. pp. 520-535.

windward of the head of the British column. Eight ships thus went by clear, but the ninth arrived at the same moment with the leading British vessel, which put her helm up and ran along close to leeward of the French line towards its rear, followed in so doing by the rest of her fleet.

The battle thus assumed the phase of two fleets passing each other in opposite directions, on parallel lines; a condition usually unproductive of results, and amounting to little more than a brush, as had been the case in two rencounters between Rodney and De Guichen in the prolonged chase of May, 1780. Chance permitted a different issue on this occasion. The wind at the moment of first collision, shortly before 8 a.m., was east, and so continued till five minutes past nine, when it shifted suddenly to the south-eastward, ahead for the French, abaft for the British. The former, being already close to the wind, could keep their sails full only by bearing away, which broke up their line ahead, the order of battle as ranged for mutual support; while the British being able to luff could stand into the enemy's line. Rodney's flag-ship, the *Formidable*, 90, was just drawing up with the *Glorieux*, 74, nineteenth from the van in the French order and fourth astern of the *Ville de Paris*, De Grasse's flag-ship. Luffing to the new wind, she passed through the French line at this point, followed by the five ships astern of her; while the sixth astern, the *Bedford*, 74, luffing on her own account, broke also through the French astern of the *César* and the *Hector*, 74's, eleventh and twelfth in their order. The twelve British vessels in rear of the *Bedford* followed in her wake. Hood was in one of these, the *Barfleur*, 90. Of the ships ahead of Rodney the nearest one imitated his example instantly and went through the line; the remainder, sixteen in all, continued northward for a space.

These sudden and unexpected movements overpowered the *César*, *Hector*, and *Glorieux* under a weight of successive broadsides that completely crushed them, separated De Grasse with six companion vessels from his van and his rear, and placed the British main body to windward of the French. Both sides were disordered, but the French were not only disordered but severed, into three formless groups, not to be united except by a good breeze and exceeding good management, neither of which was forthcoming. Even to frame a plan operative under such conditions requires in an admiral accuracy of judgment and readiness rarely bestowed; but to communicate his designs and enforce execution upon captains under such a staggering shock of disaster is even more uncommon of accomplishment. During the remainder of the day light airs from the eastward prevailed, interspersed with frequent calms; conditions unfavourable to movement of any kind, but far more to the French, deprived of concert of purpose, than to the British, whose general course was sufficiently defined by the confusion of the enemy, and the accident of a small group surrounding their commander-in-chief, to capture whom was always a recognized principal object. The very feebleness of the breeze favoured them by comparison; for they had but to go before it with all their light sails, while their opponents, in order to join, were constrained to lateral movement, which did not allow the same canvas.

There was, in short, during the rest of the day an unusual opportunity for success, on such a scale as should be not only brilliant, but really decisive of the future course of the war; opportunity to inflict a maritime blow from which the enemy could not recover. Does it need to say clearly that here the choice was between a personal triumph, already secured for the successful admiral, and the general security of the nation by the "annihilation"—the word is Nelson's—of the enemy? That Rodney thus phrased the alternative to himself is indeed most unlikely; but that he failed to act efficiently, to rise to an emergency, for the possible occurrence of which he had had ample time as well as warning to prepare, is but too certain. Even after the British had got to windward of the enemy and seen their disorder, although the signal for the line was hauled down, none was made for a general chase. That for close action, hoisted at 1 p.m., was discontinued thirty minutes later, when five full hours of daylight remained. Even in example the admiral was slack, by Hood's account.

He pursued only under topsails (sometimes his foresail set, and at other times his mizzen topsail aback) the greatest part of the afternoon, though the flying enemy had all the sail set their very shattered state would allow.

Hood, curbed by his superior's immediate presence, did what he could by putting all sail on the *Barfleur*, and signalling the various ships of his personal command to do the same; "not one but chased in the afternoon with studding sails below and aloft." It was bare poetic justice, therefore, that the *Ville de Paris*, the great prize of the day, though surrounded by numerous foes, struck formally to him.

The *Hector*, *César*, and *Glorieux*, already paralyzed ere the chase began, were the only results of this languid movement, except the French flag-ship and the *Ardent*, 64. The latter was taken because, notwithstanding her being an indifferent sailer, she gallantly tried to pass from her own division, the van, to support her commander-in-chief in his extremity. It was 6.29 p.m. when the *Ville de Paris* struck; sixteen minutes later, 6.45, Rodney made signal to bring-to for the night—to give over pursuit. Only the *Ville de Paris* and the *Ardent* can be considered to have been secured by following, after the battle proper closed.

Nor was any other attempt made to profit by the victory. On the 13th the fleet began to move very slowly towards Jamaica, the local protection of which had become imperative through the failure to annihilate the enemy, who must now go to leeward—to Haiti; but after four hours Rodney brought-to again, and on the 16th, according to Hood, was in—

> .... the exact same spot off Guadeloupe. It has indeed been calm some part of the time, but we might have been more than twenty leagues farther to the westward.

The *César* having been accidentally burned on the night of the battle, the prizes *Hector* and *Glorieux* were sent ahead in charge of three ships-of-the-line. This was a questionable disposition, as they were advancing in the direction of the enemy, without being covered by the interposition of the main fleet. The *Ville de Paris* Rodney kept close by his own side, unable to tear himself from her; so at least said Hood, who "would to God she had sunk the moment she had yielded to the arms of His Majesty," for "we would then have had a dozen better ships in lieu of her." Rodney was so tickled with her that he "can talk of nothing else, and says he will hoist his flag on board of her."

On April 17th Hood, having vainly urged his commander to improve the situation by more energetic action, represented to him that the small detachment convoying the *Hector* and *Glorieux* might fall in with a superior enemy, if not supported. Rodney then directed him to go ahead with ten ships until as far as Altavela, midway on the south side of Santo Domingo, where he was to await the main body. Hood gave a wide construction to these orders, and pushed for the Mona Passage, between Santo Domingo and Porto Rico, where on the 19th he intercepted two sixty-four gun ships, and two smaller cruisers. In reporting this incident to Rodney, he added, "It is a very mortifying circumstance to relate to you, Sir, that the French fleet which you put to flight on the 12th went through the Mona Channel on the 18th, only the day before I was in it." That sustained vigorous chase could not have been fruitless is further shown by the fact that Rodney himself, deliberately as he moved, apparently lying-to each night of the first half-dozen succeeding the battle, reached Jamaica three days only after the main body of the defeated French gained Cap François, though they had every motive to speed.

Of the reasons for such lethargic action, wholly inconsistent with true military principle, and bitterly criticised by Hood,—who affirmed that twenty ships might have been taken,—Rodney drew up an express account, which cannot be considered as adequate to his justification. In this he argued that, if he had pursued, the enemy, who—

> . . . . went off in a close connected body, might have defeated by rotation the ships that had come up with them, and thereby exposed the British fleet, after a victory, to a defeat.
> They went off in a body of twenty-six ships-of-the-line, and might, by ordering two or three of their best-sailing ships or frigates to have shown lights at times, and by

changing their course, have induced the British fleet to have followed them, while the main of their fleet, by hiding their lights, might have hauled their wind, have been far to windward before daylight, and intercepted the captured ships, and the most crippled ships of the English.

He even conceived that, as the main body of the British would at the same time have gone far to leeward, the French, regaining their own ports in Guadeloupe and Martinique, might have taken Antigua, Barbados, and Santa Lucia.

The principal impression produced by this formal summary of reasons is that of unwisdom after the event, and that it was elicited by the remonstrances of Hood to himself, which are known to have voiced discontent prevalent in the fleet, and rendered some ready reply expedient. The substance of them, when analyzed, is that war must be rendered effective by not running risks, and that calculation to that effect is to be made by attributing every chance and advantage to the enemy, and none to one's self. Further, no account is to be taken of that most notable factor, ultimate risk,—as distinguished from present risk. This phantasm, of the sudden assumption of the offensive by a beaten and disordered fleet, which, through the capture of its chief, had changed commanders at nightfall, is as purely and mischievously imaginative as the fiction, upon which it rests, of the close connected body. Instead of being close-connected, the French were scattered hopelessly, utterly disabled for immediate, or even proximate, resistance to a well sustained chase and attack. During the next twenty-four hours their new admiral had with him but ten ships; and only five joined in the following twelve days, to April 25th, when he reached Cap François, where four more were found. Six others had strayed to Curacao, six hundred miles distant, whence they did not rejoin the flag until May. Neither in Rodney's surmises, nor in the actual facts of the case, is to be found any reasonable excuse for failure to observe the evident military duty of keeping touch with the enemy during the dark hours,—"pursue under easy sail," to use Hood's words, "so as never to have lost sight of the enemy in the night,"—

with a view to resume the engagement next day, at farthest. This, and to regain to windward, were as feasible to the victor as to the vanquished.

A truer explanation of this grave negligence is to be found in Rodney's more casual words recorded by Hood.

> I lamented to Sir George on the twelfth that the signal for a general chase was not made when that for the line was hauled down, and that he did not continue to pursue so as to keep sight of the enemy all night; to which he only answered, 'Come, we have done very handsomely as it is.' I could therefore say no more upon the subject.

He did, however, resume the subject with Sir Charles Douglas, the chief of staff. Douglas was of the same opinion as Hood, and for making the suggestion at the proper moment had been snubbed by Rodney, who had established over him a domination of manner which precluded proper insistence, or even due representation, such as became his office. "His answer was, 'Sir George chose to pursue in a body;'" that is, in regular order, not by general chase.

"'Why, Sir Charles,' I replied, 'if that was Sir George's wish, could it have been more effectually complied with than by the signal for a general chase, with *proper attention*? Because, if a ship is too wide on the starboard wing, you have a signal to make her steer more to port. If a ship is too wide on the larboard wing, you have a signal to make her steer more to starboard. If a ship is too far ahead, you can by signal make her shorten sail,'" etc. This by daylight; while, "'if Sir George was unwilling his ships should engage in the night, there is a signal to call every ship in, and, that followed by the one for the form of sailing, the fleet might have gone on in sight of the enemy all night in the most compact and safe order for completing the business most gloriously the next day.' Sir Charles walked off without saying another word." There was in fact nothing to say. Hood's methods were not only correct, but in no respect novel. Every capable officer was familiar with them before, as well as after the battle. The trouble was that Rodney was content with a present clear success, and averse from further risk. He had reached his limitations. It is known now that Douglas agreed with Hood, but he was too loyal to his chief to say so publicly, then or afterwards; and especially, doubtless, to so irritable a talker.

As illustrative of Rodney's professional character the events of April 8th to 12th are therefore unfavourable rather than the reverse. Concerning his stronger qualities their evidence is simply cumulative; the new light thrown reveals defects, not unsuspected excellencies. The readiness in which his fleet was held at Santa Lucia, the promptness with which he followed, the general conduct of the chase as far as appears, though doubtless open to criticism in detail as in the ever censorious remarks of Hood,—all these show the same alert, accomplished, and diligent officer, resolute to the utmost of his natural and acquired faculties. It is the same after the battle joins, so long as its progress does not transcend his accepted ideas,—which were much in advance of the great mass of his contemporaries,—though under the conditions he saw no chance to apply the particular methods familiar to his thought.

But when sudden opportunity offered, of a kind he had not anticipated, he is found unequal to it. Neither natural temper, nor acquired habit of mind, respond to the call. To pass through the French line, when the wind shifted, was an instigation too sudden and a risk too great for his own initiative. The balance of evidence shows that it was due to the suggestion, and even more to the pressure, of Sir Charles Douglas. Carried beyond his habitual submission by the impulse of a great thought, and unburdened by the ultimate responsibility which must remain with the admiral, the Captain of the Fleet not only urged luffing through the enemy's line, but—so the story runs—in the excitement of the moment, and seeing the chance slipping past, even under the then sluggish breeze, he ordered the helm down. The admiral, thus faced, countermanded the order. A moment of silence followed, during which the two men stepped apart, the admiral even entering the cabin, which would be but a few paces from the wheel. Returning, he permitted Douglas to have his way; an act which, whether done courteously or grudgingly, does not bespeak professional conviction, but the simple acceptance of another's will in place of one's own indecision.

The incident is in entire keeping with the picture of Rodney's irresolution, and consequent uncertain course, drawn in successive touches by Hood in the hours and days succeeding the victory. Events had called him to deeds beyond his limitations. Age of course counted for much; fatigue, after three days of doubtful chase and one of prolonged battle, for more; but it may here be recalled that an older man, after a more wearisome and doubtful exposure, willed of his own motion to do what Rodney left undone. Sir Byam Martin has recorded:[10]

> After the battle of the 1st of June, Lord Howe was quite exhausted, as well indeed he might, considering that they had been manoeuvring and fighting for three days. Although feeble in body, and so exhausted as to be obliged to sit down in a chair on deck, he expressed a wish to pursue the flying enemy; but Sir Roger Curtis, the Captain of the Fleet (Chief of Staff, as Douglas to Rodney) said, 'I vow to God, my lord, if you do they will turn the tables upon us.' This anecdote I had from the late Admiral Bowen, who was master of the *Queen Charlotte* and a party to the conversation.

Under circumstances approaching similarity,—so far as North Atlantic fogs and weather resemble West India climate,— Howe was sixty-eight, Rodney sixty-three, at the moment of testing. The one lost the support of the man—Curtis—upon whom he must chiefly rely for observation and execution; the other was urged in vain by the officer who held the same relation to him. Nelson once spoke slightingly of "a Lord Howe's victory, take a part, and retire into port;" as a trait of official character, however, Howe's purpose was far in advance of Rodney's, as this was viewed by Nelson's ideal admiral, Hood. It is now known, by a letter of Nelson's very recently published, that he held the same opinion of Rodney's remissness

---

10. Journals of Sir T. Byam Martin, Navy Records Society, vol. iii. p. 137.

in this instance, although he cordially recognized the general obligation of the country and the navy to that eminent seaman. Writing in 1804 to his intimate friend Cornwallis, one of Rodney's captains, he used these words:

> On the score of fighting, I believe, my dear friend, that you have had your full share, and in obtaining the greatest victory, *if it had been followed up*, that our country ever saw.[11]

It was a clear case of spirit being brought into subjection to form.

Rodney's professional career may be reckoned to have ended with his arrival at Jamaica on the 29th of April. The change of ministry consequent upon Cornwallis's surrender brought into power his political opponents, and in May the new Admiralty superseded him. News of the victory reached England just too late to permit them to revoke the order; his successor, Admiral Pigot, having already sailed. On the 22nd of July Rodney left Jamaica, and on the 15th of September landed at Bristol. Although not so intended, his recall may be considered in line with his proverbial good fortune. He left his successor to grapple with difficulties, and with numbers, the continued existence of which was due chiefly to his own neglect after April 12th, and by the burden of which the conditions of peace were influenced adversely to Great Britain. To quote again Hood's apt comment, "Had Sir George Rodney's judgment, after the enemy had been so totally put to flight, bore any proportion to the high courage, zeal and exertion, shown by every captain, officer, and man under his command in battle, *all* difficulty would now have been at an end. We might have done just as we pleased, instead of being at this hour (April 30th) upon the defensive." This is ultimate risk, which is entailed by exaggerated concern for immediate apparent security, and ends in sapping endurance.

The auspicious moment at which the news of the battle reached England, and the surface brilliancy of the achievement,—especially the capture of the enemy's commander-in-chief,—diverted attention from any examination of possible shortcom-

---

11. The Blockade of Brest, Navy Records Society. Introduction, p. xvi. Author's italics.

ings. Rodney received a vote of thanks from Parliament, and was advanced to the peerage by the King. A pension of £2,000 per annum was also voted, additional doubtless to a similar sum granted after his destruction of Langara's squadron and relief of Gibraltar. Other rewards and recognition had already attended his naval career. He had been made a baronet in 1764, at the expiration of his first tenure of the Leeward Islands Station; in 1780 the order of the Bath was bestowed upon him,—the distinction being enhanced by not awaiting a vacancy, but making him a supernumerary member,—and in 1781, upon the death of Lord Hawke, he became Vice-Admiral of Great Britain, the highest professional honour in the service.

After his return to England Rodney lived generally in retirement. His latter years were harassed by law suits, growing chiefly out of his proceedings at St. Eustatius, and the attendant expenses kept him poor. He died in May, 1792, at the age of seventy-three.

Howe: 1726-1799

CHAPTER 4

Howe: 1726-1799

The name of Howe, albeit that of a stranger to the land, has a special claim upon the esteem and cordial remembrance of Americans. The elder brother of the subject of this sketch, during the few short months in which he was brought into close contact with the colonists of 1758, before the unlucky campaign of Ticonderoga, won from them not merely the trust inspired by his soldierly qualities and his genius for war,—the genius of sound common sense and solidity of character,—but got a deep hold upon their affections by the consideration and respect shown to them by him, traits to which they had been too little accustomed in the British officers of that day. Nor was this attitude on his part only a superficial disguise assumed by policy to secure a needed support. The shrewd, suspicious provincials would soon have penetrated a veil so thin, that covered only the usual supercilious arrogance which they had heretofore encountered. Lord Howe, almost alone among his military contemporaries, warmly greeted them as fellow-countrymen, men of no alien or degenerate blood. He admitted at once the value of their experience, sought their advice, and profited by both; thus gaining, besides the material advantage of methods adapted to the difficulties before him, the adhesion of willing hearts that followed enthusiastically, confident in their leader's wisdom, and glowing with the unaccustomed sense of being appreciated, of receiving recognition long withheld, but now at last ungrudgingly accorded.

The army felt him, from general to drummer boy. He was its soul; and while breathing into it his own energy and ardour, he broke through the traditions of the service, and gave it new shapes to suit the time and place.... He made himself greatly beloved by the provincial officers, and he did what he could to break down the barriers between the colonial soldiers and the British regulars.[12]

In campaign, Lord Howe adopted the tried expedients of forest warfare, associating with himself its most practised exponents; and on the morning of his death, in one of those petty skirmishes which have cut short the career of so many promising soldiers, he discussed the question of Ticonderoga and its approaches, lying on a bearskin beside the colonial ranger, John Stark, to whose energy, nineteen years later, was due the serious check that precipitated the ruin of Burgoyne's expedition. Endeared as he was to American soldiers by the ties of mutual labours and mutual perils gladly shared, and to all classes by genial bearing and social accomplishments, his untimely end was followed throughout the Northern colonies by a spontaneous outburst of sorrow, elicited not only by the anticipated failure of the enterprise that hung upon his life, but also by a sense of personal regret and loss. Massachusetts perpetuated the memory of her grief by a tablet in Westminster Abbey, which hands down to our day "the affection her officers and soldiers bore to his command."

Captain Richard Howe of the Royal Navy, afterwards Admiral and Earl, succeeded him in the Irish viscounty which had been bestowed upon their grandfather by William III. Of a temperament colder, at least in external manifestation, than that of his brother, the new Lord Howe was distinguished by the same fairness of mind, and by an equanimity to which perturbation and impulsive injustice were alike unknown. There seems to have been in his bearing something of that stern, impassive gravity that marked Washington, and imposed a constraint upon bystanders; but whatever apparent harshness there was in the face only concealed a genuine warmth of heart, which at times broke with an

---

12. Parkman's *Montcalm and Wolfe*, vol. ii. p. 90.

illumining smile through the mask that covered it, and was always ready to respond to the appeals of benevolence. If, as an officer, he had a fault conspicuously characteristic, it was a reluctance to severity, a tendency to push indulgence to undue extremes, into which may perhaps have entered not merely leniency of disposition, but the weakness of loving popularity. To be called by the seamen, as Howe was, the "sailor's friend," is in the experience of navies a suspicious encomium, involving more of flattery to a man's foibles than of credit to his discretion and his judgment. But at the time when the quarrel between Great Britain and her colonies was fast becoming embittered, the same kindliness, coupled with a calm reasonableness of temper, ruled his feelings and guided his action. Although by political creed a moderate Tory, he had none of the wrong-headedness of the party zealot; and the growing alienation between those whom he, like his brother, regarded as of one family, caused only distress and an earnest desire to avert coming evils. Influenced by these sentiments, he sought the acquaintance of Franklin, then in London as a commissioner from the colonies; and the interviews between them, while resultless by reason of the irreconcilable differences of opinion severing the two parties to the dispute, convinced the wary American of the good will and open-mindedness of the already distinguished British seaman. The same qualities doubtless suggested the selection of Howe for the mission of conciliation to America, in 1776, where his associate was his younger brother, Sir William, in whom the family virtues had, by exaggeration, degenerated into an indolent good humour fatal to his military efficiency. The admiral, on the contrary, was not more remarkable for amiability and resolute personal courage than he was for sustained energy and untiring attention to duty,—traits which assured adequate naval direction, in case conciliation should give place, as it did, to coercive measures.

 It is to be regretted that the methods, or the opportunities, of naval biographers and historians of the past century have preserved to us little, in personal detail and anecdote, of a period the peculiarities of which, if not exactly picturesque, were at least grotesque and amusing. The humour of Smollett has indeed drawn in broad caricature some of the salient features of the seaman of his day, which was that of Howe's entrance into the navy; and those who are familiar with the naval light literature based upon the times of Nelson can recognize in it characteristics so similar, though evidently softened by advancing civilization and increased contact with the world, as to vouch for the accuracy of the general impression conveyed by the earlier novelist. It is, however, correct only as a *general* impression, in which, too, allowance must be made for the animus of an author who had grievances to exploit, and whose great aim was to amuse, even if exact truthfulness were sacrificed at the shrine of exaggerated portrayal. Though not wholly without occasional gleams of light, shed here and there by recorded incident and anecdote upon the strange life of the seamen of that period, the early personal experiences of individuals have had scant commemoration; and with the exception of St. Vincent, who fortunately had a garrulous biographer, we learn little of men like Hawke, Howe, Hood, and Keppel, until, already possessors of naval rank, they stand forth as actors in events rather historical than biographical.

Of Howe's first services, therefore, not much record remains except a bare summary of dates,—of promotions, and of ships to which he was attached,—until 1755, the beginning of the Seven Years War, when he was already a post-captain. Born in 1726, he entered the navy in 1739, at the outbreak of the war with Spain which initiated a forty years' struggle over colonies and colonial trade. With short intervals of peace, this contest was the prominent characteristic of the middle of the eighteenth century, and terminated in the conquest of Canada, the independence of the United States, and the establishment of British predominance in India and upon the ocean. This rupture of a quiet that had then endured a quarter of a century was so popular with the awakened intelligence of England, aroused at last to the imminent importance of her call to expansion by sea, that it was greeted by a general pealing of the bells, which drew from the reluctant prime minister, Walpole, that bitter gibe, "Ay, today they are ringing their bells, and tomorrow they will be wringing their hands." Howe embarked with Anson's squadron, celebrated for its sufferings, its persistence, and its achievements, to waste the Spanish colonies of the Pacific; but the ship in which he had started was so racked in the attempt to double Cape Horn that she was forced to return to England. The young officer afterwards served actively in the West Indies and in home waters. On the 1st of May, 1746, being then in command of a small sloop of war, he was severely wounded in action with a superior enemy's force off the coast of Scotland. A few days before that, on the 10th of April, he had been promoted post-captain, being barely turned twenty. Thus early he was securely placed on the road to the highest honours of his profession, which, however, were not to prove beyond the just claim of his already established personal merit.

During the first thirty months of the Seven Years War, Howe was closely engaged with, and at times in command of, the naval part of combined expeditions of the army and navy, fitted out to harass the French coasts. The chief, though not the sole aim in these undertakings was to effect diversions in favour of Frederick the Great, then plunged in his desperate struggle with the allied forces of Russia, Austria, and France. It was believed that the last would be compelled, for the defence of her own shores against those raids,—desultory, it is true but yet uncertain as to the time and place where the attack would fall,—to withdraw a number of troops that would sensibly reduce the great odds then overbearing the Prussian king. It is more than doubtful whether this direction of British power, in partial, eccentric efforts, produced results adequate to the means employed. In immediate injury to France they certainly failed, and it is questionable whether they materially helped Frederick; but they made a brisk stir in the Channel ports, their operations were within easy reach of England in a day when news travelled slowly, and they drew the attention of the public and of London society in a degree wholly disproportionate to their importance relatively to the great issues of the war. Their failures, which exceeded their achievements, caused general scandal; and their occasional triumphs aroused exaggerated satisfaction at this earlier period, before the round of unbroken successes under the first Pitt had accustomed men, to use Walpole's lively phrase, to come to breakfast with the question, "What new victory is there this morning?" The brilliant letter-writer's correspondence is full of the gossip arising from these usually paltry affairs; and throughout, whether in success or disaster, the name of Howe appears frequently, and always as the subject of praise.

> Howe, brother of the lord of that name, was the third on the naval list. He was undaunted as a rock, and as silent, the characteristics of his whole race. He and Wolfe soon contracted a friendship like the union of cannon and gunpowder.

"Howe," he says in another place, "never made a friendship except at the mouth of a cannon."

Of his professional merits, however, professional opinions will be more convincing. A Frenchman, who had acted as pilot of his ship, the *Magnanime*, when going into action, was asked if it were possible to take a lighter vessel, the *Burford*, close to the walls of another fort farther in. "Yes," he replied, "but I should prefer to take the *Magnanime*."

"But why?" it was rejoined; "for the *Burford* draws less water."

"True," he said, "*mais le capitaine Howe est jeune et brave*."

Sir Edward Hawke, the most distinguished admiral of that generation, gave a yet higher commendation to the "young and brave" captain, who at this time served under his orders,—one that must cause a sigh of regretful desire to many a troubled superior. Several years later, when First Lord of the Admiralty, he nominated Howe, in October, 1770, to command a squadron destined to the Mediterranean, when hostilities with Spain were expected. The appointment was criticised on the ground that he was a junior admiral in the fleet, having been very recently promoted; but Hawke, doubtless mindful that the same objection had been made to him at a similar period of his career, answered, in the spirit of St. Vincent defending his choice of Nelson:

> I have tried Lord Howe on most important occasions. He never asked me *how* he was to execute any service entrusted to his charge, but always went straight forward and *did it*.

Some quaint instances are recorded of the taciturnity for which he was also noted. Amid the recriminations that followed the failure at Rochefort, Howe neither wrote nor said anything. At last the Admiralty asked why he had not expressed an opinion. In the somewhat ponderous style that marked his utterances, he replied, "With regard to the operations of the troops I was silent, as not being at that time well enough informed thereof, and to avoid the mention of any particulars that might prove not exactly agreeable to the truth."

The next year, an army officer of rank, putting questions to him and receiving no answer, said, "Mr. Howe, don't you hear me? I have asked you several questions."

Howe answered curtly, "I don't like questions,"—in which he was perhaps not peculiar.

It was during the continuance of these petty descents upon the French coast, in 1758, that Howe was directed to receive on board, as midshipman, and for service in the fleet, the Duke of York, a grandson of the reigning monarch; in connection with whom arose a saying that was long current, perhaps is still current, in the British navy. The young lad of nineteen, before beginning his routine duties, held a reception on board Commodore Howe's ship, at which the captains of the squadron were presented to him. The seamen, unpractised in ceremonial distinctions other than naval, saw with wonder that the midshipman kept on his hat, while the rest uncovered. "The young gentleman," whispered one, "isn't over civil, as I thinks. Look if he don't keep his hat on before all the captains!"

"Why," another was heard to reply, "where should he learn manners, seeing as how he was never at sea before?"

It is likewise from this period of Howe's career that two of the rare personal anecdotes have been transmitted, illustrative of his coolness and self-possession under all circumstances of danger, as well as when under the enemy's fire; one of them also touched with a bit of humour,—not a usual characteristic of his self-contained reticence. The service involved considerable danger, being close in with the enemy's coast, which was indifferently well known and subject to heavy gales of wind blowing dead on shore. On one such occasion his ship had anchored with two anchors ahead, and he had retired to his cabin, when the officer of the watch hurriedly entered, saying, "My lord, the anchors are coming home,"—the common sea expression for their failure to grip the bottom, whereupon the ship of course drags toward the beach. "Coming home, are they?" rejoined Howe. "I am sure they are very right. I don't know who would stay abroad on such a night, if he could help it."

Yet another time he was roused from sleep by a lieutenant in evident perturbation: "My lord, the ship is on fire close to the magazine; but don't be frightened; we shall get it under shortly."

"Frightened, sir!" said Howe. "What do you mean? I never was frightened in my life." Then, looking the unlucky officer in the face, he continued, "Pray, Mr.——, how does a man *feel* when he is frightened? I need not ask how he *looks*."

The even, unaffected self-possession indicated by these anecdotes of the early prime of life remained with him to the end, as is shown by another incident collected by a biographer who knew many of his contemporaries.

> When Howe was in command of the Channel Fleet, after a dark and boisterous night, in which the ships had been in some danger of running foul of each other, Lord Gardner, then the third in command, the next day went on board the *Queen Charlotte* and inquired of Lord Howe how he had slept, for that he himself had not been able to get any rest from anxiety of mind. Lord Howe said he had slept perfectly well, for as he had taken every possible precaution he could before dark, he laid himself down with a conscious feeling that everything had been done, which it was in his power to do, for the safety of the ships, and the lives of those entrusted to his care, and this conviction set his mind at ease.
>
> The apprehensiveness with which Gardner was afflicted—
>
> .... is further exemplified by an anecdote told by Admiral Sir James Whitshed, who commanded the *Alligator*, next him in the line. Such was his anxiety, even in ordinary

weather, that, though each ship carried three poop lanterns, he always kept one burning in his cabin, and when he thought the *Alligator* was approaching too near he used to run out into the stern gallery with the lantern in his hand, waving it so as to be noticed.

From Gardner's rank at the time, the conversation narrated must have occurred during the early years of the French Revolution, when Howe was over sixty-seven. As illustrative of character it is particularly interesting, for Gardner was not only a much younger man, but one whose gallantry and competence had been eminently proved as a captain in several hard fought battles, while as an admiral in chief command he later acquired considerable reputation as a tactician.

Composure under suspense is chiefly a matter of temperament; of the constitutional outfit with which Nature favours some, and does not others. It may be cultivated by its happy possessor; but when wanting, the sufferer can supply its place only by laborious self-control, the tension of which by itself expends the energies it seeks to maintain, and so imposes limitations of strength that are often insuperable obstacles to achievement, especially if prolonged. The strain of this endurance is prominent among those borne by commanders-in-chief, who can at no moment afford to be lax, nor yet precipitate; and it increases with time at compound interest. Howe's native imperturbability was therefore one of the chief factors in his great professional powers, making possible the full exercise of all the others. By dint of it principally he reached the eminence which must be attributed to him as a general officer; for it underlay the full, continuous, and sustained play of the very marked faculties, personal and professional, natural and acquired, which he had. It insured that they should be fully developed, and should not flag; for it preserved his full command over them by delivering him from the factitious burdens of the imagination.

This quality not only entered into his external professional life, but characterized the habitual temper of his mind. "He divested himself in a remarkable manner," says his biographer, "of every approach to a state of anger or resentment"—instancing herein, it may be noted, the improvement of a natural gift; "and he carefully abstained from all irritating language, whether in speaking or writing. In the perusal of the four hundred letters and upwards that have been mentioned, embracing opinions of, and unreserved discussions upon, the merits or otherwise of many and various characters, of all classes of individuals, it did not fail forcibly to strike the reader of them, how invariably, with one single exception, he takes the good natured and favourable side of every question. In the whole series, the harshest word employed is 'blockhead,' bestowed on his steward for not taking care of his *own* interests."

This equable frame of mind was thus a fundamental trait in Howe, private as well as public, personal as well as professional; not assumed for the moment, but constant in operation. He had none of the irritability attributed to genius, as also he gives no sign of its inspiration,—of originality. He is seen at his strongest in dealing stage by stage with difficult situations created for him, following step by step, and step by step checking, the lead of another; his action being elicited by successive circumstances, not deriving from some creative, far-reaching conception of his own. The temperament is one eminently practical, capable on due opportunity of very great deeds, as Howe showed; for, having improved much native capacity by the constant cultivation of professional knowledge, and with the self-confidence which naturally springs from such acquisition, he rose readily to the level of exertion demanded by any emergency not in excess of his abilities, and so long as the need lasted maintained himself there easily, without consciousness of exhaustive effort, or apprehension of improbable contingencies. "Never hasting, never resting," might be safely affirmed of him.

He is seen therefore at his best in a defensive campaign, such as that against D'Estaing in the summer of 1778, which in the writer's opinion was his greatest achievement; or again in a great deliberate operation like the relief of Gibraltar,—the one of his deeds most esteemed, it is said, by himself,—protracted over a month in its performance, and essentially defensive in character, not only because of the much superior fleet of the enemies, but because the adverse forces of nature and the obstinate incapacity of the captains of supply ships had to be counteracted by unremitting watchfulness, foresight, and skill, dealing however with conditions determined for him, not imposed by his own initiative; or, finally, in the chase and partial actions of May 28 and 29, 1794, in which persistence, endurance, and aptitude are alike and equally displayed, assuring to him beyond dispute the credit of a great tactician. Accordingly, in direct consequence of what has been noted, it is as a tactician, and not as a strategist, that he can claim rank; for whatever may be the fundamental identity of principles in the military art, whether applied to strategy or to tactics, it in the end remains true that the tactician deals with circumstances immediately before him and essentially transient, while the strategist has to take wider views of more lasting conditions, and into them to introduce his own conceptions to be modifying factors. Creative thought and faculty of initiation are therefore more characteristic of the natural endowments of the born strategist. There is also more room for them in his work, because in the larger and more complicated field there is greater elasticity and opportunity to effect new combinations, to contrive which makes a greater call upon originative power.

In the chain of eminent typical names which leads up to that of Nelson, there will be found between Howe and his next conspicuous successor,—conspicuous, that is, not only by merit, as was Hood, but by achievement, which was denied to Hood,—between Howe and Jervis, just that difference which essentially separates the tactician from the strategist: the lifting of the eye from the moves of the game immediately before one, to glance over the whole board, to view the wider field, and from its possibilities to form conceptions directive of immediate action for distant ends. In both these distinguished general officers,—for such both were,—there is seen a similar close attention to details, based upon and guided by an acquaintance with their profession profound as well as extensive, minute as well as general; in both the same diligence and iron equanimity in difficult situations, although in Jervis the impression received is rather that of a burden borne with resolute fortitude, whereas in Howe the burden is thrown off by a placid, unforeboding temper; but in the adoption of measures, those of Howe will be found generally not to extend beyond the situation immediately before him, by which they are dictated, whereas Jervis seeks to bend circumstances to his will, according to a conception he has formed of what the situation ought to be, and can be forced to become.

The idiosyncrasy of either officer is emphasized in their respective plans of campaign, while commanding the Channel Fleet during the French Revolution. Howe will maintain a certain station in port, keeping his fleet there in hand, well conditioned, and as far as may be well drilled; then, when the French do something, he also will do something to counteract them. Jervis, on the contrary, confronting substantially the same conditions, frames his measures with a view to prevent the enemy from doing anything, and all the details of his plan rest upon this one idea, to the fulfilment of which they contribute. He puts the fleet at once into the position of action, instead of that of awaiting, as Howe does. Both are charged with the same duty,—the defence of Great Britain,—and by the same Government, which evidently in each case frames its instructions upon the ascertained views of the eminent officer entrusted with the work. To carry out this defensive campaign, Howe of his own choice narrows his strategic plan to the sheer defensive, which follows the initiative of the enemy; Jervis of set purpose seeks the same object by offensive dispositions, by which the enemy is to be forced to regulate his movements. Howe sees the defence of the empire in the preservation of his own fleet; Jervis in the destruction of the enemy. The one view is local, narrow, and negative; the other general, broad, and positive. As often happens—and very naturally—Jervis's preoccupation with considerations wider than his own command found expression, twice at least, in phrases which pithily summed up his steadfast enduring habit of mind. On the morning of St. Vincent he was overheard to mutter, "A victory is very necessary to England at this time." The present odds to his own fleet, twenty-seven against fifteen, disappeared in the larger needs of the country. Again, when wrestling with the perplexities and exigencies of the wild Brest blockade in midwinter, in January, 1801, he wrote concerning repairs to his own vessels at Torbay, an open though partially sheltered roadstead:

> Under the present impending storm from the north of Europe, and the necessity there is of equipping every ship in the royal ports that can swim, no ship under my command must have anything done to her at Plymouth or Portsmouth that can be done at this anchorage.

Here again is seen the subordination of the particular and personal care to the broad considerations of a great strategic emergency.

The series of diversions upon the French coast in which Howe was employed during 1758, terminated with that season, and he returned to his own ship, the *Magnanime*, rejoining with her the main fleet under Hawke in the great Brest blockade of 1759. The French Government, after four years of disaster upon the continent, of naval humiliation, and of loss of maritime and colonial power, had now realized that its worst evils and chief danger sprang from the sea power of Great Britain, and, like Napoleon a half-century later, determined to attempt an invasion. Its preparations and Hawke's dispositions to counteract them, have been described in the life of that admiral, as have Rodney's bombardment of Havre and interception of coastwise communications; all directed to the same general end of confounding designs against England, but no longer as mere diversions in favour of Frederick. Howe was still a private captain, but he bore a characteristically conspicuous part in the stormy final scene at Quiberon, when Hawke drove Conflans before him to utter confusion. When the French fleet was sighted, the *Magnanime* had been sent ahead to make the land. She was thus in the lead in the headlong chase which ensued, and was among the first in action; at 3 p.m., by Howe's journal, the firing having begun at 2.30, according to Hawke's despatch. The foreyard being soon shot away, the consequent loss of manoeuvring power impeded her captain's designs in placing her, but she remained closely engaged throughout, compelling one French vessel to strike and anchor alongside her. The bad weather prevented taking possession that night of the prize, which, in consequence, availed herself of her liberty by running ashore, and so was lost to her captors. The *Magnanime* was reported as having thirteen killed and sixty-six wounded, out of a total of hurt not much exceeding three hundred in the entire fleet. The casualty list proves exposure to fire, doubtless; but is no sure test of the effectiveness of a vessel's action. The certainty of Howe's conduct in this affair, otherwise imperfectly described, rests on a broader and firmer basis of reputation, won by unvarying efficiency in many differing capacities and circumstances.

He continued to serve, but without further noteworthy incident, up to the peace made in the winter of 1762-63. From that time until the difficulties with the American colonies came to a head in 1775, he was not actively employed afloat, although continuously engaged upon professional matters, especially as a close student of naval tactics and its kindred subjects, to which he always gave sympathetic attention. During this period, also, he became a member of the House of Commons, and so continued until transferred from the Irish peerage to that of Great Britain, in 1782. In 1770, at the age of forty-five, he became a rear-admiral, and, as has been already stated, received at once a proof of Hawke's high confidence, by being appointed to the command of the squadron destined for the Mediterranean, when hostilities concerning the Falkland Islands threatened with Spain; a dispute chiefly memorable as the means of bringing into the navy both Nelson and Exmouth. In 1775 he was promoted to vice-admiral, and in February of the following year was appointed commander-in-chief of the North American station. Together with his military duties, he was, as has before been said, given powers, conjointly with his brother, to treat for the settlement of existing troubles.

Although his habitual reticence restrained his sentiments from finding expression in positive words, there can be little doubt that the necessity of raising his hand against the Americans caused Howe keener regret than it did to many of his brother officers. He took instant occasion to address to Franklin a personal note, recalling their former association, and expressing an earnest hope that their friendship might contribute something to insure the success of his official mission. In the five years that had elapsed, however, Franklin had been in the heat of the political struggle, and, philosopher though he was, he had not Howe's natural phlegm. Hence, his reply, while marked by respect and even formal cordiality toward the admiral himself, displayed a vivacity of resentment and a bitterness for which the latter had scarcely looked. Still, his habitual equanimity was not ruffled, and he read the letter with the simple comment, "My old friend expresses himself very warmly."

Howe's arrival antedated the signature of the Declaration of Independence by less than a week. During the period of attempted negotiation, while scrupulously faithful to his instructions, he showed to his late fellow-countrymen all the courtesy and consideration that the most cordial esteem could extend. The incident of the official communication addressed by the Howes to Washington, in which they sought to evade giving him the title of "General," is sufficiently familiar; but it is more rarely recalled that, in verbal intercourse with American officers, the admiral habitually styled him "General Washington," and sent complimentary messages to him as such. He even spoke of the colonies as "states," and at the same time dwelt with evident emotion upon the testimonials of respect and affection which had been shown to his brother's memory by the colonists.

To narrate Howe's share in the operations by which New York in 1776, and Philadelphia in 1777, fell into the hands of the British, would be only to repeat well-known historical episodes, enlivened by few or no incidents personal to himself. In them the navy played a part at once subordinate and indispensable, as is the office of a foundation to its superstructure. The cause of the Americans was hopeless as long as their waters remained in the undisputed control of the enemy's ships; and it was the attempt of Great Britain to cast aside this essential support, and to rely upon the army alone in a wild and intricate country, that led to her first great disaster,—Burgoyne's surrender at Saratoga. Upon this, France at once recognized the independence of the colonies, and their alliance with that kingdom followed. A French fleet of twelve ships-of-the-line under the Count D'Estaing, left Toulon April 15, 1778, for the American coast. This force far exceeded Howe's; and it was no thanks to the British Government, but only to the admiral's sleepless vigilance and activity, seconded, as such qualities are apt to be, by at least an average degree of supineness on the part of his antagonist, that his scanty squadron was not surprised and overpowered in Delaware Bay, when Sir Henry Clinton evacuated Philadelphia to retreat upon New York. Howe, who had the defects of his qualities, whose deliberate and almost stolid exterior evinced a phlegmatic composure of spirit which required the spur of imminent emergency to rouse it into vehement action, never in his long career appeared to greater advantage, nor achieved military results more truly brilliant, than at this time, and up to the abandonment of the attack on Rhode Island by the Americans under Sullivan, three months later. Then only, if ever, did he rise above the level of an accomplished and resolute general officer, and establish a claim to genius, of that order, however, which is not originative in character, but signalized by an infinite capacity for taking pains; and that not for a short time merely, but through a long, protracted period of strain. The display, nevertheless, does not assure him a place in the front rank of great commanders, whose actions find their source in the living impulse of their own creative energy; for it is elicited by extreme circumstances alone, by obvious pressure, to which he must adapt himself. This he does with unfailing adequacy, indeed; resolutely checkmating, but never initiating. Steady as a rock, like a rock, also, Howe only gave forth sparks under blows that would have broken weaker men.

D'Estaing was twelve weeks in coming from Toulon to Cape May, but Howe knew nothing of his sailing until three weeks after he had started. Then orders were received to abandon Philadelphia and concentrate upon New York. The naval forces were scattered, and had to be collected; the supplies of the army, except those needed for the march across Jersey, were to be embarked at Philadelphia, and the great train of transports and ships of war moved over a hundred miles down a difficult river, and thence to New York. Despite every effort, a loss of ten days was incurred, through calms, in the mere transit from Philadelphia to the sea; but during this momentous crisis D'Estaing did not appear. Two days more sufficed to bring the fleet into New York Bay on June 29th; but yet the grave admiral, roused to the full tension of his great abilities, rested not. With a force little more than half that coming against him, he knew that all depended upon the rapidity with which his squadron took the imposing position he had in mind. Still D'Estaing tarried, giving to his untiring enemy twelve more precious days, during which the army of Sir Henry Clinton, reaching Navesink beach the day after the fleet, was snatched by it from the hot pursuit of the disappointed Washington, and carried safely to New York.

In the expected French squadron were eight ships of seventy-four guns or over, with three sixty-fours. To confront these, for the defence of the port, Howe disposed of six, none heavier than a sixty-four; but they were ranged to command the entrance of the harbour upon a tactical plan that evinced both a careful study of the ground and the resources of a thorough seaman. This instance alone, had Howe never done anything else, would have established his reputation as a tactician. The ships, placed in echelon, and enabled to turn their batteries in any direction, by the provision of springs and adaptation to the tide conditions at the moment when alone attack would be possible, could concentrate their entire force of guns upon the enemy, raking them as they advanced up channel; while, if they succeeded in coming abreast, then also the broadsides would be turned upon them. When D'Estaing at last came, all was ready; the energy that had improved every fleeting moment then gave place to the imperturbable resolution which was Howe's greatest attribute, and against which, seconded by his careful preparation, success could be won only by a desperate and sanguinary struggle. The attempt was not made. Ten days after arriving, the French admiral again put to sea, heading to the southward. By combined energy and skill Howe had won the first move in the game. Clinton's army and New York were saved. As Washington wrote a little later:

The arrival of the French fleet is a great and striking event; but the operations of it have been injured by a number of unforeseen and unfavourable circumstances, which have lessened the importance of its services to a great degree. The length of the passage, in the first instance, was a capital misfortune; for, had even one of common length taken place, Lord Howe, with the British ships of war and all the transports in the river Delaware, must inevitably have fallen; and Sir Henry Clinton must have had better luck than is commonly dispensed to men of his profession under such circumstances, if he and his troops had not shared at least the fate of Burgoyne.

If this narration of events is so carefully worded as not to imply a censure upon D'Estaing, it none the less, however unintentionally, measures the great military merit of Lord Howe.

Nor did this end his achievements. Two or three days after the French departed a small reinforcement from England reached New York, and in the course of a week Howe, who had not failed to keep touch with the enemy's fleet till it was ninety miles at sea, heard that it had been seen again, heading for Narragansett Bay, then controlled by a British garrison on Rhode Island. This was in pursuance of a prearranged plan to support the American forces under General Sullivan, which had already advanced against the place. Adapting anew his action to the circumstances of the enemy's movements, Howe, though still much inferior, hurried to the spot, arriving and anchoring off Point Judith, at the entrance to Newport, on August 9th, the day after D'Estaing had run the fire of the British works and entered the harbour. With correct strategic judgment, with a flash of insight which did not usually distinguish him when an enemy was not in view, and contrary to his avowed policy when commander of the Channel Fleet, he saw that the true position for his squadron was in face of the hostile port, ready to act as circumstances might dictate. His mere presence blocked this operation also. D'Estaing, either fearing that the British admiral might take the offensive and gain some unexpected advantage, or tempted by the apparent opportunity of crushing a small hostile division, put to sea the next day. Howe, far superior as a seaman to his antagonist, manoeuvred to avoid a battle with a force superior by a half to his own; and this purpose was effected by his skilful management of his fleet, aided by his adversary's irresolution, notwithstanding that the unusual action of the wind thwarted his effort to control the situation by gaining the weather gage. Both the general manoeuvres, and the special dispositions made of his ships to meet the successive intentions of the enemy, as they became apparent, showed a mind fortified by previous preparation as well as by the natural self-possession for which he was conspicuous. It was eminently a tactical triumph.

A tremendous gale followed, scattered both fleets, and dismasted several of the French. D'Estaing appeared again off Rhode Island only to notify Sullivan that he could no longer aid him; and the latter, deprived of an indispensable support, withdrew in confusion. The disappointment of the Americans showed itself by mobbing some French seamen in Boston, whither their fleet retired. Washington continues, in the letter above quoted:

> After the enterprise upon Rhode Island had been planned, and was in the moment of execution, that Lord Howe with the British ships should interpose merely to create a diversion, and draw the French fleet from the island, was again unlucky, as the Count had not returned on the 17th to the island, though drawn from it on the 10th; by which the whole was subjected to a miscarriage.

What Washington politically calls bad luck was French bad management, provoked and baffled by Howe's accurate strategy, untiring energy, consummate seamanship, and tactical proficiency. Clinton's army delivered, the forcing of New York frustrated, Rhode Island and its garrison saved, by a squadron never more than two thirds of that opposed to it, were achievements to illustrate any career; and the more so that they were effected by sheer scientific fencing, like some of Bonaparte's greatest feats, with little loss of blood. They form Howe's highest title to fame, and his only claim as a strategist. It will be observed, however, that the characteristic of his course throughout is untiring and adequate adaption to the exigencies of the situation, as momentarily determined by the opponent's movements. There is in it no single original step. Such, indeed, is commonly the case with a strictly defensive campaign by a decisively inferior force. It is only the rare men who solve such difficulties by unexpected exceptional action.

It is indicative of Howe's personal feelings about the colonial quarrel, during the two years in which he thus ably discharged his official duties, that both he and his brother determined to ask relief from their commands as soon as it appeared that all hopes of conciliation were over. The appointment of other commissioners hastened their decision, and the permission to return was already in the admiral's hands when the news of D'Estaing's coming was received. Fighting a traditional foreign foe was a different thing from shedding the blood of men between whom and himself there was so much in common; nor was Howe the man to dodge responsibility by turning over an inferior force, threatened by such heavy odds, to a junior officer before the new commander-in-chief came. His resolution to remain was as happy for his renown as it was creditable to his character. After the brief campaign just sketched, true to his steady previous policy, he followed the French fleet to Newport when he heard of its reappearance there, and thence to Boston, coming off that port only three days after it; but finding it now sheltered under shore batteries, impregnable to his still inferior numbers, and learning that it was in need of extensive repairs, he resigned the command in New York to a rear-admiral, and departed to Newport to meet his successor, Vice-Admiral Byron. Upon the latter's arrival he sailed for England, towards the end of September, 1778. General Howe had preceded him by four months.

The two brothers went home with feelings of great resentment against the ministry. The course of the war had so far been unfortunate. The loss of Boston, the surrender of Burgoyne, the evacuation of Philadelphia, and finally the entrance of France into the contest, constituted a combination of mishaps which certainly implied fault somewhere. As usual, no one was willing to accept blame, and hot disputes, with injurious imputations, raged in Parliament. There is here, happily, no necessity for apportioning the responsibility, except in the case of Lord Howe; and as to him, it is reasonably clear that all was done that could be up to the coming of the French, while it is incontestable that afterwards, with a force utterly inadequate, for which the Government was answerable, he had averted imminent disaster by most masterly management. His words in the House of Commons were bitter.

> He had been deceived into his command, and he was deceived while he retained it. Tired and disgusted, he had desired permission to resign it; and he would have returned as soon as he obtained leave, but he could not think of doing so while a superior enemy remained in American seas; that, as soon as that impediment was removed, he gladly embraced the first opportunity of returning to Europe. Such, and the recollection of what he had suffered, were his motives for resigning the command, and such for declining any future service so long as the present ministry remained in office.

In terms like these could officers holding seats in Parliament speak concerning the Government of the day. It was a period in which not only did party feeling run high, but corruption was an almost avowed method of political management. The navy itself was split into factions by political bias and personal jealousies, and there was a saying that "if a naval officer were to be roasted, another officer could always be found to turn the spit." The head of the Admiralty, Lord Sandwich, was a man of much ability, but also of profligate character, as well public as private. He doubtless wished the success of his department,—under the terrible chances of war no chief can do otherwise, for the responsibility of failure must fall upon his own head; but through corrupt administration the strength of the navy, upon the outbreak of war, had been unequal to the work it had to do. Some one must suffer for this remissness, and who more naturally than the commander of a distant station, who confessed himself "no politician"? Hence, Howe certainly thought, the neglect with which he had been treated. "It would not be prudent to trust the little reputation he had earned by forty years' service, his personal honour and everything else he held dear, in the hands of men who have neither the ability to act on their own judgment, nor the integrity and good sense to follow the advice of others who might know more of the matter." A year later, it was roundly charged that the Channel Fleet had been brought home at a most critical moment, losing an exceptional opportunity for striking the enemy, in order to affect the elections in a dockyard town. Admiral Keppel considered that he had been sacrificed to party feeling; and a very distinguished officer, Barrington, refused to take a fleet, although willing to serve as second, even under a junior. "Who," he wrote, "would trust himself in chief command with such a set of scoundrels as are now in office?" Even a quarter of a century later, Earl St. Vincent gave to George III. himself the same reason for declining employment. After eliciting from him an unfavourable opinion as to the discipline and efficiency of the Channel Fleet, the king asked, "Where such evils exist, does Lord St. Vincent feel justified in refusing his conspicuous ability to remedy them?"

"My life," replied the old seaman, "is at your Majesty's disposal, and at that of my country; but my honour is in my own keeping, and I will not expose myself to the risk of losing it by the machinations of this ministry, under which I should hold command." To such feelings it was due that Howe, Keppel, and Barrington did not go to sea during the anxious three years that followed the return of the first. The illustrious Rodney, their only rival, but in himself a host, was the one distinguished naval chief who belonged heart and soul to the party with which Sandwich was identified.

Thus it happened that Rodney's period of activity during the war of the American Revolution coincided substantially with that of Howe's retirement. The same change of administration, in the spring of 1782, that led to the recall of the older man, brought Howe again into service, to replace the mediocrities who for three campaigns had commanded the Channel Fleet, the mainstay of Great Britain's safety. Upon it depended not only the protection of the British Islands and of the trade routes converging upon them, but also the occasional revictualling of Gibraltar, now undergoing the third year of the famous siege. Its operations extended to the North Sea, where the Dutch, now hostile, flanked the road to the Baltic, whence came the naval stores essential to the efficiency of the British fleet; to the Bay of Biscay, intercepting the convoys despatched from France to her navies abroad; and to the Chops of the Channel, where focussed the trade routes from East and West, and where more than once heavy losses had been inflicted upon British commerce by the allies. All these services received conspicuous and successful illustration during Howe's brief command, at the hands either of the commander-in-chief or of his subordinates, among whom were the very distinguished Barrington and Kempenfelt. Howe himself, with twenty-five sail-of-the-line, in July encountered an allied fleet of forty off Scilly. By an adroit tactical movement, very characteristic of his resolute and adequate presence of mind, he carried his ships between Scilly and Land's End by night, disappearing before morning from the enemy's view. He thus succeeded in meeting to the westward a valuable Jamaica convoy, homeward bound, and taking it under his protection. The allies being afterwards driven south by a heavy gale, the vessels of war and trade slipped by and reached England safely. Thus does good luck often give its blessing to good management.

To relieve Gibraltar, however, was the one really great task, commensurate to his abilities, that devolved upon Howe during this short command. In the summer of 1782, the Spaniards were completing ten heavy floating batteries, expected to be impervious to shot and to combustion, and from an attack by which upon the sea front of the works decisive results were anticipated. At the same time prolonged blockade by land and sea, supported by forty-nine allied ships-of-the-line anchored at Algeciras, the Spanish port on the opposite side of the Bay, was producing its inevitable results, and the place was now in the last extremity for provisions and munitions of war. To oppose the hostile fleets and introduce the essential succours, to carry which required thirty-one sail of supply ships, Great Britain could muster only thirty-four of-the-line, but to them were adjoined the superb professional abilities of Lord Howe, never fully evoked except when in sight of an enemy, as he here must act, with Barrington and Kempenfelt as seconds; the one the pattern of the practical, experienced, division commander, tested on many occasions, the other an officer much of Howe's own stamp, and like him a diligent student and promoter of naval manoeuvres and naval signals, to the development of which both had greatly contributed. To the train of supply ships were added for convoy a number of merchant vessels destined to different parts of the world, so that the grand total which finally sailed on September 11th was 183. While this great body was gathering at Spithead, there occurred the celebrated incident of the oversetting of the *Royal George* at her anchors, on August 29th—

When Kempenfelt went down
With twice four hundred men.

Howe thus lost the man upon whom principally he must have relied for the more purely tactical development of the fleet, opportunity for which he anticipated in the necessarily slow and graduated progress of so large an assemblage.

The occasion was indeed one that called for deliberation as well as for calculated audacity, both controlled by a composure and ability rarely conjoined to the same great extent as in Howe. Circumstances were more imminent than in the two previous reliefs by Rodney and Darby; for the greatly superior numbers of the allies were now not in Cadiz, as before, but lying only four miles from the anchorage which the supply vessels must gain. True, certainly, that for these a certain portion of their path would be shielded by the guns of the fortress, but a much greater part would be wholly out of their range; and the mere question of reaching his berth, a navigational problem complicated by uncertain winds, and by a very certain current sweeping in from the Atlantic, was extremely difficult for the merchant skipper of the day, a seaman rough and ready, but not always either skilful or heedful. The problem before Howe demanded therefore the utmost of his seamanlike qualities and of his tactical capacity.

The length of the passage speaks for the deliberate caution of

Howe's management, as his conduct at the critical moment of approach, and during the yet more critical interval of accomplishing the entrance of the supply ships, evinces the cool and masterful self-control which always assured the complete and sustained exertion of his great professional powers at a required instant. Thirty days were consumed in the voyage from Spithead to Gibraltar, but no transport was dropped. Of the huge convoy even, it is narrated that after a heavy gale, just before reaching Cape Finisterre, the full tally of 183 was counted. After passing that cape, the traders probably parted for their several destinations, each body under a suitable escort. The stoppages for the rounding-up of straying or laggard vessels, or for re-establishing the observance of order which ever contributes to regulated movement, and through it to success, were not in this case time lost. The admiral made of them opportunities for exercising his ships-of-the-line in the new system of signals, and in the simple evolutions depending upon them, which underlie flexibility of action, and in the day of battle enable the fleet to respond to the purposes of its commander with reasonable precision, and in mutual support.

Such drill was doubly necessary, for it not only familiarized the intelligence of the captains with ideas too generally neglected by seamen until called upon to put them into practice, and revealed to them difficulties not realized until encountered, but also enforced recognition of the particular qualities of each vessel, upon the due observance of which substantial accuracy of manoeuvre depends. The experience gained during this cruise, going and returning, probably opened the eyes of many officers to unsuspected deficiencies in themselves, in handling a ship under the exigencies of fleet tactics. Howe certainly was in this respect disappointed in his followers, but probably not greatly surprised. At the same time it is but fair to note that the service was performed throughout without any marked hitch traceable to want of general professional ability. A French writer has commented upon this.

> There occurred none of those events, so frequent in the experiences of a squadron, which often oblige admirals to take a course wholly contrary to the end they have in view.

It is impossible not to recall the unhappy incidents which, from the 9th to the 12th of April, of this same year, befell the squadron of the Count De Grasse. If it is just to admit that Lord Howe displayed the highest talent, it should be added that he had in his hands excellent instruments.

On the 10th of October the fleet and store ships drew nigh the Straits of Gibraltar. On that day it was rejoined by a frigate, which forty-eight hours before had been sent ahead to communicate the approach of the relief, and to concert action. She brought the cheering news of the victorious repulse by the British of the grand attack by sea and land upon September 13th, with the entire destruction of the trusted floating batteries. Under this flush of national triumph, and with a fair westerly wind, the great expedition entered the straits on October 11th, in ranged order for action. The convoy went first, because, sailing before the wind, it was thus to leeward of the ships of war, in position to be immediately defended, if attacked. Two squadrons of the fleet succeeded them, in line-of-battle ahead, formed thus for instant engagement, Howe leading in the *Victory*; while the third of the squadrons followed in reserve, in an order not stated, but probably in a line abreast, sweeping a broader belt of sea, and more nearly under the eye of the Commander-in-chief, who, for the purposes of the present operation, had left his traditional post in the centre. Howe's reasons for this change of position, if ever stated, have not come under the eyes of the writer; but analysis shows that he was there close to the store ships, whose safe entrance to the port was at once the main object of the enterprise and the one most critically uncertain of achievement, because of the general bad behaviour of convoys. There he could control them more surely, and at the same time by his own conduct indicate his general purposes to subordinates, who, however deficient in distinctly tactical proficiency, had the seamanship and the willingness adequately to support him.

At 6 p.m. the supply ships were off the mouth of the bay, with the wind fair for their anchorage; but, although full and particular instructions had been issued to them concerning currents and other local conditions, all save four missed the entrance and were swept to the eastward of the Rock. The fleet of course had to follow its charge, and by their failure a new task confronted Howe's professional abilities and endurance. Fortunately he had an able adviser in the captain of the fleet, who had had long experience of the locality, invaluable during the trying week that ensued. The allies had not yet stirred. To move near fifty sail-of-the-line in pursuit of an enemy, inferior indeed, but ranged for battle, and the precise moment of whose appearance could not have been foreseen, was no slight undertaking, as Nelson afterwards said. It may be recalled that before Trafalgar over twenty-four hours were needed for the allied thirty-three to get out of Cadiz Bay. On the 13th, however, the combined French and Spaniards sailed, intent primarily, it would seem, not on the true and vital offensive purpose of frustrating the relief, but upon the very secondary defensive object of preserving two of their own numbers, which in a recent gale had been swept to the eastward. Thus trivially preoccupied, they practically neglected Howe, who on his part stripped for action by sending the supply vessels to the Zaffarine Islands, where the vagarious instincts of their captains would be controlled by an anchor on the bottom. On the 14th the allies bore north from the British, close under the Spanish coast, and visible only from the mastheads. On the 15th the wind came east, and the convoy and fleet began cautiously to move towards Gibraltar, the enemy apparently out of sight, and certainly to the eastward. On the evening of the 16th eighteen supply ships were at the mole, and on the 18th all had arrived. Gibraltar was equipped for another year's endurance.

We have less than could be wished of particulars touching this performance of Howe's, from the day of leaving England to that of fulfilment, five full weeks later. Inference and comment has to be built up upon incidents transmitted disconnectedly, interpreted in connection with the usual known conditions and the relative strength of the two opposing parties. To professional understanding, thus far supplemented, much is clear; quite enough, at the least, to avouch the deliberation, the steadiness, the professional aptitude, the unremitting exertion that so well supplies the place of celerity,—never resting, if never hasting,—

the calculated daring at fit moments, and above all the unfailing self-possession and self-reliance which at every instant up to the last secured to the British enterprise the full value of the other qualities possessed by the Commander-in-chief. A biographical notice of Howe cannot be complete without quoting the tribute of an accomplished officer belonging to one of the navies then arrayed against him. "The qualities displayed by Lord Howe during this short campaign," says Captain Chevalier of the French service, "rose to the full height of the mission which he had to fulfil. This operation, one of the finest in the War of American Independence, merits a praise equal to that of a victory. If the English fleet was favoured by circumstances,—and it is rare that in such enterprises one can succeed without the aid of fortune,—it was above all the Commander-in-chief's quickness of perception, the accuracy of his judgment, and the rapidity of his decisions that assured success."

Having accomplished his main object and landed besides fifteen hundred barrels of powder from his own ships, Howe tarried no longer. Like Nelson, at Gibraltar on his way to St. Vincent, he would not trifle with an easterly wind, without which he could not leave the Straits against the constant inset; neither would he adventure action, against a force superior by a third, amid the currents that had caused him so trying an experience. There was, moreover, the important strategic consideration that if the allied fleets, which were again in sight, followed him out, they would thereby be drawn from any possible molestation of the unloading of the supply ships, which had been attempted, though with no great success, on the occasion of the relief by Darby, in 1781. Howe therefore at once headed for the Atlantic. The allies pursued, and engaged partially on the afternoon and evening of October 20th; but the attack was not pushed home, although they had the advantage of the wind and of numbers. On the 14th of November the British fleet regained Spithead. It may be remarked that Admirals Barrington and Millbank both praised their captains very highly, for the maintenance of the order in their respective divisions during this action; the former saying it "was the finest close connected line I ever saw during my service at sea." Howe, who held higher ideals, conceived through earnest and prolonged study and reflection, was less well satisfied. It seems, however, reasonable to infer that the assiduity of his efforts to promote tactical precision had realized at least a partial measure of success.

Another long term of shore life now intervened, carrying the gallant admiral over the change-fraught years of failing powers from fifty-six to sixty-seven, at which age he was again called into service, in the course of which he was to perform the most celebrated, but, it may confidently be affirmed, not the most substantial, nor even the most brilliant, action of his career. During much of this intermediate period, between 1783 and 1788, Howe occupied the Cabinet position of First Lord of the Admiralty, the civil head and administrator of the Navy. Into the discharge of this office he carried the same qualities of assiduous attention to duty, and of close devotion to details of professional progress, which characterized him when afloat; but, while far from devoid of importance, there is but little in this part of his story that needs mention as distinctive. Perhaps the most interesting incidents, seen in the light of afterwards, are that one of his earliest appointments to a ship was given to Nelson; and that the cordiality of his reception at the end of the cruise is said to have removed from the hero an incipient but very strong disgust for the service. The future admiral wrote to his brother:

> You ask me by what interest did I get a ship? I answer, having served with credit was my recommendation to Lord Howe. Anything in reason that I can ask, I am sure of obtaining from his justice.

At the outbreak of the French Revolution, Howe stood conspicuously at the head of the navy, distinguished at once for well-known professional accomplishments and for tried capacity in chief command. His rivals in renown among his contemporaries—Keppel, Barrington, and Rodney—had gone to their rest. Jervis, Duncan, Nelson, Collingwood, and their compeers, had yet to show what was in them as general officers. Lord Hood alone remained; and he, although he had done deeds of great promise, had come to the front too late in the previous war for his reputation to rest upon sustained achievement as well as upon hopeful indication. The great commands were given to these two: Hood, the junior, going to the Mediterranean with twenty ships-of-the-line, Howe taking the Channel Fleet of somewhat superior numbers.

The solid, deliberate, methodical qualities of the veteran admiral were better adapted to the more purely defensive role, forced upon Great Britain by the allied superiority in 1782, than to the continuous, vigilant, aggressive action demanded by the new conditions with which he now had to deal, when the great conflagration of the Revolution was to be hemmed in and stamped out by the unyielding pressure and massive blows of the British sea power. The days of regulated, routine hostilities between rulers had passed away with the uprising of a people; the time foretold, when nation should rise against nation, was suddenly come with the crash of an ancient kingdom and of its social order. An admirable organizer and indefatigable driller of ships, though apparently a poor disciplinarian, Howe lacked the breadth of view, the clear intuitions, the alacrity of mind, brought to bear upon the problem by Jervis and Nelson, who, thus inspired, framed the sagacious plan to which, more than to any other one cause, was due the exhaustion alike of the Revolutionary fury and of Napoleon's imperial power. Keenly interested in the material efficiency of his ships, as well as in the precision with which they could perform necessary evolutions and maintain prescribed formations, he sought to attain these ends by long stays in port, varied by formal cruises devoted to secondary objects and to fleet tactics. For these reasons also he steadfastly refused to countenance the system of close-watching the enemy's ports, by the presence before each of a British force adequate to check each movement at its beginning.

Thus nursing ships and men, Howe flattered himself he should insure the perfection of the instrument which should be his stay in the hour of battle. Herein he ignored the fundamental truth, plainly perceived by his successor, St. Vincent, that the effectiveness of a military instrument consists more in the method of its use, and in the practised skill of the human element that wields it, than in the material perfection of the weapon itself. It may justly be urged on his behalf that the preparation he sought should have been made, but was not, by the Government in the long years of peace. This is true; but yet the fact remains that he pursued his system by choice and conviction repeatedly affirmed; that continuous instead of occasional cruising in the proper positions would better have reached the ends of drill; and that to the material well being of his ships he sacrificed those correct military dispositions before the enemy's ports, instituted and maintained by Hawke, and further developed and extended by Jervis, who at the same time preserved the efficiency of the vessels by increased energy and careful prevision of their wants. The brilliant victory of the 1st of June has obscured the accompanying fact, that lamentable failure characterized the general strategic use of the Channel Fleet under Howe and his immediate successor.

Once in sight of the enemy, however, the old man regained the fire of youth, and showed the attainments which long study and careful thought had added to his natural talent for war, enabling him to introduce distinct advances upon the tactical conceptions of his predecessors. The battle of June 1, 1794, was brought about in the following manner. Political anarchy and a bad season had combined to ruin the French harvests in 1793, and actual famine threatened the land. To obviate this, at least partially, the Government had bought in the United States a large quantity of breadstuffs, which were expected to arrive in May or June, borne by one hundred and eighty merchant vessels. To insure the safety of this valuable convoy, the Brest Fleet was sent to meet it at a designated point; five ships going first, and twenty-five following a few days later. Robespierre's orders to the admiral, Villaret-Joyeuse, were to avoid battle, if possible, but at all hazards to secure the merchant fleet, or his head would answer for it.

About the same time, Howe, who had kept his vessels in port during the winter, sailed from the Channel with thirty-two ships-of-the-line. These he soon divided into two squadrons; one of which, numbering six, after performing a specific service, was not ordered to rejoin the main body, but to cruise in a different spot. These ships were sadly missed on the day of battle, when they could have changed a brilliant into a crushing victory. Howe himself went to seek the French, instead of taking a position where they must pass; and after some running to and fro, in which the British actually got to the westward of their foes, and might well have missed them altogether, he was lucky enough, on the 28th of May, some four hundred miles west of the island of Ushant, to find the larger of their two detachments. This having been meanwhile joined by one ship from the smaller, both opponents now numbered twenty-six heavy vessels.

The French were to windward, a position which gives the power of refusing or delaying decisive action. The average speed of any fleet, however, must fall below the best of some of the force opposed to it; and Howe, wishing to compel battle, sent out six of his fastest and handiest ships. These were directed to concentrate their fire upon the enemy's rear, which, from the point of view of naval tactics, was the weakest part of a line-of-battle of sailing ships; because, to aid it, vessels ahead must turn round and change their formation, performing a regular evolution, whereas, if the van be assailed, the rear naturally advances to its help. If this partial attack crippled one or more of the French, the disabled ships would drift towards the British, where either they would be captured, or their comrades would be obliged to come to their rescue, hazarding the general engagement that Howe wanted. As it happened, the French had in the rear an immense ship of one hundred and ten guns, which beat off in detail the successive attacks of her smaller antagonists; but in so doing she received so much injury that she left the fleet after nightfall, passing the British unmolested, and went back to Brest. One of her assailants, also, had to return to England; but, as the relative force of the units thus clipped from the respective opponents was as three to two, the general result was a distinct material gain for Howe. It is to be scored to his credit as a tactician that he let this single enemy go, rather than scatter his fleet and lose ground in trying to take her. He had a more important object.

The next morning, May 29th, the French by poor seamanship had lost to leeward, and were consequently somewhat nearer. Both fleets were heading south-easterly, with the wind at south-southwest; both, consequently, on the starboard tack. Howe saw that, by tacking in succession, his column would so head that several of his vessels in passing could bring the hostile rear under their guns, and that it was even possible that three or four might be cut off, unless reinforced; to attempt which by the enemy would involve also tactical possibilities favourable to the British. The necessary movement was ordered; and the French admiral, seeing things in the same light, was justly so alarmed for the result that he turned his head ships, and after them his whole column in succession, to run down to help the rear. Judicious, and indeed necessary, as this was, it played right into Howe's hands, and was a tribute to his tactical skill, by which it was compelled; for in doing this the French necessarily gave up much of their distance to windward, and so hastened the collision they wished to avoid. Although the attack upon their rear was limited to a few desultory broadsides, the two fleets were at last nearly within cannon shot, whereas the day before they had been eight or ten miles apart. Both were now on the port tack, running west in parallel lines.

Towards noon, Howe saw that the morning's opportunity of directing his whole column upon the enemy's rear again offered, but with a far better chance; that if his ships manoeuvred well half a dozen of the French must be cut off, unless their admiral, to save them, repeated his previous manoeuvre of running down to their assistance, which would infallibly entail the general engagement sought by the British. The signal to tack in succession was again made, and to pass through the enemy's line; but here Howe's purpose was foiled, as Rodney's on April 17th, by the failure of his leading vessel. Her captain, like Carkett, was of considerable seniority, having commanded a ship-of-the-line under Howe at New York, in 1778. His conduct during this brief campaign was so unfavourably noticed by his admiral that he asked a Court-Martial, which dismissed him from his ship, though clearing him of cowardice. Upon the present occasion he for some time delayed obedience; and, when he did go about, wore instead of tacking, which lost ground and caused confusion by going to leeward. The second ship acted well, and struck the French column some distance from its rear, proving Howe right in judging that the enemy's order could there be pierced. As this vessel was not closely supported, she received such injuries from successive fires, that, when she at last found an opening through which to pass, she was unable to manoeuvre.

Seeing that the van was failing him, Howe, whose flag-ship, the *Queen Charlotte*, was tenth from the head of his column, now took the lead himself, tacked his own vessel, though her turn was not yet come, and, accompanied by his next ahead and astern,—another striking instance of the inspiring influence of a high example,—stood straight for the hostile order. The three broke through astern of the sixth ship from the French rear, and cut off two of the enemy, which were speedily surrounded by others of the British. Villaret-Joyeuse then repeated his former evolution, and nothing could have saved a general engagement except the disorder into which the British had fallen, and Howe's methodical abhorrence of attacks made in such confusion as prevailed. Moreover, the decisive result of this last brush was that the French entirely lost the windward position, and the British admiral knew that he now had them where they could not escape; he could afford to postpone the issue. Accordingly, fighting ceased for the day; but the French had been so mauled that three more ships had to go into port, leaving them but twenty-two to the enemy's twenty-five.

To appreciate Howe's personal merit as a tactician, reflection should be bestowed upon the particulars of his conduct on these two days, with which the First of June is not to be compared; for in them culminated, so to speak, a long course of preparation in the study of tactical possibilities, and of the system of signals needed to insure necessary evolutions. His officers, as a body, do not appear to have deserved by their manoeuvring the encomium passed by Rodney upon his, during the long chase to windward in May, 1780; and, as Howe had now held command for a year, this failure may probably be assigned to lack of that punctilious severity to which Rodney attributed his own success. But in the matter of personal acquirement Howe shows a distinct advance upon Rodney's ideas and methods. There is not to be noted in Rodney's actions any foreshadowing of the judicious attack upon the enemy's rear, on May 28th, by a smart flying squadron. This doubtless presents some analogy to a general chase, but there is in it more of system and of regulated action; in short, there is development. Again, although Rodney doubtless tacked in succession repeatedly, between May 9th and May 20th, in his efforts to reach the enemy to windward, there does not then appear, nor did there appear on either of the two occasions when he succeeded in striking their column from to leeward, any intention, such as Howe on the 29th communicated by signal and enforced by action, of breaking through the enemy's line even at the cost of breaking his own. Not even on April 12th had Rodney, as far as appears, any such formulated plan. There is here, therefore, distinct progress, in the nature of reflective and reasoned development; for it is scarcely to be supposed that Howe's assiduity and close contact with the navy had failed to note, for future application, the incidents of Rodney's battles, which had been the subject of animated discussion and censure by eye-witnesses.

It will be recognized that the conception in Howe's mind, maintained unchangeably and carried consistently into effect during these two days, was to attack continually, as opportunity offered, the rear end of the enemy's column, which corresponds precisely with the attack upon the flank of a line of battle on shore. Merit does not depend upon result, but fortunate result should be noted for the encouragement and guidance of the future. In consequence of these sustained and judiciously directed movements, and of the steps found necessary by the French admiral because of injuries received, the enemy had lost from their line four ships, of which one was of one hundred and twenty guns, another of eighty; while of those retained one had lost all her spars save the lower masts, and had thenceforth to be towed in action. Against this was to be set only one British seventy-four, disabled on the 28th and returned to port; their other damaged vessels refitted at sea and stayed with the fleet. On the other hand, Howe's separated division of six remained separated, whereas four fresh French ships joined their main fleet on the 30th. Admirable tactics were thus neutralized by defective strategy; and therefore it may with substantial accuracy be said that Howe's professional qualities and defects were both signally illustrated in this, his last conspicuous service.

The French admiral on the evening of the 29th saw that he now must fight, and at a disadvantage; consequently, he could not hope to protect the convoy. As to save this was his prime object, the next best thing was to entice the British out of its path. With this view he stood away to the northwest; while a dense fog coming on both favoured his design and prevented further encounter during the two ensuing days, throughout which Howe continued to pursue. In the evening of May 31st the weather cleared, and at daybreak the next morning the enemies were in position, ready for battle, two long columns of ships, heading west, the British twenty-five, the French again twenty-six through the junction of the four vessels mentioned. Howe now had cause to regret his absent six, and to ponder Nelson's wise saying, "Only numbers can annihilate."

The time for manoeuvring was past. Able tactician as he personally was, and admirable as had been the direction of his efforts in the two days' fighting, Howe had been forced in them to realize two things, namely, that his captains were, singly, superior in seamanship, and their crews in gunnery, to the French; and again, that in the ability to work together as a fleet the British were so deficient as to promise very imperfect results, if he attempted any but the simplest formation. To such, therefore, he resorted; falling back upon the old, unskilful, sledge-hammer fashion of the British navy. Arranging his ships in one long line, three miles from the enemy, he made them all go down together, each to attack a specified opponent, coming into action as nearly as might be at the same instant. Thus the French, from the individual inferiority of the units of their fleet, would be at all points overpowered. The issue justified the forecast; but the manner of performance was curiously and happily marked by Howe's own peculiar phlegm. There was a long summer day ahead for fighting, and no need for hurry. The order was first accurately formed, and canvas reduced to proper proportions. Then the crews went to breakfast. After breakfast, the ships all headed for the hostile line, under short sail, the admiral keeping them in hand during the approach, as an infantry officer dresses his company. Hence the shock from end to end was so nearly simultaneous as to induce success unequalled in any engagement conducted on the same primitive plan.

Picturesque as well as sublime, animating as well as solemn, on that bright Sunday morning, was this prelude to the stern game of war about to be played: the quiet summer sea stirred only by a breeze sufficient to cap with white the little waves that ruffled its surface; the dark hulls gently rippling the water aside in their slow advance, a ridge of foam curling on either side of the furrow ploughed by them in their onward way; their massive sides broken by two, or at times three, rows of ports, whence, the tompions drawn, yawned the sullen lines of guns, behind which, unseen, but easily realized by the instructed eye, clustered the groups of ready seamen who served each piece. Aloft swung leisurely to and fro the tall spars, which ordinarily, in so light a wind, would be clad in canvas from deck to truck, but whose naked trimness now proclaimed the deadly purpose of that still approach. Upon the high poops, where floated the standard of either nation, gathered round each chief the little knot of officers through whom commands were issued and reports received, the nerves along which thrilled the impulses of the great organism, from its head, the admiral, through every member to the dark lowest decks, nearly awash, where, as farthest from the captain's own oversight, the senior lieutenants controlled the action of the ships' heaviest batteries.

On board the *Queen Charlotte*, Lord Howe, whose burden of sixty-eight years had for four days found no rest save what he could snatch in an arm-chair, now, at the prospect of battle, "displayed an animation," writes an eye-witness, "of which, at his age, and after such fatigue of body and mind, I had not thought him capable. He seemed to contemplate the result as one of unbounded satisfaction." By his side stood his fleet-captain, Curtis, of whose service among the floating batteries, and during the siege of Gibraltar, the governor of the fortress had said, "He is the man to whom the king is chiefly indebted for its security;" and Codrington, then a lieutenant, who afterwards commanded the allied fleets at Navarino. Five ships to the left, Collingwood, in the *Barfleur*, was making to the admiral whose flag she bore the remark that stirred Thackeray: "Our wives are now about going to church, but we will ring about these Frenchmen's ears a peal which will drown their bells." The French officers, both admirals and captains, were mainly unknown men, alike then and thereafter. The fierce flames of the Revolution had swept away the men of the old school, mostly aristocrats, and time had not yet brought forward the very few who during the Napoleonic period showed marked capacity. The commander-in-chief, Villaret-Joyeuse, had three years before been a lieutenant. He had a high record for gallantry, but was without antecedents as a general officer. With him, on the poop of the *Montagne*, which took her name from Robespierre's political supporters, stood that anomalous companion of the generals and admirals of the day, the Revolutionary commissioner, Jean Bon Saint-André, about to learn by experience the practical working of the system he had advocated, to disregard all tests of ability save patriotism and courage, depreciating practice and skill as unnecessary to the valour of the true Frenchman.

As the British line drew near the French, Howe said to Curtis, "Prepare the signal for close action."

"There is no such signal," replied Curtis.

"No," said the admiral, "but there is one for closer action, and I only want that to be made in case of captains not doing their duty." Then closing a little signal book he always carried, he continued to those around him, "Now, gentlemen, no more book, no more signals. I look to you to do the duty of the *Queen Charlotte* in engaging the flag-ship. I don't want the ships to be bilge to bilge, but if you can lock the yardarms, so much the better; the battle will be the quicker decided."

His purpose was to go through the French line, and fight the *Montagne* on the far side. Some doubted their succeeding, but Howe overbore them.

"That's right, my lord!" cried Bowen, the sailing-master, who looked to the ship's steering. "The *Charlotte* will make room for herself." She pushed close under the French ship's stern, grazing her ensign, and raking her from stern to stem with a withering fire, beneath which fell three hundred men. A length or two beyond lay the French *Jacobin*. Howe ordered the *Charlotte* to luff, and place herself between the two. "If we do," said Bowen, "we shall be on board one of them."

"What is that to you, sir?" asked Howe quickly.

"Oh!" muttered the master, not inaudibly. "D——n my eyes if I care, if you don't. I'll go near enough to singe some of our whiskers." And then, seeing by the *Jacobin*'s rudder that she was going off, he brought the *Charlotte* sharp round, her jib boom grazing the second Frenchman as her side had grazed the flag of the first.

From this moment the battle raged furiously from end to end of the field for nearly an hour,—a wild scene of smoke and confusion, under cover of which many a fierce ship duel was fought, while here and there men wandered, lost, in a maze of bewilderment that neutralized their better judgment. An English naval captain tells a service tradition of one who was so busy watching the compass, to keep his position in the ranks, that he lost sight of his antagonist, and never again found him. Many a quaint incident passed, recorded or unrecorded, under that sulphurous canopy. A British ship, wholly dismasted, lay between two enemies, her captain desperately wounded. A murmur of surrender was somewhere heard; but as the first lieutenant checked it with firm authority, a cock flew upon the stump of a mast and crowed lustily. The exultant note found quick response in hearts not given to despair, and a burst of merriment, accompanied with three cheers, replied to the bird's triumphant scream. On board the *Brunswick*, in her struggle with the *Vengeur*, one of the longest and fiercest fights the sea has ever seen, the cocked hat was shot off the effigy of the Duke of Brunswick, which she bore as a figurehead. A deputation from the crew gravely requested the captain to allow the use of his spare chapeau, which was securely nailed on, and protected his grace's wig during the rest of the action. After this battle with the ships of the new republic, the partisans of monarchy noted with satisfaction that, among the many royal figures that surmounted the stems of the British fleet, not one lost his crown. Of a harum-scarum Irish captain are told two droll stories. After being hotly engaged for some time with a French ship, the fire of the latter slackened, and then ceased. He called to know if she had surrendered. The reply was, "No."

"Then," shouted he, "d——n you, why don't you fire?" Having disposed of his special antagonist without losing his own spars, the same man kept along in search of new adventures, until he came to a British ship totally dismasted and otherwise badly damaged. She was commanded by a captain of rigidly devout piety.

"Well, Jemmy," hailed the Irishman, "you are pretty well mauled; but never mind, Jemmy, whom the Lord loveth he chasteneth."

The French have transmitted to us less of anecdote, nor is it easy to connect the thought of humour with those grimly earnest republicans and the days of the Terror. There is, indeed, something unintentionally funny in the remark of the commander of one of the captured ships to his captors. They had, it was true, dismasted half the French fleet, and had taken over a fourth; yet he assured them it could not be considered a victory, "but merely a butchery, in which the British had shown neither science nor tactics." The one story, noble and enduring, that will ever be associated with the French on the 1st of June is in full keeping with the temper of the times and the enthusiasm of the nation. The seventy-four-gun ship *Vengeur*, after a three hours' fight, yardarm to yardarm, with the British *Brunswick*, was left in a sinking state by her antagonist, who was herself in no condition to help. In the confusion, the *Vengeur*'s peril was for some time not observed; and when it was, the British ships that came to her aid had time only to remove part of her survivors. In their report of the event the latter said:

> Scarcely had the boats pulled clear of the sides, when the most frightful spectacle was offered to our gaze. Those of our comrades who remained on board the *Vengeur du Peuple*, with hands raised to heaven, implored, with lamentable cries, the help for which they could no longer

hope. Soon disappeared the ship and the unhappy victims it contained. In the midst of the horror with which this scene inspired us all, we could not avoid a feeling of admiration mingled with our grief. As we drew away, we heard some of our comrades still offering prayers for the welfare of their country. The last cries of these unfortunates were, 'Vive la République!' They died uttering them.

Over a hundred Frenchmen thus went down. Seven French ships were captured, including the sunk *Vengeur*. Five more were wholly dismasted, but escaped,—a good fortune mainly to be attributed to Howe's utter physical prostration, due to his advanced years and the continuous strain of the past five days. He now went to bed, completely worn out. Lieutenant Codrington, an officer who was present wrote:

> We all got round him, indeed, I saved him from a tumble, he was so weak that from a roll of the ship he was nearly falling into the waist. 'Why, you hold me up as if I were a child,' he said good-humouredly.

Had he been younger, there can be little doubt that the fruits of victory would have been gathered with an ardour which his assistant, Curtis, failed to show. The fullest proof of this is the anecdote, already quoted in the sketch of Rodney,[13] which has been transmitted by Admiral Sir Byam Martin direct from the sailing-master of the *Queen Charlotte*, afterwards Admiral Bowen; but his account is abundantly confirmed by other officers, eye and ear witnesses. Taken in connection with these, Codrington's story of his physical weakness bears the note, not of pathos only, but of encouragement; for the whole testifies assuredly to the persistence, through great bodily debility, of a strong quality diligently cultivated in the days of health and vigour. In truth, it was impossible for Howe to purpose otherwise. Having been continuously what he was in his prime, it could not be that he would not intend, with all the force of his will, to persevere to the utmost in the duty before him. The faithfulness of a lifetime does not so forsake a man in his end. What he lacked in that

---

13. *Ante*, p. 250.

critical hour was not the willing mind, but the instrument by which to communicate to the fleet the impulse which his own failing powers were no longer able directly to impart.

Lord Howe's career practically ended with this battle and the honours that followed it. Infirmities then gained rapidly upon him, and it would have been well had his own wish to retire been granted by the Government. He remained in nominal command of the Channel Fleet, though not going to sea, until the occurrence of the great mutinies of 1797. The suppression—or, more properly, the composing—of this ominous outbreak was devolved upon him by the ministry. He very wisely observed that "preventive measures rather than corrective are to be preferred for preserving discipline in fleets and armies;" but it was in truth his own failure to use such timely remedies, owing to the lethargy of increasing years, acting upon a temperament naturally indulgent and inapprehensive, that was largely responsible for disorders of whose imminence he had warning. From the military standpoint, the process of settlement had much the air of *opéra bouffe*,—a consummation probably inevitable when just grievances and undeniable hardships get no attention until the sufferers break through all rules, and seek redress by force. The mutinous seamen protested to Howe the bitterness of their sorrow at the sense of wrong doing, but in the same breath insisted that their demands must be conceded, and that certain obnoxious officers must be removed from their ships. The demands were yielded, Howe gently explaining to the men how naughty they had been; and that, as to the unpopular officers, they themselves asked relief from so unpleasant a situation. In his curiously involved style, he wrote:

> This request has been complied with, under the pretext of an equal desire on the part of the officers not to be employed in ships where exception, without specification of facts, has been taken to their conduct. However ineligible the concession, it was become indispensably necessary." Under this thin veil, men persuaded themselves that appearances were saved, as a woman hides a smile behind her fan. Admiral Codrington, a firm admirer of Howe, justly

said: "It was want of discipline which led to the discontent and mutiny in the Channel Fleet. Lord Howe got rid of the mutiny by granting the men all they asked; but discipline was not restored until the ships most remarkable for misconduct had been, one after the other, placed under the command of Lord St. Vincent."

With the settlement of this mutiny Lord Howe's long career of active service closed. Immediately afterwards he retired formally, as he sometime before had actually, from the command of the Channel Fleet, and on the 5th of August, 1799, he died full of years and honours; having lived just long enough to welcome the rising star of Nelson's glory as it burst upon men's sight at Cape St. Vincent and the Nile.

Jervis: 1735–1823

CHAPTER 5

Jervis: 1735-1823

The renown of Nelson is part of the heritage of the world. His deeds, although their full scope and real significance have been but little understood, stand out conspicuous among a host of lesser achievements, and are become to mankind the symbol of Great Britain's maritime power in that tremendous era when it drove the French Revolution back upon itself, stifling its excesses, and so insuring the survival of the beneficent tendencies which for a time seemed well nigh lost in the madness of the nation.

The appearance of a prodigy like Nelson, however, is not an isolated event, independent of antecedents. It is the result of a happy meeting of genius and opportunity. The hour has come, and the man. Other men have laboured, and the hero enters into their labours; not unjustly, for thereto he also has been appointed by those special gifts which fit him to reap as theirs fitted them to sew. In relation to Nelson and his career, the illustrious officer whose most distinguishing characteristics we have now to trace stood pre-eminent among many forerunners. It was he, above all others, who made the preparation indispensable to the approaching triumphal progress of the first of British naval heroes, so that his own work underlies that of his successor, as foundation supports superstructure. There is not between them the vital connection of root to branch, of plant to fruit. In the matter of professional kinship Nelson has far more in common with Hood. Between these there is an identity of kind, an orderly sequence of development, an organic bond, such as knits together the series of a progressive evolution. It is not so with

Jervis. Closely conjoined as the two men long were in a common service, and in mutual admiration and sympathy, it would be an error to think of the elder as in any sense the professional progenitor of the younger; yet he was, as it were, an adoptive father, who from the first fostered, and to the last gloried in, the genius which he confessed unparalleled. "It does not become me to make comparisons," he wrote after Copenhagen; "all agree that there is but one Nelson." And when the great admiral had been ten years in his grave, he said of an officer's gallant conduct at the Battle of Algiers, "He seems to have felt Lord Nelson's eye upon him;" as though no stronger motive could be felt nor higher praise given.

John Jervis was born on the 20th of January, 1735, at Meaford, in Staffordshire. He was intended for his father's profession, the law; but, by his own account, a disinclination which was probably natural became invincible through the advice of the family coachman. "Don't be a lawyer, Master Jacky," said the old man; "all lawyers are rogues." Sometime later, his father receiving the appointment of auditor to Greenwich Hospital, the family removed to the neighbourhood of London; and there young Jervis, being thrown in contact with ships and seamen, and particularly with a midshipman of his own age, became confirmed in his wish to go to sea. Failing to get his parents' consent, he ran away towards the close of the year 1747. From this escapade he was brought back; but his father, seeing the uselessness of forcing the lad's inclinations, finally acquiesced, though it seems likely, from his after conduct, that it was long before he became thoroughly reconciled to the disappointment.

In January, 1748, the future admiral and peer first went afloat in a ship bound to the West Indies. The time was inauspicious for one making the navy his profession. The war of the Austrian succession had just been brought to an end by the Peace of Aix-la-Chapelle, and the monotonous discomfort of hard cruising, unrelieved by the excitements of battle or the flush of prize-taking, was the sole prospect of one whose narrow means debarred him from such pleasures as the station afforded and youth naturally prompted him to seek. His pay was little over twenty pounds a year, and his father had not felt able to give more than that sum towards his original outfit. After being three years on board, practising a rigid economy scarcely to be expected in one of his years, the lad of sixteen drew a bill upon home for twenty pounds more. It came back dishonoured. The latent force of his character was at once aroused. To discharge the debt, he disposed of his pay tickets at a heavy discount; sold his bed, and for three years slept on the deck; left the mess to which he belonged, living forward on the allowance of a seaman, and making, mending, and washing his own clothes, to save expense. Doubt has been expressed as to the reality of these early privations, on the ground that his father's office at Greenwich, and the subsequent promotions of the young officer, show the existence of a family influence, which would have counteracted such extreme restriction in money matters. The particulars, however, have been so transmitted as to entitle them to acceptance, unless contradicted by something more positive than circumstantial inference from other conditions, not necessarily contradictory.

This sharp experience was singularly adapted to develop and exaggerate his natural characteristics, self-reliance, self-control, stern determination, and, it must be added, the exacting harshness which demanded of others all that he had himself accepted. His experience of suffering and deprivation served, not to enlarge his indulgence, but to intensify his severity. Yet it may be remarked that Jervis was at all periods in thorough touch with distinctively naval feeling, sympathizing with and respecting its sensibilities, sharing its prejudices, as well as comprehending its weaknesses. Herein he differed from Rodney, who in the matter of community of sentiment stood habitually external to his profession; in it, but in heart not of it; belonging consciously and willingly to a social class which cherished other ideals of life and action. His familiarity with the service quickened him to criticise more keenly and accurately than a stranger, to recognize failings with harsher condemnation; but there appears no disposition to identify himself with it further than as an instrument of personal advancement and distinction.

Upon Jervis's naval future, the results of his early ordeal were wholly good. Unable to pursue pleasure ashore, he stuck to seagoing ships; and the energies of a singularly resolute mind were devoted to mastering all the details of his profession. After six years in the Caribbean, he returned to England in the autumn of 1754. The troubles between France and Great Britain which issued in the Seven Years War had already begun, and Jervis, whose merit commanded immediate recognition from those under whom he served, found family influence to insure his speedy promotion and employment. Being made lieutenant early in 1755, he was with Boscawen off the Gulf of St. Lawrence when that admiral, although peace yet reigned, was ordered to seize the French fleet bearing reinforcements to Quebec. At the same time, Braddock's unfortunate expedition was miscarrying in the forests of Pittsburgh. A year later, in 1756, Jervis went to the Mediterranean with Admiral Hawke, sent to relieve Byng after the fiasco at Minorca which brought that unhappy commander to trial and to death.

Before and during this Mediterranean cruise Jervis had been closely associated with Sir Charles Saunders, one of the most distinguished admirals of that generation, upon whom he made so favourable an impression that he was chosen for first lieutenant of the flag-ship, when Saunders, in 1758, was named to command the fleet to act against Quebec. The gallant and romantic General Wolfe, whose death in the hour of victory saddened the triumph of the conquerors, embarked in the same ship; and the long passage favoured the growth of a close personal intimacy between the two young men, who had been at school together as boys, although the soldier was several years older than the sailor. The relations thus formed and the confidences exchanged are shown by a touching incident recorded by Jervis's biographer. On the night before the battle on the Heights of Abraham, Wolfe went on board the *Porcupine*, a small sloop of war to whose command Jervis had meanwhile been promoted, and asked to see him in private. He then said that he was strongly impressed with the feeling that he should fall on the morrow, and therefore wished to entrust to his friend the miniature of the lady, Miss Lowther, to whom he was engaged, and to have from him the promise that, if the foreboding proved true, he would in person deliver to her both the portrait and Wolfe's own last messages. From the interview the young general departed to achieve his enterprise, to which daring action, brilliant success, and heroic death have given a lustre that time itself has not been able to dim, whose laurels remain green to our own day; while Jervis, to whose old age was reserved the glory that his comrade reaped in youth, remained behind to discharge his last request,—a painful duty which, upon returning to England, was scrupulously fulfilled.

Although the operations against Quebec depended wholly upon the control of the water by the navy, its influence, as often happens, was so quietly exerted as to draw no attention from the general eye, dazzled by the conspicuous splendour of Wolfe's conduct. To Jervis had been assigned the distinguished honour of leading the fleet with his little ship, in the advance up river against the fortifications of the place; and it is interesting to note that in this duty he was joined with the afterwards celebrated explorer, James Cook, who, as master of the fleet, had special charge of the pilotage in those untried waters. Wolfe, Cook, and Jervis form a striking trio of names, then unknown, yet closely associated, afterwards to be widely though diversely renowned.

When the city fell, Commander Jervis was sent to England, probably with despatches. There he was at once given a ship, and ordered to return with her to North America. Upon her proving leaky, he put in to Plymouth, where, as his mission was urgent, he was directed to take charge of a sloop named the *Albany*, then lying at anchor near by, and to proceed in her. To this moment has been attributed an incident which, as regards time and place, has been more successfully impeached than the story of his early privations, in that no mention of it is found in the ship's log; and there are other discrepancies which need reconcilement. Nevertheless it is, as told, so entirely characteristic, that the present writer has no doubt it occurred, at some time, substantially as given by his biographer, who was son to a secretary long in close relations with him when admiral. It would be entirely in keeping with all experience of testimony that the old man's recollections, or those of his secretary, may have gone astray on minor circumstances, while preserving accurately the fundamental and only really important facts, which are perfectly consistent with, and illustrative of, the stern decision afterwards shown in meeting and suppressing mutiny of the most threatening description. The crew of the *Albany*, it is said, from some motives of discontent refused to sail. Jervis had brought with him a few seamen from his late command. These he ordered to cut the cables which held the ship to her anchors, and to loose the foresail. Daunted more, perhaps, by the bearing of the man than by the mere acts, the mutineers submitted, and in twenty-four days, an extraordinarily short passage for that time, the *Albany* was at New York. Here Jervis was unfortunately delayed, and thus, being prevented from rejoining Sir Charles Saunders, lost the promotion which a British commander-in-chief could then give to an officer in his own command who had merited his professional approval. It was not until October, 1761, when he was twenty-six, that Jervis obtained "post" rank,—the rank, that is, of full, or post, captain. By the rule of the British navy, an officer up to that rank could be advanced by selection; thenceforth he waited, through the long succession of seniority, for his admiral's commission. This Jervis did not receive until 1787, when he was fifty-two.

It was as a general officer, as an admiral commanding great fleets and bearing responsibilities unusually grave through a most critical period of his country's history, that Jervis made his high and deserved reputation. For this reason, the intervening years, though pregnant with the finished character and distinguished capacity which fitted him for his onerous work, and though by no means devoid of incident, must be hastily sketched. The Treaty of Paris, which in 1763 closed the Seven Years War, was followed by twelve years of peace. Then came the American Revolution, bringing in its train hostilities with France and Spain. During the peace, Jervis for nearly four years commanded a frigate in the Mediterranean. It is told that while his ship was at Genoa two Turkish slaves escaped from a Genoese galley, and took refuge in a British boat lying at the mole, wrapping its flag round their persons. Genoese officers took them forcibly from the boat and restored them to their chains. Jervis resented this, as being not only an insult to the British flag, but also an enforcement of slavery against men under its protection; and so peremptory was his tone that an apology was made, the two captives were given up on the frigate's quarter-deck, and the offending officers punished. The captain's action, however, was not sustained by his own government. It is curious to note that, notwithstanding his course in this case, and although he was not merely nominally, but strenuously, a Whig, or Liberal, in political faith, connected by party ties with Fox and his coterie of friends, Jervis was always opposed to the abolition of the slave trade and to the education of the lower orders. Liberty was to him an inherited worship, associated with certain stock beliefs and phrases, but subordination was the true idol of his soul.

In 1775 Captain Jervis commissioned the *Foudroyant*, of eighty-four guns, a ship captured in 1758 from the French, and thereafter thought to be the finest vessel in the British fleet. To this, her natural superiority, Jervis added a degree of order, discipline, and drill which made her the pride and admiration of the navy. He was forty when his pennant first flew from her masthead, and he held the command for eight years, a period covering the full prime of his own maturity, as well as the entire course of the American Revolution. It was also a period marked for him, professionally, less by distinguished service than by that perfection of military organization, that combination of dignified yet not empty pomp with thorough and constant readiness, which was so eminently characteristic of all the phases of Jervis's career, and which, when the rare moments came, was promptly transformed into unhesitating, decisive, and efficient action. The *Foudroyant*, in her state and discipline, was the type in miniature of Jervis's Mediterranean fleet, declared by Nelson to be the finest body of ships he had ever known; nay, she was the precursor of that regenerate British navy in which Nelson found the instruments of his triumphs. Sixty years later, old officers recalled the feelings of mingled curiosity and awe with which, when sent to her on duty from their own ships, they climbed on board the *Foudroyant*, and from the larboard side of her quarter-deck gazed upon the stern captain, whose qualities were embodied in his vessel and constituted her chief excellences.

During Jervis's command, the *Foudroyant* was continuously attached to the Channel Fleet, whose duty, as the name implies, was to protect the English Channel and its approaches; a function which often carried the ships far into the Bay of Biscay. Thus he took a prominent part in Keppel's battle off Ushant in 1778, in the movements occasioned by the entrance into the Channel of an overpowering Franco-Spanish fleet in 1779 and 1781, and in the brilliant relief of Gibraltar by Admiral Howe towards the end of 1782. His most distinguished service, however, was taking, single-handed, the French seventy-four *Pégase*, in the spring of the latter year. The capture was effected after an action of fifty minutes, preceded by a chase of twelve hours, running before a half-gale of wind. The *Foudroyant* was unquestionably superior in battery to her enemy, who, moreover, had but recently been commissioned; but, as has justly been remarked of some of the victories of our own ships over those of the British in the War of 1812, although there was disparity of forces, the precision and rapidity with which the work was done bore incontrovertible testimony to the skill and training of the captain and crew. Single combats, such as this, were rare between vessels of the size of the *Foudroyant* and *Pégase*, built to sail and fight in fleets. That one occurred here was due to the fact that the speed of the two opponents left the British squadron far astern. The exploit obtained for Jervis a baronetcy and the ribbon of the Order of the Bath.

Sir John Jervis did not serve afloat during the ten years of peace following 1783, although, from his high repute, he was one of those summoned upon each of the alarms of war that from time to time arose. Throughout this period he sat in Parliament, voting steadily with his party, the Whigs, and supporting Fox in his opposition to measures which seemed to tend towards hostilities with France. When war came, however, he left his seat, ready to aid his country with his sword in the quarrel from which he had sought to keep her.

Having in the mean time risen from the rank of captain to that of rear-admiral and of vice-admiral, Jervis's first service, in 1794, was in the Caribbean Sea, as commander of the naval part of a joint expedition of army and navy to subdue the French West India islands. The operation, although most important and full of exciting and picturesque incident, bears but a small share in his career, and therefore may not be dwelt upon in so short a sketch as the present aims to be. Attended at first by marked and general success, it ended with some severe reverses, occasioned by the force given him being less than he demanded, and than the extent of the work to be done required. A quaintly characteristic story is told of the admiral's treatment of a lieutenant who at this period sought employment on board his ship. Knowing that he stood high in the old seaman's favour, the applicant confidently expected his appointment, but, upon opening the "letter on service," was stunned to read:

> *Sir*,—You, having thought fit to take to yourself a wife, are to look for no further attentions from
> Your humble servant,
> *J. Jervis*

The supposed culprit, guiltless even in thought of this novel misdemeanour, hastened on board, and explained that he abhorred such an offence as much as could the admiral. It then appeared that the letter had been sent to the wrong person. Jervis was himself married at this time; but his well-regulated affections had run steadily in harness until the mature age of forty-eight, and he saw no reason why other men should depart from so sound a precedent. "When an officer marries," he tersely said, "he is d———d for the service."

Returning to England in February, 1795, Jervis was in August nominated to command the Mediterranean station, and in November sailed to take up his new duties. At the end of the month, in San Fiorenzo Bay, an anchorage in the north of Corsica, he joined the fleet, which continued under his flag until June, 1799. He had now reached the highest rank in his profession, though not the highest grade of that rank as it was then subdivided; being a full Admiral of the Blue. The crowning period of his career here began. Admirable and striking as had been his previous services, dignified and weighty as were the responsibilities borne by him in the later part of a life prolonged far beyond the span of man, the four years of Jervis's Mediterranean command stand conspicuous as the time when preparation flowered into achievement, solid, durable, and brilliant. It may be interesting to Americans to recall that his age was nearly the same as that of Farragut when the latter assumed the charge in which, after long years of obscure preparation, he also reaped his harvest of glory. It is likewise worthy of note that this happy selection was made wholly independent of the political bias, which till then had so often and unworthily controlled naval appointments. Jervis belonged to the small remnant of Whigs who still followed Fox and inveighed against the current war, as unnecessary and impolitic. It was a pure service choice, as such creditable alike to the Government and the officer.

Though distinguished success now awaited him, a period of patient effort, endurance, and disappointment had first to be passed, reproducing in miniature the longer years of faithful service preceding his professional triumphs. Jervis came to the Mediterranean too late for the best interests of England. The year 1795, just ending, was one in which the energies of France, after the fierce rush of the Terror, had flagged almost to collapse. Not only so, but in its course the republic, discouraged by frequent failure, had decided to abandon the control of the sea to its enemy, to keep its great fleets in port, and to confine its efforts to the harassment of British commerce. To this change of policy in France is chiefly to be ascribed the failure of naval achievement with which Macaulay has reproached Pitt's earlier ministry. Battles cannot be fought if the foe keeps behind his walls. Prior to this decision, two fleet battles had been fought in the Mediterranean in the spring and summer of 1795, in which the British had missed great successes only through the sluggishness of their admiral. "To say how much we wanted Lord Hood" (the last commander-in-chief), wrote Nelson, "is to ask, 'Will you have all the French fleet or no battle?'" Could he have foreseen all that Jervis was to be to the Mediterranean, his distress must have been doubled to know that the fortunes of the nation thus fell between two stools.

His predecessor's slackness in pushing military opportunities, due partly to ill health, was mainly constitutional, and therefore could not but show itself by tangible evidences in the more purely administrative and disciplinary work. Jervis found himself at once under the necessity of bringing his fleet—in equipment, in discipline, and in drill—sharply up to that level of efficiency which is essential to the full development of power when occasion offers. This his perfect achievement, of organization and administration, in its many intricate details, needs at least to be clearly noted, even though space do not admit many particulars; because his capacity as administrator at the head of the Admiralty a few years later has been seriously impugned, by a criticism both partial and excessive, if not wholly unjust. Nelson, a witness of his Mediterranean service from beginning to end, lauded to the utmost the excellence there reached, and attributed most of the short-coming noted in the later office to the yielding of a man then advanced in years, to advisers, in trusting whom fully he might well believe himself warranted by experience.

Although, when taking command, his fleet reached the seemingly large proportions of twenty-five ships-of-the-line and some fifty cruisers, heavy allowance must be made for the variety of services extending over the two thousand miles of the Mediterranean, from east to west. Seven of-the-line had to be kept before Cadiz, though still a neutral port, to check a French division within. One of the same class was on the Riviera with Nelson; and other demands, with the necessities of occasional absences for refit, prevented the admiral from ever assembling before Toulon, his great strategic care, much more than a round dozen to watch equal French numbers there. The protection of Corsica, then in British hands; the convoy of commerce, dispersed throughout the station; the assurance of communications to the fortress and Straits of Gibraltar, by which all transit to and from the Mediterranean passes; diplomatic exigencies with the various littoral states of the inland sea; these divergent calls, with the coincident necessity of maintaining every ship in fit condition for action, show the extent of the administrative work and of the attendant correspondence. The evidence of many eye-witnesses attests the successful results.

Similar attention, broad yet minute, was demanded for the more onerous and invidious task of enforcing relaxed discipline and drill. Concerning these, the most pregnant testimony, alike to the stringency and the persistence of his measures, may be found in the embittered expressions of enemies. Five years later, when the rumour spread that he was to have the Channel Fleet, the toast was drunk at the table of the man then in command, "May the discipline of the Mediterranean never be introduced into the Channel."

"May his next glass of wine choke the wretch," is a speech attributed to a captain's wife, wrathful that her husband was kept from her side by the admiral's regulations. For Jervis's discipline began at the top, with the division and ship commanders. One of the senior admirals under him persisting in a remonstrance, beyond the point which he considered consistent with discipline, was sent home. "The very disorderly state of His Majesty's ship under your command," he writes to a captain, "obliges me to require that neither yourself nor any of your officers are to go on shore on what is called pleasure."

"The commander-in-chief finds himself under the painful necessity of publicly reprimanding Captains——and——for neglect of duty, in not maintaining the stations assigned to their ships during the last night." In a letter to a lieutenant he says:

> If you do not immediately make a suitable apology to Commissioner Inglefield for the abominable neglect and disrespect you have treated him with, I will represent your behaviour to the Lords Commissioners of the Admiralty, and recommend your name to be struck off the list of lieutenants.

Captains of vessels were not only subject to strict regulation as to their personal proceedings, compelled to sleep on board, for instance, even in home ports; but duties customarily left to subordinates, with results to discipline that might not now obtain but which were in those days deplorable, were also assigned to them.

> The commander-in-chief has too exalted an opinion of the respective captains of the squadron to doubt their being upon deck when the signal is made to tack or wear *in the night,* and he requires all lieutenants then to be at their stations, except those who had the watch immediately preceding.

Nor did he leave this delicately worded, but pointed, admonition, issued in the Mediterranean, to take care of itself. In after years, when he was nigh seventy, his secretary tells that on a cold and rainy November night off Brest, the signal to tack being made, he hurried to the cabin to persuade the old man not to go on deck, as was his custom. He was not, however, in his cot, nor could he for a long time be found; but at last a look into the stern gallery discovered him, in flannel dressing-gown and cocked hat, watching the movements of the fleet. To remonstrance he replied, "Hush, I want to see how the evolution is performed on such a night, and to know whether Jemmy Vashon (commanding the ship next astern) is on deck;" but soon hearing the captain's well-known shrill voice, crying, "Are you all ready forward?" he consented then to retire.

Post-captains and commanders were required to attend at points on shore where the boats and crews of ships congregated on service; at landing places and watering places,—scenes fruitful in demoralization,—to maintain order and suppress disturbance.

> The Masters and Commanders are to take it in turn, according to rank, to attend the duty on shore at the ragged staff, from gun-fire in the morning to sunset, to keep order and prevent disputes, and to see that boats take their regular turns. They are never to be absent from the spot except at regular meal times.
>
> When the squadron is at anchor in Torbay, a captain of a ship-of-the-line is to command at the watering place at Brixham, taking to his assistance his commanding officer

of marines with a party of his men. He also may take with him a lieutenant of the ship and as many midshipmen as he thinks fit; *but he himself* is not to quit his command until regularly relieved.

A greater stringency is observable at this later date, in the Channel Fleet, than in the Mediterranean; for at the earlier period the spirit of mutiny had not openly broken out, and he had besides on the distant station better captains than those who had clung to the home fleet under its lax discipline. "Old women in the guise of young men," he affirmed many of them to be.

There was in fact an imminent necessity that naval rank should be made to feel its responsibilities, and to exert its predominance; to be restored to prestige, not by holding aloof in its privileges, but by asserting itself in act. The preponderance of political and family influence in determining promotion of officers, unbalanced by valid tests of fitness such as later days imposed, had not only lowered the competency of the official body as a whole, but impaired the respect which personal merit alone can in the long run maintain. On the other hand, the scarcity of seamen in proportion to the heavy demands of the war, and the irregular methods of impressment and recruiting then prevailing, swept into the service a vast number of men not merely unfit, but of extremely bad character,—"miscreants," to use Collingwood's word,—to be ruled only by fear of the law and of their officers, supported by the better element among the crews. But these better men also were becoming alienated by the harsh restrictions of the times, and by the procrastination of superiors—Howe, the Sailor's Friend, among others—to heed their just complaints. The stern Jervis, whom none suspected of fatherly tenderness, if less indulgent to culprits, was far more attentive to meet the reasonable demands of those under him. While quelling insubordination mercilessly, he ever sought to anticipate grievance; exhibiting thus the two sides of the same spirit of careful, even-handed justice.

Jervis's work during the first eighteen months of his command was therefore not only necessary, but most timely. By improving that period of comparative internal quiet, he educated his officers and men to pass steadfastly, though not unmoved, through the awful crisis of the mutinies in 1797-98. Professional self-respect, a most powerful moral force, was more than restored; it was intensified by the added dignity and power manifest in the surroundings of daily life, as well as in the military results obtained. Seamen, like others, deal more conservatively with that of which they are proud because it reflects honour upon themselves; and they obey more certainly men who share their labours and lead them capably in danger, as did Jervis's Mediterranean captains. With himself, severity was far from being the only instrument. Thoroughly capable professionally, and thereby commandful of respect, he appealed also to men's regard by intelligent and constant thought for the wants and comfort of those under him; by evidence of strong service feeling on his own part; by clear and clearly expressed recognition of merit, wherever found; by avoidance of misunderstandings through explanation volunteered when possible,—not apologetically, but as it were casually, yet appealing to men's reason. Watchfulness and sympathetic foresight were with him as constant as sternness, though less in evidence.

Of this prevalence of kindly naval feeling amid the harshness which seemed superficially the chief characteristic of his rule, many instances could be cited. Passing by the frequent incidental praise of distinguished captains, Nelson, Troubridge, and others, he thus advocates the claims of one of the humble, hopeless class of sailing-masters, out of the line of promotion. After an act of brilliant merit in the West Indies—

> Mr. White was ambitious to become a lieutenant; but not having served six years in the navy, and being a master, I could not then comply with his wishes. He is now Master of the *Defence*, and his captain speaks in the highest terms of him; and it is a tribute *due to the memory* of Captain Faulknor,—whose certificate of that matchless service is enclosed,—and *to the gallantry of his officers and crew*, to state the claims of Mr. White to your Lordship, who is the protector of us all.

The present and the past, the merits of the living, the memory of the glorious dead, the claims of the navy to see well-doers rewarded, are all pressed into service to support a just request, and with a manifest heartiness which in virtue of its reality approaches eloquence.

> I have given an order to Mr. Ellis to command as a lieutenant, he being the son of a very old officer whom I knew many years; and coming very strongly recommended from his last ship, I place him under your Lordship's protection as *a child of the service*.

When a man thus bears others' deserts and the profession on his heart, he can retain the affections of his subordinates even though he show all the unbending severity of Jervis, and despite the numerous hangings, which, for that matter, rarely fell except on the hopelessly bad. A most significant feature of his rule as a disciplinarian was his peculiar care of health, by instructed sanitary measures, by provision of suitable diet, and by well-ordered hospital service. This was not merely a prudential consideration for the efficiency of the fleet; he regarded also the welfare of the sufferers. He made it a rule to inspect the hospitals himself, and he directed a daily visit by a captain and by the surgeons of the ships from which patients were sent, thus keeping the sick in touch with those they knew, and who had in them a personal interest. An odd provision, amusingly illustrative of the obverse side of the admiral's character, was that the visiting captain should be accompanied by a boatswain's mate, the functionary charged with administering floggings, and, "if they find the patients do not conduct themselves properly and orderly, they are to punish them agreeably to the rules of the Navy." It was, however, on his care of health, in its various exposures, that the admiral specially valued himself; it was, he said, his proudest boast among the services to which he laid claim.

But while he laboured thus for the welfare of the seamen, it was naturally upon the professional tone of his officers that his chief reliance must be placed; and the leaders among them he grappled to his soul with hooks of steel, as they recognized the wisdom and force of his measures, and the appreciation given to them and others. Whatever beneficent influence might issue from him as a fountain-head must through them be distributed, and by them reinforced and sustained. "The discipline of the fleet," he said, "is in the ward-room;" and greatly did he lament the loose insubordinate talk, the spirit of irresponsible criticism that found voice at mess-tables, within the hearing of servants, by whom it was disseminated throughout the body of the ship. Not only he, but many, attributed to this hot-bed the fomenting of discontent into organized mutiny. This could not be stopped by direct measures, but only by imposing a feeling of fear, and nurturing that of officer-like propriety, by stringent prescription of forms of respect and rigid exaction of their observance. To stand uncovered before a superior, instead of lightly touching the hat, to pay outward reverence to the national flag, to salute the quarter-deck as the seat of authority, were no vain show under him. "Discipline," he was fond of quoting, "is summed up in the one word, 'Obedience;'" and these customs were charged with the observance which is obedience in spirit. They conduced to discipline as conventional good manners, by rendering the due of each to each, knit together the social fabric and maintain the regularity and efficiency of common life; removing friction, suppressing jars, and ministering constantly to the smooth and even working of the social machinery.

By measures such as these, extending to all ranks and every detail, exemplifying, in spirit and in form, the extremes of cordial reward, iron restraint, and weighty punishment, Jervis patiently fashioned the fleet which was to be both a pattern for coming days, and the highly tempered instrument to achieve his own victory of Cape St. Vincent and the earlier triumphs of Nelson; as well as to sustain and to crush the onset of mutiny which soon afterwards shook the Navy to its centre. For purely military action of an aggressive character no opportunity was afforded him. His coming to the Mediterranean coincided with that of Napoleon Bonaparte to the Army of Italy. During 1795, wrote Nelson, if the British fleet had done its duty, the French army could not have moved along the Riviera of Genoa. It failed, and the Austrian general, its ally, also failed to act with vigour. So the year had ended, for the Austrians, with a disastrous defeat and a retreat behind the Apennines. To the Riviera they never returned to receive the co-operation which Jervis stood eager to give. At their first move to cross the mountains, Bonaparte struck, and followed up his blows with such lightning-like rapidity that in thirty days they were driven back over a hundred miles, behind the Adige; their chief fortress, Mantua, was blockaded; all northwest Italy with its seaboard, including Leghorn, was in the power of France; and Naples also had submitted. Jervis, powerless to strike a blow when no enemy was within reach, found his fleet without a friendly port nearer than Gibraltar, while Corsica, where alone he could expect anchorage and water, was seething with revolt against the British crown, to which, by its own vote, it had been annexed but two years before.

Amid these adverse circumstances, the only large operation possible to him was the close watching of the port of Toulon, conducted on the same general plan that was afterwards more illustriously exhibited before Brest, between 1800 and 1805, under conditions of surpassing difficulty. All contemplated movements of the French fleet were thus dammed at the source, for it must first fight the British, after which there was little hope of being in a state to fulfil any further mission. For six months, from April to October, Jervis held his fleet close up to the port, the advanced body two miles from the entrance. The effort was admirable as a pattern, and for disciplinary purposes. The ships, forced to self-dependence, became organically self-reliant. Their routine life of seamanship and military exercise perfected habit and efficiency, and difficulties to others insuperable were as the light burdens which a giant carries unwittingly.

Further than this, achievement could not then go. During the summer Bonaparte held Mantua by the throat, and overthrew one after another the Austrian forces approaching to its relief. Two French armies, under Jourdan and Moreau, penetrated to the heart of Germany; while Spain, lately the confederate of Great Britain, made an offensive and defensive alliance with France, and sent a fleet of over twenty ships-of-the-line into the

Mediterranean. Staggered by these reverses, the British ministry ordered Corsica evacuated and the Mediterranean abandoned. Jervis was cruelly embarrassed. A trusted subordinate of high reputation had been before Cadiz with seven ships-of-the-line, watching a French division in that port. Summoned, in view of the threatening attitude of Spain, to reinforce the main fleet in San Fiorenzo Bay, he lost his head altogether, hurried past Gibraltar without getting supplies, and brought his ships destitute to the admiral, already pressed to maintain the vessels then with him. Although there were thirty-five hostile ships in Toulon and the British had only twenty-two, counting this division, there was nothing to do but to send it back to Gibraltar, under urgent orders to return with all speed. With true military insight and a correct appreciation of the forces opposed to him, Jervis saw the need of fighting the combined enemies then and there.

Unfortunately, the division commander, Admiral Mann, on reaching Gibraltar, became infected with the spirit of discouragement then prevailing in the garrison, called a council of naval captains, and upon their advice, which could in no wise lessen his own responsibility, decided to return to England. This culpably unwarrantable act aptly illustrates the distinction, rarely appreciated, between an error of judgment and an error of conduct. Upon arrival, he was at once deprived of his command, a step of unquestionable justice, but which could not help Jervis. Collingwood, then a captain in the fleet, wrote:

> We were all eyes, looking westward from the mountain tops, but we looked in vain. The Spanish fleet, nearly double our number, was cruising almost in view, and our reconnoitring frigates sometimes got among them, while we expected them hourly to be joined by the French fleet.

Jervis himself wrote:

> I cannot describe to your lordship the disappointment my ambition and zeal to serve my country have suffered by this diminution of my force; for had Admiral Mann sailed from Gibraltar on the 10th of October, the day he received my orders, and fulfilled them, I have every reason

to believe the Spanish fleet would have been cut to pieces. The extreme disorder and confusion they were observed to be in, by the judicious officers who fell in with them, leave no doubt upon my mind that a fleet so trained and generally well commanded as this is would have made its way through them in every direction.

Nelson shared this opinion, the accuracy of which was soon to be tested and proved. He wrote to his wife:

They at home do not know what this fleet is capable of performing; anything and everything. The fleets of England are equal to meet the world in arms; and of all the fleets I ever saw, I never beheld one, in point of officers and men, equal to Sir John Jervis's, who is a commander-in-chief able to lead them to glory.

To a friend he wrote:

Mann is ordered to come up; we shall then be twenty-two sail-of-the-line such as England hardly ever produced, commanded by an admiral who will not fail to look the enemy in the face, be their force what it may. I suppose it will not be more than thirty-four of-the-line.

"The admiral is firm as a rock," wrote at the same moment the British viceroy of Corsica. Through all doubts and uncertainties he held on steadily, refusing to leave the rendezvous till dire necessity forced him, lest Mann, arriving, should be exposed alone and lost. At last, with starvation staring him in the face if delaying longer, he sailed for Gibraltar, three men living on the rations of one during the passage down.

Mann's defection had reduced the fleet from twenty-two vessels to fifteen. A series of single accidents still further diminished it. In a violent gale at Gibraltar three ships-of-the-line drove from their anchors. One, the *Courageux*, stretching over toward the Barbary coast, ran ashore there and was totally wrecked, nearly all her crew perishing. Her captain, a singularly capable seaman named Hallowell, was out of her upon a court-martial, and it was thought she would not have been lost had he been on board. Another, the *Gibraltar*, struck so heavily on a reef that she had to be sent to England. Upon being docked, a large piece of rock was found to have penetrated the bottom and stuck fast in the hole. Had it worked out, the ship would have foundered. The third vessel, the *Zealous*, was less badly hurt, but she had to be left behind in Gibraltar when Jervis, by orders from home, took his fleet to Lisbon. There, in entering the Tagus, a fourth ship was lost on a shoal, so that but eleven remained out of twenty-two. Despite these trials of his constancy, the old man's temper still continued "steady as a rock." He wrote to the Admiralty:

> Whether you send me a reinforcement or not, I shall sleep perfectly sound,—not in the Tagus, but at sea; for as soon as the *St. George* has shifted her topmast, the *Captain* her bowsprit, and the *Blenheim* repaired her mainmast, I will go out.

"Inactivity in the Tagus," he wrote again, "will make cowards of us all." This last expression summed up much of his naval philosophy. Keep men at sea, he used to say, and they cannot help being seamen, though attention will be needed to assure exercise at the guns. And it may be believed he would thus contemn the arguments which supported Howe's idea of preserving the ships by retaining them in port. Keep them at sea, he would doubtless have replied, and they will learn to take care of themselves.

In quitting the river another vessel took the ground, and had to be left behind. This, however, was the last of the admiral's trials for that time. A few days later, on the 6th of February, 1797, there joined him a body of five ships-of-the line, detached from England as soon as the government had been freed from the fear of the invasion of Ireland, which the French had attempted on a large scale in December. On the 13th, Nelson, a host in himself, returned from an adventurous mission up the Mediterranean. The next day, February 14th, Jervis with his fifteen ships met a Spanish fleet of twenty-seven some thirty miles from Cape St. Vincent, which has given its name to the battle.

The Spaniards were running for Cadiz, to the east-southeast,—say, across the page from left to right, inclining a little downward,—while Jervis's fleet was approaching nearly at right angles from the north, or top of the page. It was in two close, compact columns, of seven and eight ships respectively. The Spaniards, on the contrary, were in disorder and dispersed. Six of their ships were far ahead of the others, an interval of nearly eight miles separating the two groups. The weather, which was foggy, cleared gradually. Jervis was walking back and forth on the poop with Hallowell, lately captain of the wrecked *Courageux*, and he was heard to say, "A victory is very essential to England at this moment." As ship after ship of the enemy loomed up through the haze, successive reports were made to him.

"There are eight sail-of-the-line, Sir John."

"There are twenty sail-of-the-line, Sir John."

"There are twenty-five of-the-line, Sir John."

Finally, when the full tale of twenty-seven was made out, the captain of the fleet remarked on the greatness of the odds. "Enough of that, sir," retorted the admiral, intent on that victory which was so essential to England; "if there are fifty sail, I will go through them." This reply so delighted Hallowell, an eccentric man, who a year later gave Nelson the coffin made from the mainmast of the *Orient*, that he patted his august superior on the back. "That's right, Sir John," said he, "and, by G——, we'll give them a d——d good licking!"

When the weather finally cleared, toward 10 a.m., the British were near to the enemy and heading direct for the gap, which the Spaniards, too late, were trying to close. Almost at the moment of meeting, Jervis formed his two columns into one—the order of battle—"with the utmost celerity;" thus doubling the length of the line interposed between the two divisions of the enemy. Soon opened the guns of the leading ship, the *Culloden*, Captain Troubridge; the reports following one another in regular succession, as though firing a salute by watch. The *Culloden*'s course led so direct upon a Spanish three-decker, that the first lieutenant reported a collision imminent. "Can't help it, Griffiths," replied Troubridge; "hardest fend off." But the Spaniard, in confusion, put his helm up and went clear. By this time the Spanish division on the right, or west, of the British had changed its course and was steering north, parallel but opposite to its foes. As the *Culloden* went through, the admiral signalled her to put about and follow it. Troubridge, fully expecting this order, obeyed at once; and Jervis's signal was scarce unfurled when, by the flapping of the *Culloden*'s sails, he saw it was receiving execution. "Look at Troubridge!" he shouted. "Doesn't he handle his ship as though the eyes of all England were on him? I would to God they were, that she might know him as I know him!" But here a graver matter drew the admiral's care. The Spanish division from the left, steering across his path of advance, approached, purposing in appearance to break through the line. The *Victory* stopped, or, as seamen say, hove-to; and as the Spanish admiral came near within a hundred yards, her broadside rang out, sweeping through the crowded decks and lofty spars a storm of shot, to which, in the relative positions, the foe could not reply. Staggered and crippled he went about, and the *Victory* stood on.

Meanwhile, the ships which Troubridge and his followers were pursuing drew toward the tail of the British column, and as they did so made a movement to pass round it, and so join their friends who had just been so severely handled in making the attempt to pass through. But Nelson was in this part of the order, there being but two ships behind him. Now, as far as signals went, he should continue on, and, like the others, follow in due succession behind the *Culloden*. He saw that if this were done the Spaniards would effect their junction, so he instantly turned his ship toward the rear, out of her place, and threw her alone across the enemy's advance. It is said that the Captain of the Fleet drew Jervis's attention to this breach of discipline. "Ay," replied the old seaman, "and if ever you offend in the same way, I promise you my forgiveness beforehand." For a while Nelson took the brunt of the hostile fire from half a dozen ships, but not for long. Soon Troubridge, his dearest friend, came up with a couple of others; and Collingwood, the close associate of early days, who had the rear ship, was signalled to imitate Nelson's act. In doing this, he silenced the fire of two enemies; but, wrote Nelson—

.... disdaining the parade of taking possession of beaten ships, Captain Collingwood most gallantly pushed on to save his old friend and messmate, who appeared to be in a critical state, being then fired upon by three first-rates, and the *San Nicolas*, eighty.

To get between Nelson's ship and the *San Nicolas*, Collingwood had to steer close, passing within ten feet of the latter; so that, to use his own expression, "though we did not touch sides, you could not put a bodkin between us." His fire drove the *San Nicolas* upon one of the first-rates, the *San Josef*; and when, continuing on to seek other unbeaten foes, he left the field again clear for Nelson, the latter, by a movement of the helm, grappled the *San Nicolas*. Incredible as it may appear, the crew of this one British seventy-four carried, sword in hand, both the enemy's ships, though of far superior force. Nelson wrote:

> Extravagant as the story may seem, on the quarter-deck of a Spanish first-rate I received the swords of the vanquished Spaniards, which, as I received, I gave to William Fearney, one of my bargemen, who placed them with the greatest *sang-froid* under his arm.

Four Spanish ships, two of them of the largest size, were the trophies of this victory; but its moral effect in demonstrating the relative values of the two navies, and the confidence England could put in men like Jervis, Nelson, and the leading captains, was far greater. The spirit of the nation, depressed by a long series of reverses, revived like a giant refreshed with wine. Jervis had spoken truth when he said a victory was essential to England at that time. The gratitude of the state was shown in the profusion of rewards showered upon the victors. Promotions and honours were liberally distributed. The Government had already purposed to recognize Jervis's previous services by raising him to the lower ranks of the peerage; but this timely triumph procured him at one step a higher elevation. He was created Earl of St. Vincent, with a pension of three thousand pounds per annum.

The tactical decisions made by Jervis on this momentous occasion were correct as far as they went; but, except the initial determination to attack the larger body of the enemy, because to windward, there is no evidence of tactical originality in him, no innovation comparable to Howe's manoeuvres on May 28 and 29,—and there was undoubted oversight in not providing by signal against that move of the weather Spanish division which it became Nelson's opportunity and glory to counteract. It is also possible that the signal to tack in succession, a wholly routine proceeding, might have been made earlier to advantage; but the writer does not think that the body of the fleet should then have tacked together, as some criticism would have it. Until the British van approached on the new tack, the broadsides of the centre were better ranged on the original line to counteract the efforts, actually made, by the lee Spanish division to break through. As regards the decision not to follow the victory further, which has been censured in the instances of Rodney and Howe, the conditions here differed in much. The disparity of numbers was very great; if many of the enemy had suffered greatly, many also had not suffered at all; they were now reunited; above all Jervis's strategic and political insight—far superior to his tactical equipment—had rightly read the situation when he said that what England needed was a victory,—moral effect. The victory was there, undeniable and brilliant, it was better not risked.

The rest of the Spaniards, many of them badly crippled, took refuge in Cadiz, and there Jervis, after repairing damages, held them blockaded for two years, from April, 1797, to May, 1799. For the greater part of this time the operation was conducted by anchoring the British fleet, a resource which the character of the ground permitted, and which, though not everywhere possible, St. Vincent declared the only way of assuring the desired end of holding a position in all weathers. During this period was rendered the other most signal service done by him to the state, in suppressing the mutinous action of the seamen, which there, as everywhere else in the British navy at that time, sought to overthrow the authority of the officers.

The cause of the mutinies of 1797 is not here in question. Suffice it to say that, in their origin, they alleged certain tangible material grievances which were clearly stated, and, being undeniable, were redressed. The men returned to their duty; but, like a horse that has once taken the bit between his teeth, the restive feeling remained, fermenting in a lot of vicious material which the exigencies of the day had forced the navy to accept. Coinciding in time with the risings in Ireland, 1796-1798, there arose between the two movements a certain sympathy, which was fostered by the many Irish in the fleets, where agents were in communication with the leaders of the United Irishmen on shore.

In the Channel and the North Sea, the seamen took the ships, with few exceptions, out of the hands of their officers. In the former, they dictated their terms; in the latter, after a month of awful national suspense, they failed: the difference being that in the one case the demands, being reasonable, carried conviction, while in the other, becoming extravagant, the Government's resistance was supported by public opinion. It remained to be seen how the crisis would be met in a fleet so far from home that the issue must depend upon the firmness and judgment of a man of adamant. It was no more than prudent to expect that the attempt would be made there also; and the watchfulness of the superior officers of the fleet soon obtained certain information of its approach, though as yet without proof adequate to the arrest of individuals. The policy of the admiral, broadly stated, was that of isolating ship from ship—*divide et impera*—to prevent concerted action; a measure effected to all practical purpose by his unremitting vigilance, and by the general devotion to his policy among his leading officers. On the other hand, evidence was not wanting that in the ships long under his orders his own character was now fairly understood, and obtained for him a backing among the seamen themselves, without which his severity alone might have failed.

The first overt sign of trouble was the appearance of letters addressed to the leading petty officers of the different ships of the Mediterranean fleet. These were detected by a captain, who held on to them, and sent to St. Vincent to ask if they should be delivered. Careful to betray no sign of anxiety, the admiral's reply was a general signal for a lieutenant from each ship to come to him; and by them word was sent that all letters should be delivered as addressed, unopened. "Should any disturbance arise," he added, "the commander-in-chief will know how to repress it."

Disturbance soon did arise, and it is significant to note that it appeared in a ship which, by taking the ground when leaving Lisbon, had not shared in the Battle of St. Vincent. In July, 1797, two seamen of the *St. George* had been condemned to death for an infamous crime. Their shipmates presented a petition, framed in somewhat peremptory terms, for their liberation, on the ground that execution for such an offence would bring disgrace upon all. The admiral refusing to pardon, the occasion was seized to bring mutiny to a head. A plot to take possession of the ship was formed, but was betrayed to the captain. The outburst began with a tumultuous assembling of the crew, evidently, however, mistrustful of their cause. After vainly trying to restore order, the captain and first lieutenant rushed among them, each collaring a ringleader. The rest fell back, weakened, as men of Anglo-Saxon traditions are apt to be, by the sense of law-breaking. The culprits were secured, and at once taken to the flag-ship. A court-martial was ordered for the next day, Saturday; and as the prisoners were being taken to the court, St. Vincent, with a hard bluntness of speech which characterized him,—a survival of the frank brutality of the past century,—said, "My friends, I hope you are innocent, but if you are guilty make your peace with God; for, if you are condemned, and there is daylight to hang you, you will die this day."

They were condemned; but the trial ended late, and the president of the court told them they should have Sunday to prepare.

"Sir," said the earl, "when you passed sentence, your duty was done; you had no right to say that execution should be delayed;" and he fixed it for eight the next morning.

One of the junior admirals saw fit to address him a remonstrance upon what he termed a desecration of the Sabbath. Nelson, on the contrary, approved, he wrote:

> Had it been Christmas instead of Sunday I would have hanged them. Who can tell what mischief would have been brewed over a Sunday's grog?

Contrary to previous custom, their own shipmates, the partners and followers in their crime, were compelled to hang them, manning the rope by which the condemned were swayed to the yardarm. The admiral, careful to produce impression, ordered that all the ships should hold divine service immediately upon the execution. Accordingly, when the bell struck eight, the fatal gun was fired, the bodies swung with a jerk aloft, the church flags were hoisted throughout the fleet, and all went to prayers. Ere yet the ceremony was over, the Spanish gunboats came out from Cadiz and opened fire; but St. Vincent would not mar the solemnity of the occasion by shortening the service. Gravely it was carried to its end; but when the flags came down, all boats were ordered manned. The seamen, with nerves tense from the morning's excitement, gladly hurried into action, and the enemy were forced back into port.

One such incident was far from ending the ordeal through which the admiral had to pass, and which was prolonged throughout the period of the Cadiz blockade. In May, 1798, when Nelson was sent into the Mediterranean to win the Battle of the Nile, the detachment committed to him was replaced by a dozen ships-of-the-line from the Channel, seething with the mutinous temper which at home had been humoured rather than scotched. Immediately on their joining, request was made for a Court Martial on some men of the *Marlborough*, on board which two violent mutinies had occurred,—one on the passage out. St. Vincent, having known beforehand that this ship had been pre-eminent for insubordination, had ordered her anchored in the centre of the fleet, between the two lines in which it was ranged; and the Court met without delay. The remainder of the incident is quoted substantially from one of St. Vincent's biographers, for it illustrates most forcibly the sternness of his action, as well when dealing with weakness in officers as with mutiny in crews. The written order to the commander of the division of launches appears among the earl's papers, as does also a similar one in the case of a mutiny on board the *Defence* some months earlier. The ulterior object of parading these boats was kept profoundly secret. They appeared to be only part of the pageantry, of the solemn ceremonial, with which the wisdom of the great commander-in-chief providently sought to invest all exhibitions of authority, in order to deepen impression.

The object of the last mutiny on board the *Marlborough* had been to protect the life of a seaman forfeited by a capital crime. No sooner was one sentenced to die than the commander-in-chief ordered him to be executed on the following morning—

.... and by the crew of the *Marlborough* alone, no part of the boats' crews from the other ships, as had been used on similar occasions, to assist in the punishment,—his lordship's invariable order on the execution of mutineers. On the receipt of the necessary commands for this execution, Captain Ellison of the *Marlborough* waited upon the commander-in-chief, and reminding his lordship that a determination that their shipmates should not suffer capital punishment had been the very cause of the ship's company's mutiny, expressed his conviction that the *Marlborough*'s crew would never permit the man to be hanged on board that ship.

Receiving the captain on the *Ville de Paris*'s quarter-deck, before the officers and ship's company hearkening in breathless silence to what passed, and standing with his hat in his hand over his head, as was his lordship's invariable custom during the whole time that any person, whatever were his rank, even a common seaman, addressed him on service, Lord St. Vincent listened very attentively till the captain ceased to speak; and then after a pause replied,—

'Do you mean to tell me, Captain Ellison, that you cannot *command* his Majesty's ship, the *Marlborough*? for if that is the case, sir, I will immediately send on board an officer who can.'

The captain then requested that, at all events, the boats' crews from the rest of the fleet might, as always had been customary in the service, on executions, attend at this also, to haul the man up; for he really did not expect the *Marlborough*'s would do it.

Lord St. Vincent sternly answered: 'Captain Ellison, you

are an old officer, sir, have served long, suffered severely in the service, and have lost an arm in action, and I should be very sorry that any advantage should be now taken of your advanced years. That man shall be hanged, at eight o'clock tomorrow morning, *and by his own ship's company*: for not a hand from any other ship in the fleet shall touch the rope. You will now return on board, sir; and, lest you should not prove able to command your ship, an officer will be at hand who can.'

Without another word Captain Ellison instantly retired. After he had reached his ship, he received orders to cause her guns to be housed and secured, and that at daybreak in the morning her ports should be lowered. A general order was then issued to the fleet for all launches to rendezvous under the *Prince* at seven o'clock on the following morning, armed with carronades and twelve rounds of ammunition for service; each launch to be commanded by a lieutenant, having an expert and trusty gunner's-mate and four quarter gunners, exclusive of the launch's crew. The whole were to be under the command of Captain Campbell, of the *Blenheim*, to whom, on presenting to him the written orders under which he was to act, Lord St. Vincent further said, 'he was to attend the execution, and if any symptoms of mutiny appeared in the *Marlborough*, any attempt to open her ports, or any resistance to the hanging of the prisoner, he was to proceed close touching the ship, and to fire into her, and to continue to fire until all mutiny or resistance should cease; and that, should it become absolutely necessary, he should even sink the ship in face of the fleet.'

Accordingly, at seven the next morning, all the launches, thus armed, proceeded, from the *Prince* to the *Blenheim*, and thence, Captain Campbell having assumed the command, to the *Marlborough*.

Having lain on his oars a short time alongside, the captain then formed his force in a line athwart her bows, at rather less than pistol shot distance off, and then he ordered the tompions to be taken out of the carronades, and to load. At half-past seven, the hands throughout the fleet having been turned up to witness punishment, the eyes of all bent upon a powerfully armed boat as it quitted the flag-ship; every one knowing that there went the provost-marshal conducting his prisoner to the *Marlborough* for execution. The crisis was come; now was to be seen whether the *Marlborough's* crew would hang one of their own men.

The ship being in the centre between the two lines of the fleet, the boat was soon alongside, and the man was speedily placed on the cathead and haltered. A few awful minutes of universal silence followed, which was at last broken by the watch bells of the fleet striking eight o'clock. Instantly the flag-ship's gun fired, and at the sound the man was lifted well off; but then, and visibly to all, he dropped back again; and the sensation throughout the fleet was intense. For, at this dreadful moment, when the eyes of every man in every ship was straining upon this execution, as the decisive struggle between authority and mutiny, as if it were destined that the whole fleet should see the hesitating unwillingness of the *Marlborough's* crew to hang their rebel, and the efficacy of the means taken to enforce obedience, by an accident on board the ship the men at the yard-rope unintentionally let it slip, and the turn of the balance seemed calamitously lost; but then they hauled him up to the yard arm with a run. The law was satisfied, and, said Lord St. Vincent at the moment, perhaps one of the greatest of his life, 'Discipline is preserved, sir!'

Again a year later, in May, 1799, when twenty-five French ships-of-the-line broke through the wretchedly inefficient guard at that time kept before Brest, and entered the Mediterranean, a reinforcement of over a dozen was sent from the Channel to Lord St. Vincent, who was found then in Port Mahon, Minorca. Sir Edward Pellew, captain of one of the new-comers, asked a Court-Martial upon a mutiny that had occurred just before leaving the home port. St. Vincent at first demurred, startled, according to Pellew's biographer, by the extent of the plot then revealed, and thinking it politic to suppress the facts; but it is alleged with equal probability that he was indignant at being continually called upon to remedy evils due to the general indiscipline of the Channel Fleet. "What do they mean by invariably sending the mutinous ships to me? Do they think that I will be hangman to the fleet?"

Both versions are likely enough to be correct. There is a limit to all human endurance, and the earl was now broken in health; he was sixty-four, had borne his load for three years, and was on the point of resigning his command to Lord Keith. The Court, however, was ordered, and three men were sentenced to be hanged. Pellew then interceded for one, on the ground of previous good character.

"No," replied St. Vincent. "Those who have suffered hitherto have been so worthless before that their fate was of little use as an example. I shall now convince the seamen that no character, however good, shall save a man who is guilty of mutiny."

But St. Vincent was not content with mere repression. Outwardly, and indeed inwardly, unshaken, he yet unwearyingly so ordered the fleet as to avoid occasions of outbreak. With the imposing moral control exerted by his unflinching steadiness, little trouble was to be apprehended from single ships; ignorant of what might be hoped from sympathizers elsewhere, but sure of the extreme penalty in case of failure, the movements lacked cohesion and were easily nipped. Concerted action only was to be feared, and careful measures were taken to remove opportunities. Captains were forbidden to entertain one another at dinner,—the reason, necessarily unavowed, being that the boats from various ships thus assembling gave facilities for transmitting messages and forming plans; and when ships arrived from England they underwent a moral quarantine, no intercourse with them being permitted until sanctioned by the admiral. When the captain reported to him, his boat, while waiting, was shoved off out of earshot. It is said that on one occasion a seaman in such a boat managed to call to one looking out of a port of the flag-ship, "I say, there, what have you fellows been doing out here, while we have been fighting for your beef and pork?" To which the other replied, "You'd best say nothing at all about that out here, for if old Jarvie hears ye he'll have ye dingle-dangle at the yardarm at eight o'clock tomorrow morning."

The severe strain of this prolonged watchfulness told on even his iron hardihood, and it would almost appear that some of the rough practical jokes told of this period must represent reaction from the tension under which he necessarily was through the grave anxieties pressing upon him. Humour he certainly had, but at this time it often showed itself in horse-play, so fantastic as to suggest some unusual exciting cause. Thus, for one such prank he seemed to draw his inspiration from the Sunday celebration of Divine Service. Upon its conclusion, he framed and published a new signal, for "all chaplains," the employment of which, however, was postponed to an occasion suited to his lordship's fun.

> A few days after it blew great guns from west-southwest, which is directly into the Bay of Cadiz. The inshore squadron lay six miles from the flag-ship, directly to leeward, and up went the signal for all chaplains. It was a hard pull for the rowers, and no luxury for the sitters. When they reached the quarter-deck of the *Ville de Paris*, literally drenched with salt-water, the admiral presented them to 'Bishop Morgan,' as he called the chaplain of the flag-ship, and desired that they would go down into the ward-room and hold a conclave.

One who has had a pull of that kind, as most officers have in their day, can understand that the humour was less appreciable to the victims than to the author.

> He sometimes amused himself by paying a visit to the quarter-deck at what most people would deem very unseasonable hours. Coming up one morning at half-past two, in the middle watch, he sent for Colonel Flight, the commanding officer of marines. Up came the colonel, armed at all points, supposing that some enterprise was in hand. 'I have sent for you,' said the Chief, in the quiet and gentlemanly style which he could always command, 'I have sent for you, Colonel, that you might smell, for the

first time in your life, the delicious odours brought off by the land wind from the shores of Andalusia. Take a good sniff, and then you may go and turn in again.'

A lieutenant one day came on board to answer a signal. Lord St. Vincent thought there was about him too much *embonpoint* for an officer of that rank. 'Calder,' said he to the captain of the fleet, 'all the lieutenants are running to belly; they have been too long at anchor (for the fleet was still off Cadiz); block up the entering port, except for admirals and captains, and make them climb over the hammocks.' The entering port in a three-decked ship being on the middle deck, the difference between going into that and climbing over the hammocks may be compared to entering the drawing-room by the balcony window, or mounting to the parapet and taking the attics by storm. There was also great inconvenience, and even expense, attending this painful operation, since in those days all officers wore white knee-breeches, or shorts, as they were called, and many useful garments which could not readily be replaced, were torn and spoiled in this attempt at juvenile activity, and many oaths probably sworn, which but for this needless exertion would not have been elicited.

A more pleasing, and it may well be believed much more characteristic, instance of his playfulness has also been transmitted; one illustrative too of his deep fund of kindliness which was shown in many acts, often of large pecuniary liberality, and tinged especially with a certain distinct service colouring, with sympathy for the naval officer and the naval seaman, which must have gone far to obtain for him the obedience of the will as well as submission of conduct. He wisely believed in the value of forms, and was careful to employ them, in this crisis of the mutinies, to enforce the habit of reverence for the insignia of the state and the emblems of military authority. Young lieutenants— for there were *young* lieutenants in those days—were directed to stand cap in hand before their superiors, and not merely to touch their hats in a careless manner. "The discipline of the cabin and ward-room officers is the discipline of the fleet," said the admiral; and savage, almost, were the punishments that fell upon officers who disgraced their cloth. The hoisting of the colours, the symbol of the power of the nation, from which depended his own and that of all the naval hierarchy, was made an august and imposing ceremony. The marine guard, of near a hundred men, was paraded on board every ship-of-the-line. The national anthem was played, the scarlet-clad guard presented, and all officers and crews stood bareheaded, as the flag with measured dignity rose slowly to the staff-head. Lord St. Vincent himself made a point of attending always, and in full uniform; a detail he did not require of other officers. Thus the divinity that hedges kings was, by due observance, associated with those to whom their authority was delegated, and the very atmosphere the seaman breathed was saturated with reverence.

The presence of Lord St. Vincent on these occasions, and in full uniform, gave rise to an amusing skit by one of the lieutenants of the fleet, attributing the homage exacted, not to the flag, but to the great man himself; and this, becoming known to the admiral, elicited from him in turn the exhibition of practical humour to which allusion has just been made. Parodying the scriptural story of Nebuchadnezzar's golden image, the squib began:

"I. The Earl of St. Vincent, the commander-in-chief, made an Image of blue and gold, whose height was about five feet seven inches, and the breadth thereof was about twenty inches" (which we may infer were the proportions of his lordship). "He set it up every ten o'clock a.m. on the quarter-deck of the *Ville de Paris*, before Cadiz."

Passing from hand to hand, it can be understood that this effusion, which was characterized throughout by a certain sprightliness, gave more amusement to men familiar with the local surroundings, and welcoming any trifle of fun in the dullness of a blockade, than it does to us. At last it reached the admiral, who knew the author well. Sending for him on some pretext, an hour before the time fixed for a formal dinner to the captains of the fleet, he detained him until the meal was served, and then asked him to share it. All passed off quietly until the cloth was removed, and then the host asked aloud, "What shall be done to the man whom the commander-in-chief delights to honour?"

"Promote him," said one of the company.

"Not so," replied St. Vincent, "but set him on high among the people. So, Cumby," addressing the lieutenant, "do you sit there,"—on a chair previously arranged at some height above the deck,—"and read this paper to the captains assembled."

Mystified, but not yet guessing what was before him, Cumby took his seat, and, opening the paper, saw his own parody. His imploring looks were lost upon the admiral, who sat with his stern quarter-deck gravity unshaken, while the abashed lieutenant, amid the suppressed mirth of his audience, stumbled through his task, until the words were reached, "Then the Earl of St. Vincent was full of fury, and the form of his visage was changed against the poor Captain of the Main-Top," who had not taken off his hat before the Image of blue and gold. Here a roar of laughter from the head of the table unloosed all tongues, and Cumby's penance ended in a burst of general merriment.

"Lieutenant Cumby," said the admiral, when quiet was restored, "you have been found guilty of parodying Holy Writ to bring your commander-in-chief into disrespect; and the sentence is that you proceed to England at once on three months' leave of absence, and upon your return report to me to take dinner here again."

Compelled by general break-down of health to seek rest at home, St. Vincent returned to England in August, 1799. He was not left long in repose. The condition of the Channel Fleet as regards discipline has already appeared, and the very recent incident of the escape of the great French fleet from Brest, coupled with the equally humiliating and even more threatening experience of the same character in 1796, when the invasion of Ireland was attempted,—both which occurred under the same British commander-in-chief,—showed the urgent necessity of placing in control the only man of suitable rank, whose complete adequacy to such a post had been demonstrated. St. Vincent accordingly hoisted his flag in April, 1800.

In the effort to restore discipline, he here encountered not only opposition, intensified by the greater desire for shore privileges that always attends a home station and the proximity of wives and children, but something very like an attempt at combination against his orders—a very grave military offence—on the part of the captains. All this he trampled down with severity amounting to ruthlessness. The insubordinate toast—"May the discipline of the Mediterranean never be introduced into the Channel Fleet"—was met face to face by republishing every order and restriction upon which the discipline of the Mediterranean had rested. In the more distinctly military part of his task, the closing of the port of Brest to evasions by the enemy, such as those just mentioned, he achieved a noteworthy success. Modelling his scheme upon that of Hawke, forty years before, he gave to it a development, a solidity, and an extension which his distinguished forerunner had not been able to impart. Hawke had not the advantage, which St. Vincent had, of following a period of inefficiency, the remembrance of which compelled the Admiralty vigorously to support all measures of the commander-in-chief, if they desired to replace the interminable uncertainties and anxieties of the last administration of the fleet by a sense of security, and consequent popular content.

St. Vincent's institution and maintenance of the Brest blockade must be regarded under two principal heads. There is, first, the usefulness of the blockade as an instrument to the general ends of the current war, which is the strategic point of view, involving a conception permanent in character; and there are again the local dispositions, arising from the local conditions, that may rightly be styled tactical, and vary from port to port thus watched. The former, the strategic, was more directly in line with his natural gifts; and in the possession which the idea took of him is to be found the germ of the system that thenceforward began to throttle the power of the French Revolution, whether under the Republic or the Empire. The essence of the scheme was to cut loose from the beach, and keep to the sea; ever watchful, with the same watchfulness that had not only crushed mutiny, but by diligent care forestalled occasions of revolt. "Our great reliance," he said,—not directly in reference to the blockade, but to the general thought of which the blockade, as instituted by him, was the most illustrious exemplification,—"is on the vigilance and activity of our cruisers at sea, any reduction in the number of which, by applying them to guard our ports, inlets, and beaches, would in my judgment tend to our destruction." Amplified as the idea was by him, when head of the Admiralty, to cover not only Brest but all ports where hostile divisions lay, it became a strategic plan of wide sweep, which crushed the vitality of the hostile navies, isolated France from all support by commerce, and fatally sapped her strength. To St. Vincent, more than to any one man, is due the effective enforcement and maintenance of this system; and in this sense, as practically the originator of a decisive method, he is fairly and fully entitled to be considered the organizer of ultimate victory.

The local dispositions before Brest will not here be analyzed.[14] Suffice it to say that, as revealed in Jervis's correspondence, they show that equipment of general professional knowledge, that careful study of conditions,—of what corresponds to "the ground" of a shore battle-field,—and the thoughtful prevision of possibilities, which constitute so far the skilful tactician. The defence and the attack of seaports, embracing as they do both occupation of permanent positions and the action of mobile bodies, are tactical questions; differing much, yet not radically, from field operations, where positions are taken incidentally, but where movement of armed men is the principal factor. In the one sense St. Vincent displayed a high degree of aptitude for ordered permanent dispositions, which is the side of tactics most akin to strategy. On the more distinctively tactical side, in the movements of a fleet in action, he had little opportunity. As far as shown by his one battle, Cape St. Vincent, it would not appear that either by nature or cultivation he possessed to any great extent the keen insight and quick appreciation that constitute high tactical ability.

Earl St. Vincent rendered three great services to England. The

---

14. This has been done by the author elsewhere (*Influence of Sea Power upon the French Revolution and Empire*, Vol. I. pp. 371-377).

first was the forming and disciplining the Mediterranean fleet into the perfection that has been mentioned. Into it, thus organized, he breathed a spirit which, taking its rise from the stern commander himself, rested upon a conviction of power, amply justified in the sequel by Cape St.Vincent and the Nile, its two greatest achievements. The second was the winning of the Battle of St.Vincent at a most critical political moment. The third was the suppression of mutiny in 1797 and 1798. But, in estimating the man, these great works are not to be considered as isolated from his past and his future. They were the outcome and fruitage of a character naturally strong, developed through long years of patient sustained devotion to the ideals of discipline and professional tone, which in them received realization. Faithful in the least, Jervis, when the time came, was found faithful also in the greatest. Nor was the future confined to his own personal career. Though he must yield to Nelson the rare palm of genius, which he himself cannot claim, yet was the glory of Nelson, from the Nile to Trafalgar, the fair flower that could only have bloomed upon the rugged stalk of Jervis's navy. Upon him, therefore, Nelson showered expressions of esteem and reverence, amounting at times almost to tenderness, in his early and better days. In later years their mutual regard suffered an estrangement which, whatever its origin, appears as a matter of feeling to have been chiefly on the part of the younger man, whose temper, under the malign influence of an unworthy passion, became increasingly embittered, at strife within itself and at variance with others. The affectionate admiration of St.Vincent for his brilliant successor seems to have remained proof against external differences.

It was poetic justice, then, that allotted to St.Vincent the arrangement of the responsible expedition which, in 1798, led to the celebrated Battle of the Nile; in its lustre and thorough workmanship the gem of all naval exploits. To him it fell to choose for its command his brilliant younger brother, and to winnow for him the flower of his fleet, to form what Nelson after the victory called "his band of brothers."

"The Battle of the Nile," said the veteran admiral, Lord Howe, "stands singular in this, that every captain distinguished himself."

The achievement of the battle was Nelson's own, and Nelson's only; but it was fought on St. Vincent's station, by a detachment from St. Vincent's fleet. He it was who composed the force, and chose for its leader the youngest flag-officer in his command. Bitter reclamations were made by the admirals senior to Nelson, but St. Vincent had one simple sufficient reply,—"Those who are responsible for measures must have the choice of the men to execute them."

When St. Vincent, in 1799, quitted the Mediterranean, he had yet nearly a quarter of a century to live. His later years were distinguished by important services, but they embody the same spirit and exemplify the same methods that marked his Mediterranean command, which was the culminating period of his career. In 1801, when Pitt's long term of office came to an end, he became First Lord of the Admiralty,—the head of naval affairs for the United Kingdom,—and so continued during the Addington administration, till 1804. In 1806, at the age of seventy-two, he was again for a short time called to command the Channel fleet; but in 1807 he retired from active service, and the square flag that had so long flown with honour was hauled down forever.

The rest of his life was spent chiefly at his country-seat, Rochetts, in Essex, sixteen miles from London. Having a handsome income, though not wealthy, he entertained freely; and his retreat was cheered by frequent visits from his old naval subordinates and political friends. Generous in the use of money, and without children for whom to save, the neighbourhood learned to love him as a benefactor. In cases of necessity, his liberality rose to profusion, and he carried into the management of his estate a carelessness he never showed in administering a fleet. It is told that he once undertook to raise a sum by mortgage, in entire forgetfulness of a much larger amount in bank. Far into old age he retained the active habits of his prime. To say that he rose at four, asserts a biographer, would be to understate the case; he was frequently in the fields at half-past two in the early summer dawn of England,—always before his labourers,—and he was not pleased if his male guests did not appear by six. To ladies he was more tolerant. With mind unclouded and unweakened to the last, he retained his interest in public affairs and in the navy, contributing to the conversation which animated his home the judgment of an acute intellect, though one deeply tinged by prejudices inseparable from so strong a character. Thus honoured and solaced by the companionship of his friends, he awaited in calm dignity the summons, which came on the 13th of March, 1823. He was two months over eighty-eight when he passed away, the senior admiral of Great Britain.

Saumarez: 1757-1836

Chapter 6

Saumarez: 1757-1836

"These were honourable among the thirty," says the ancient Hebrew chronicler, "yet they attained not unto the first three." Since that far-away day, when the three mighty men broke through the host of the Philistines that they might bring their chieftain water from the well of Bethlehem, to how many fighters, land and sea, have these words been applicable!—men valiant in deed, wise in council, patient in endurance, yet lacking that divine somewhat which, for want of a better name, we call genius. Of such an one now, and, in contrasted sequence, of another of his peers, we are about to give an account; men who in their respective careers illustrated more conspicuously, the one the distinctively military, the other the more purely nautical, aspects, in the due blending of which the excellence of the profession is realized; foremost, both, among the ocean warriors whose pennants flew through the wild scenes where England's flag was called to brave the battle and the breeze—

Till danger's troubled night depart,
And the star of peace return.

James Saumarez was born on the 11th of March, 1757, in Guernsey, one of the Channel group of islands that still remain attached to the English crown,—the sole remaining fragment of the Norman duchy to which the kingdom itself was for a while but an appendage. In Saumarez's childhood, French was still so generally spoken there that, despite the very early age at which he went to sea, he always retained a perfect mastery of that language; and it is recorded that one of his uncles, being intended for the sea service, was sent to school in England when ten years old, in order to acquire the use of English. From such a stock, whose lineage among the gentry of the island can be traced to the fourteenth century, sprang three distinguished officers of this name, destined to illustrate the British flag by their deeds in several wars, in which their chief opponent was the French navy. Among these, the subject of this article attained the most brilliant renown. Eighteen months older than Nelson, not even Nelson saw more or harder fighting than did James Saumarez, nor bore himself more nobly throughout their day and generation.

Having early shown a taste for the navy, his father, who had six sons and a restricted income, obtained of a naval captain to have his name borne on the books of a ship of war at the early age of ten; a curious custom of that day allowing such constructive service to be counted in the time prescribed for attaining a lieutenant's commission. The boy did not actually go afloat until 1770, when a little over thirteen. This first employment kept him from home continuously for five years, a period spent wholly in the Mediterranean, and for the most part in the Levant; the active naval war then existing between Turkey and Russia, in the waters of Asia Minor, necessitating a special protection to British interests. It is a singular circumstance that this sea, esteemed so important to Great Britain, was never again visited by him, with the exception of the few brief months from May to October, 1798, when, as second in command, he followed Nelson's flag during the pursuit of Bonaparte's fleet which ended in its destruction at the Battle of the Nile.

Returning to England in 1775, his actual and constructive service permitted Saumarez to appear for examination for a lieutenancy. This he passed, but was not at once promoted. The troubles with the American colonies had now become open hostilities, and he was appointed, as master's mate or passed midshipman, to the *Bristol* of fifty guns, selected as flag-ship for the expedition against Charleston. This duty, which, by bringing him immediately under the eyes of the naval commander-in-chief, placed him also on the highway to advancement, he owed to Admiral Keppel, then one of the leading flag officers of the British navy. His uncle, Philip Saumarez, and Keppel had shared the perils and sufferings of Anson's well-known expedition to the South Seas in 1740. Together they had buffeted the wild weather off Cape Horn, with ships' companies more than decimated by scurvy; together they had spread terror among the Spanish colonies of the Pacific; together they had captured the great galleon off Manila; and Keppel still retained an affectionate interest in the kinsman of his old shipmate, who had long since fallen gloriously on the deck of his ship, in close action with a French vessel of far superior force.

The squadron, which was commanded by Commodore Sir Peter Parker, assembled at Cork, whence it sailed in January, 1776. Embarked on board the *Bristol* was Lord Cornwallis, afterwards so closely, and for himself disastrously, associated with the course of the American Revolution. Struck by Saumarez's activity and efficiency, he offered him a commission in his own regiment, with the position of aide-de-camp to himself. The young seaman, having a naturally strong military bent, which at that moment seemed more likely to receive satisfaction on shore than at sea, and swayed doubtless also by the prospect of a powerful patron, in the days when patronage had so much to do with men's careers, was on the point of accepting; but his messmates chaffed him so mercilessly upon adopting a profession which habitually supplied them with derisive illustrations and comparisons, that he finally declined. Many years later, when Saumarez was among the senior captains of the navy, the two gentlemen met as guests at the table of the head of the Admiralty, who upon hearing the incident from Cornwallis remarked that he would have deprived the navy of one of its best officers.

Owing partly to delays inseparable from sailing vessels, and partly to the dilatoriness with which war was most often waged before the days of the French Revolution, the British expedition did not appear off Charleston until the beginning of June, 1776. To Americans who know their own history, the stirring story of Fort Moultrie and its repulse of the British fleet has been familiar from childhood. Few are the American boys to whom the names of Jasper, of Marion, and of their brave commander, Moultrie himself, are unknown. But while all honour is due to the band of raw provincials who at this critical moment—one week before the Declaration of Independence was signed—withstood the enemy, and for the moment saved the province, the steady, obstinate valour shown by the seamen of kindred race, who contended with them, was no less brilliant, and was even more severely tested. The loss of the fort was thirty-seven killed and wounded; that of the *Bristol* alone was one hundred and eleven out of a crew of three hundred and fifty; and during much of the action, which lasted thirteen hours, she was powerless to return the raking fire of the enemy, in consequence of shot severing the ropes that kept her broadside in position. Saumarez was here for the first time engaged, and had two narrow escapes. Once, when pointing a gun, a cannon-ball entering the port swept away seven of the eight men who served the piece; and somewhat later another ball struck off the head of a messmate by whom he was standing, covering him with blood.

In this, his maiden action, Saumarez gave full proof of the steady courage which ever distinguished him; and it is worthy of passing remark that, in the doggedness of the fighting and the severity of the slaughter, the battle was typical of a great part of his after experience. Several death vacancies resulting among the officers, he was promoted to be lieutenant a fortnight later; and when the *Bristol* went north he was again actively engaged in the operations on Long Island, and along the East and Hudson rivers, up to the evacuation of New York by the Americans. His conspicuous activity at length obtained for him the command of a galley, with which he was sent to Rhode Island in February, 1778. The judgment of the illustrious Rodney, as well as the repeated efforts of the Americans to regain control of Narragansett Bay, may be cited against the opinion expressed by Bancroft, that the seizure of this important naval centre by the British was a mistake. The tenure of the island, however, depended upon the control of the surrounding waters, and upon the active destruction of the American means of transport. Saumarez's galley was one of the force stationed in the eastern, or Seakonnet, passage; and in the five months thus employed it is recorded that he was forty-seven times under fire.

Sullivan was at this time preparing for his attack upon the British lines, expecting co-operation by the French fleet. This arrived on the 29th of July, and six days later Seakonnet Channel was entered by a detachment superior in force to the British there. The latter burned their ships and retreated to Rhode Island, where the officers and seamen, Saumarez among them, continued actively engaged in the defence of the works. On August 8th, the main French fleet, under the Count d'Estaing, ran the batteries of the principal channel, and anchored off the north end of the island, seriously increasing the perils of the defenders; but next day the appearance of Lord Howe with an inferior squadron lured the French admiral out of the bay, his vessels were crippled by a storm, and he abandoned the coast. Sullivan, deprived of an essential factor in his scheme, had then to fall back; and the British captains, with their crews, being no longer needed, returned to England to seek other ships.

Both by fortune and by choice, Saumarez's lot throughout life was thrown with the line-of-battle force of the navy, that body of heavy fighting ships which constitute the true backbone of a sea service, because their essential function is to fight, not singly, but in masses, co-operating with others like themselves. In that respect they correspond to the solid masses of infantry, which, however disposed tactically, form the strength of armies. The aptitudes of brilliant officers differ. Some are born frigate-captains, partisan warriors, ever actively on the wing, and rejoicing in the comparative freedom and independence of their movements, like the cavalry raider and outpost officer. Of this type was Pellew, Lord Exmouth, a seaman inbred, if ever there was one, who in this sphere won the renown most distinctively associated with his name, while giving proof throughout a long career of high professional capacity in many directions. But while Saumarez, in his turn, was occasionally employed in frigate and light cruiser service, and always with great credit, his heart was with the ship-of-the-line, whose high organization, steady discipline, and decisive influence upon the issues of war appealed to a temperament naturally calm, methodical, and enduring. "He always preferred the command of a ship-of-the-line to a frigate," says his biographer, who knew him well,—"notwithstanding the chances of prize-money are in favour of the latter;" and he himself confirmed the statement, not only by casual utterance,—"My station as repeating frigate is certainly more desirable than a less conspicuous one, at the same time I would rather command a seventy-four,"—but by repeated formal applications. In variety and interest of operations, as well as in prize-money, did a cruising frigate have advantages; for much of the time of ships-of-the-line passed necessarily in methodical routine and combined movements, unfavourable to individual initiative. Nevertheless, their functions are more important and more military in character. In accordance with this preference Saumarez is found, whether by his own asking or not, serving the remaining three years of his lieutenant's time upon vessels of that class; and in one of them he passed through his next general action, a scene of carnage little inferior to the Charleston fight, illustrated by the most dogged courage on the part of the combatants, but also, it must be said, unrelieved by any display of that skill which distinguishes scientific warfare from aimless butchery. This, however, was not Saumarez's fault.

Towards the end of 1780, Great Britain, having already France, Spain, and America upon her hands, found herself also confronted by a league between the Baltic states to enforce by arms certain neutral claims which she contested. To this league, called the Armed Neutrality, Holland acceded, whereupon England at once declared war. Both nations had extensive commercial interests in the Baltic, and it was in protecting vessels engaged in this trade, by a large body of ships of war, that the only general action between the two navies occurred. This was on the 5th of August, 1781, in the North Sea, off the Dogger-Bank, from which it has taken its name.

At the time of meeting, the British, numbering six ships-of-the-line, were returning from the Baltic; the Dutch, with seven ships, were bound thither. Despite the numerical difference, no great error is made in saying that the two squadrons were substantially of equal force. Each at once ordered the merchant vessels under its protection to make the best of their way towards port, while the ships of war on either side began to form in order of battle between the enemy and their own convoy. The lists being thus cleared and the lines ranged, the British vessels, which were to windward, stood down together, after what was then the time-honoured and unintelligent practice of their service, each to attack one of the Dutch; disdaining to attempt doubling upon any part of the hostile line. Their ideal appears to have been that of the tournament, where every advantage of numbers and combination was rejected in order to insure that the test should be that of individual courage and skill. So strong was this tradition in the British navy that its ablest contemporary chronicler, James, has sought to explain away, half apologetically, the advantage gained by Nelson in doubling on the French van at the Nile.

The Dutch, equally quixotic, refrained from taking advantage of the enemy's inability to use his broadsides while thus approaching nearly head-on. Arrayed in a close column, the ships about six hundred feet apart, the crews at the guns, and the marines drawn up on the poops, they waited in silence until the English, at 8 a.m., were in position at half musket shot. Then the battle-flag was hoisted by each admiral, and all opened together, the conflict raging with fury for nearly four hours. It was the first time since the days of the great De Ruyter, more than a century before, that these kindred people had thus met in fair fight upon the sea. Equal in courage and in seamanship, and each neglecting to seek a tactical advantage, the usual result followed. Many men were killed and wounded, no ship was taken, and the combatants separated after a drawn battle; but as one Dutch ship sank the next day, and their convoy could not proceed, the British claimed a victory. Their own merchant vessels, being on the return voyage, were able to complete it.

Saumarez had shown his usual gallantry, and was again promoted. On the 23rd of August, eighteen days after the action, he was made commander into the *Tisiphone*, a small but fast cruiser, technically called a fire-ship, and attached to the Channel fleet. In December, the British government learned that a large number of transports and supply ships were about to sail from Brest for the West Indies. These were to carry troops and stores to the fleet of Count De Grasse, who had returned to Martinique after the surrender at Yorktown, and was now about to undertake the conquest of Jamaica. It was imperative to intercept an expedition so essential to the success of the French plan, and Admiral Kempenfelt—the same who afterwards, in the *Royal George*, "went down with twice four hundred men"—was sent in pursuit with twelve ships-of-the-line. The *Tisiphone* accompanied them as lookout vessel, and on the 12th of December, 1781, being then well ahead of the fleet, she was able to signal the admiral that the enemy was in sight to leeward with seventeen of-the-line; but that the latter, instead of being between the British and the transports, were on the far side. Kempenfelt, an able tactician as well as seaman, seized his advantage, pushed between the men-of-war and the convoy, and carried off fifteen sail laden with military and naval stores, of great money value and greater military importance. More could not be done without risking a battle with a too superior force. It was essential, therefore, to apprise the British commander in the West Indies of the approach of the French reinforcements as well as of Kempenfelt's successes, and the *Tisiphone* was the same day despatched on this errand.

Although he knew it not, Saumarez was now being borne by the tide which leads on to fortune. The next step in promotion then fixed, and still fixes, the seniority of a British officer, and the *Tisiphone*'s mission led him straight to it. Easily out sailing the unwieldy mass of enemies, he reached Barbados, and there learned that the British fleet, under Sir Samuel Hood, was anchored off the island of St. Christopher, then invaded by a French army supported by De Grasse's fleet. The tenure of the island depended upon a fort on Brimstone Hill, still held by the British; and Hood, though much inferior in force, had by a brilliant tactical move succeeded in dislodging De Grasse from his anchorage ground, taking it himself, and establishing there his fleet in such order that its position remained impregnable. The French, however, continued cruising to the southward, off the adjoining island of Nevis, where they interposed between Hood and Saumarez; and the latter could reach his commander only by threading the reefs lining the passage between the two islands,—a feat considered hazardous, if not impracticable. Nevertheless, the *Tisiphone* effected it by diligent care and seamanship, joining the fleet on January 31st, 1782.

Saumarez now found himself in the midst of the most active operations, at the opening of a campaign which promised to be of singular and critical importance. But in the midst of his rejoicing at the good fortune which had transferred him from the comparative inactivity of the Channel fleet, a momentary reverse befell. Called by signal on board the flag-ship, he received a bag of despatches, with orders to sail that night for England. As he went dejectedly down the ship's side to his boat and was shoving off, the gig of a post-captain pulled alongside. "Hallo, Saumarez," said its occupant, "where are you going?"

"To England, I grieve to say."

"Grieve!" rejoined the other. "I wish I were in your place. I have been wanting this long time to go home for my health. Hold on a moment; perhaps it can be arranged."

The newcomer, named Stanhope, went at once to the admiral, who a few minutes later sent for Saumarez. Hood had learned to value the active young officer who had taken a forward part in the guerrilla enterprises of the fleet.

"Captain Saumarez," he said, "you know not how much I wish to serve you. Captain Stanhope shall go home, as he desires, and you shall have command of the *Russell*."

The same night the *Tisiphone* sailed; Saumarez remaining as an acting post-captain, with a ship of seventy-four guns under him.

Thus it happened that two months later, at the age of twenty-five, Saumarez commanded a ship-of-the-line in Rodney's renowned battle of the 12th of April; with one exception the most brilliant and decisive action fought by the British navy in a century. This circumstance alone would have insured the confirmation of his rank by the Admiralty, even had he not also eminently distinguished himself; but it was for him one of those periods when inconstant fortune seems bent upon lavishing her favours. He was near the head of the British column, as the hostile fleets passed in opposite directions, exchanging broadsides. As his ship cleared the French rear, a neighbouring British vessel, commanded by one of the senior captains, turned to pursue the enemy. Saumarez gladly imitated him; but when the other resumed his former course, because the admiral of the van, his immediate superior, had not turned, the *Russell* kept on after the French. At this moment, Rodney in the centre, and Hood in the rear, favoured by a change of wind, were breaking through the French line. The *Russell's* course carried her toward them, and consequently, in the *mêlée* which followed, she had the distinguished honour of engaging De Grasse's flag-ship, and of being in action with her when she surrendered. Indeed, although Saumarez with characteristic modesty refrained from pressing his claim, he always, when questioned on the subject, maintained that although the enemy's vessel certainly struck to Hood's flagship, she did so immediately upon the latter joining the *Russell*.

However regarded, this was a brilliant achievement for so young a captain, less than a twelvemonth having elapsed since he was but a lieutenant. Rodney, who had meanwhile signalled his van to go about, was somewhat perplexed at finding a single ship thus opportunely in the direction whence the *Russell* appeared; and, upon being informed that she belonged to the van squadron, declared that her commander had distinguished himself above all others in the fleet. It proved, in fact, the keen military sense of the demands of an occasion which constitutes the born corps or division commander. This was Saumarez's third general action, at a time when Nelson, although three years a post-captain, had commanded only frigates, and had never seen a battle between fleets. But, if Saumarez used well the singular opportunities with which fortune favoured him, it was characteristic of Nelson that his value transpired through the simplest intercourse and amid the most commonplace incidents of service. Men felt, rather than realized, that under the slight, quaint, boyish exterior there lay the elements of a great man, who would one day fulfil his own boast of climbing to the top of the tree; and he had been made a full captain in 1779, when not quite twenty-one. According to the rule of the British service, already mentioned, this assured for life his precedence over Saumarez, promoted in 1782.

The latter, however, if outstripped by a younger competitor, who was to become the greatest of British admirals, had secured a position of vantage for that great war which then lay in the womb of the future. Returning to England in 1782, he passed in retirement the ten years that preceded the outbreak of hostilities with the French republic. During this period he was twice called out for service upon occasions of war threatening,—in 1787 with France, and in 1790 with Spain; but though in each case appointed to a ship, the employment went no farther, as hostilities were timely averted. This protracted withdrawal from active pursuit of his profession, viewed in connection with his prolonged and efficient service of the twenty following years, may be taken as indicating two things: first, that to professional excellence once attained such a break is not as fatal as is commonly argued; and second, considered with his favourable entertainment of Cornwallis's proposal to exchange into the army, this contentment with shore life during the peace confirms the remark already made, that, although a thorough seaman, Saumarez was so incidentally. His quickening interest was in the military rather than the nautical side of his calling. Pellew, on the contrary, now eagerly sought duty at sea, impelled thereto by clear restless predilection as well as, possibly, by need of increased income. It was during this interval of repose, in 1788, that Saumarez married; a step which did not in his case entail the professional deterioration charged against it by the cynical criticisms of St. Vincent. At this time, also, he made a trip to France, upon the occasion of sinking the first cone of the great Cherbourg breakwater, designed to give the French navy a first-class arsenal upon the Channel,—a purpose which it now fulfils. Louis XVI. was present at this ceremony, and treated Saumarez with much attention. This was the only time that he ever set foot upon French soil, although his home was in sight of the coast and he spoke the language fluently.

When war with France again began, in 1793, Saumarez was appointed to the frigate *Crescent*, of thirty-six guns, with which he served actively in the Channel. In her, on the 20th of October, 1793, he succeeded in intercepting the French frigate *Réunion*, of substantially equal force, which he had learned was in the habit of quitting Cherbourg in pursuit of British merchant vessels every night, returning in the morning. The ensuing action called for an exhibition of seamanship which showed he had not lost aptitude during his retirement. In the beginning he placed the *Crescent* on the weather quarter of the French ship,—that is, on the windward side, but a little to the rear. This was well judged, because (1) the all-important rudder is thus less exposed, (2) in case of an unfavourable accident the adversary tends to leave rather than to approach, and (3) the vessel, moving ahead, is at once under command to stop short of the opponent. After being placed, speed was regulated by backing or filling the mizzen-topsail, thus maintaining the relative positions, and directing fire upon the enemy's rudder. In this situation the fore-topsail yard and foretopmast of the *Crescent* were shot away in quick succession, and the ship flew up head to wind, bringing all her sails aback. For a moment she was in an awkward plight, but the *Réunion*, drawing away, could not rake; and Saumarez, by adroit management of the rudder and sails, *backed* his ship round,—always a nice operation and especially when near an enemy,—till the wind came again abaft, restoring the normal conditions of moving ahead under control of the helm. The contest was then renewed, and ended in the surrender of the French vessel. The disparity of loss—1 British to 118 French—proved the discipline of the *Crescent* and the consummate seamanship of her commander. For this exploit Saumarez was knighted. Faithful to his constant preference, he as soon as possible exchanged into a ship-of-the-line, the *Orion*, of seventy-four guns. In her he again bore a foremost part, in 1795, in a fleet-battle off the Biscay coast of France, where three enemy's ships were taken; and two years later he was in the action with the Spaniards off Cape St.Vincent, of which an account has been given in the sketch of Earl St.Vincent. After this Saumarez remained on the same station, blockading Cadiz.

In the following year, 1798, it became necessary to send a small detachment into the Mediterranean, and off the chief arsenal of the enemy, Toulon, to ascertain the facts concerning a great armament, since known as Bonaparte's Egyptian expedition, which rumour said was there in preparation. The hazardous nature of the duty, which advanced three ships of medium size, unsupported, in the very teeth of over a dozen enemies, many of superior strength, demanded the utmost efficiency in each member of the little body so exposed; a consideration which doubtless led Lord St. Vincent to choose Saumarez, though one of the senior captains, for this service, of which Nelson, the junior flag officer of the fleet, was given charge.

It seems scarcely credible that, when it was afterwards decided to raise this detachment to fourteen ships-of-the-line, sufficient to cope with the enemy, both St. Vincent and Nelson wished to remove Saumarez, with his antecedents of brilliant service, so as to allow Troubridge, his junior, to be second in command. The fact, however, is certain. Nelson had orders which would have allowed him to send the *Orion* back, when thus proceeding on a service pregnant with danger and distinction, to the immeasurable humiliation of her brave commander. After making every deduction for the known partiality for Troubridge of both St. Vincent and Nelson, it is difficult to avoid the conclusion that Saumarez, with all his undoubted merit, was in their eyes inferior to Troubridge in the qualities necessary to chief command, in case of Nelson's death, at a juncture which called for the highest abilities of a general officer. The moment was too critical to permit mere favouritism to sway two such men against their judgment. As it was, however, Nelson felt he could not part with so efficient a ship; and he therefore contented himself with giving Troubridge and Saumarez each a subdivision of four vessels, keeping six under his own immediate direction.

As all know, the French, when found, were at anchor. Thus surprised, the British fleet was hurled at them in a single mass; nor was there any subordinate command exercised, by Saumarez or any other, except that of each captain over his particular ship. Nelson's first expectation was to overtake the unwieldy numbers of the enemy, amounting to over four hundred sail, at sea, and there to destroy both convoy and escort. In such an encounter there would be inestimable tactical advantage in those compact subdivisions, which could be thrown as units, under a single head, in a required direction. For such a charge Saumarez possessed most eminent capacity.

The warm family affection that was among the many winning traits of Saumarez's symmetrical and attractive character impelled him to copious letter-writing. Hence we have a record of this pursuit of the French fleet, with almost daily entries; an inside picture, reflecting the hopes, fears, and perplexities of the squadron. Bonaparte's enterprise has been freely condemned in later days as chimerical; but it did not so appear at the time to the gallant seamen who frustrated it. The preparations had been so shrouded in mystery that neither Nelson nor his government had any certainty as to its destination,—an ignorance shared by most of the prominent French officials. When, after many surmises, the truth gradually transpired, the British officers realized that much time must yet elapse before the English ministry could know it. Two months, for instance, passed before news of the Battle of the Nile reached London. Then, if India were the ultimate object, to which Egypt was but the stepping-stone, four months more, at least, would be needed to get a naval reinforcement to the threatened point. What if, meanwhile, the ally of France in the peninsula, Tippoo Saib, had been assembling transports with the secrecy observed at Toulon and the other ports whence the divisions had sailed? "I dined with Sir Horatio today," writes Saumarez on June 15th, nearly four weeks after Bonaparte's starting, "and find that his intelligence extends only to the enemy's fleet having been seen off Sicily; but we have reason to suppose them gone for Alexandria, the distance from which to the Red Sea is only three days' journey. They may soon be transported thence by water to the East Indies, with the assistance of Tippoo Saib; and with their numerous army they expect to drive us out of our possessions in India. This profound scheme, *which is thought very feasible*, we hope to frustrate by coming up with them before they reach the place of their destination." A week later, Nelson received off Sicily news of the surrender of Malta to the French. In accordance with the views above expressed, Sir James now—June 22nd—gave Nelson his written opinion, favouring the course adopted of seeking the enemy off the coast of Egypt; one of the most responsible decisions ever taken by an admiral in chief command, especially at the beginning of a career, as Nelson then was. "We are now crowding sail for Alexandria; but it is very doubtful if we fall in with them at all, as we are proceeding on the merest conjecture, and not on any positive information. If, at the end of our journey, we find we are upon the wrong scent, our embarrassment will be great indeed. Fortunately, I only act here *en second*; but did the chief responsibility rest with me, I fear it would be more than my too irritable nerves would bear." Nelson, in truth, was passing these hours in a fever of anxiety, scarce able to eat or drink. Yet at that very moment the British were crossing the enemy's wake, unseeing and unseen, and barely fifty miles separated the two fleets.

The perplexity foreshadowed by Saumarez actually fell upon the English admiral, through his reaching Alexandria three days before the French. Harassed out of his better judgment, he hurried back to the westward, touched at Sicily, and thence once more to Egypt. Meantime, the French had landed successfully. On the 1st of August the British fleet again sighted Alexandria; saw the French flag on the walls, but no ships of war. Saumarez wrote:

> When the reconnoitring squadron made the signal that the enemy was not there despondency nearly took possession of my mind, and I do not remember ever to have felt so utterly hopeless or out of spirits as when we sat down to dinner. Judge, then, what a change took place when, as the cloth was being removed, the officer of the watch hastily came in, saying, 'Sir, a signal is just now made that the enemy is in Aboukir Bay, and moored in a line of battle.' All sprang from their seats, and, only staying to drink a bumper to our success, we were in a moment on deck.

As the captain appeared, the crew hailed him with three hearty cheers, a significant token of the gloom which had wrapped the entire squadron through the recent ordeal of suspense and disappointment.

It is only with Saumarez's share in this renowned battle that we are here concerned. As is generally known, Nelson's tactics consisted in doubling upon the van and centre of the enemy, who lay at anchor in a column head to wind, or nearly so. Their rear, being to leeward, was thus thrown out of action. The French had thirteen ships-of-the-line, of which one was of one hundred and twenty guns, and two eighties. The British also had thirteen, all seventy-fours, and one of fifty guns; but one of the former going aground left them equal in numbers and inferior in force. There were two successive acts in the drama. In the first, ten British ships engaged the eight leading French; in the second, the fifty and two of the seventy-fours, which had been belated, came upon the field and strengthened the attack upon the enemy's centre. The *Orion*, being third in the order, was one of the five vessels which passed within the French, and fought on that side. In so doing, she described a wide sweep around her two predecessors. While thus standing down to her station, an enemy's frigate, the *Sérieuse*, opened fire upon her, wounding two men. It was then part of the chivalrous comity of fleet-actions that frigates should not be molested by the ships-of-the-line, so long as they minded their own business,—an immunity which of course ceased if they became aggressive. Saumarez was urged to return her fire. "No," he replied, "let her alone; she will get bolder and come nearer. Shorten sail."

She did draw nearer, and then the *Orion*, swinging sharply towards her, let drive her broadside of double-shotted guns. All the masts of the unlucky frigate went overboard, and she shortly sank, nothing but her poop being visible the next day. The helm of the British vessel was then shifted, but so much ground had been lost that she could anchor only abreast the fifth French ship; the interval left being filled by those who followed. In this position the *Orion* silenced her immediate opponent, the *Peuple Souverain*, which, being in an hour and a half totally dismasted, cut her cables and dropped out of the line; the contest being then continued with the sixth in the French order, the *Franklin*, next ahead of the flag-ship, *Orient*. The *Orion* was thus near by the latter when she blew up, but the few burning fragments which fell on board were quickly extinguished.

Twenty-four hours after the battle, Saumarez, who had been delayed till then by a severe wound from a splinter, went on board the flag-ship to call on the admiral; and to this visit we owe the knowledge of two closely related incidents, recorded by his biographer and friend, which are significant at once of his individual ideas on tactical combination, and of the lack of personal sympathy apparent between him and Nelson; he—

> .... found several of his brother officers on the quarter-deck, discussing the merits of the action. Some regret having been expressed at the escape of the two sternmost ships of the French line, Sir James said to the admiral, 'It was unfortunate we did not—' and was proceeding to say 'all anchor on the same side.' But, before he could finish the sentence, Nelson hastily interrupted him, exclaiming, 'Thank God there was no order!' Then turning the conversation, he entered his cabin and sent for Captain Ball.... We may relate the circumstances which induced Saumarez, without the least intention to offend, to make the observation at which offence was taken. It was Nelson's custom, when in communication or company with the captains under his command, to converse with them on the various modes of attacking the enemy under different circumstances; and, on one of these occasions, Sir James Saumarez, who had seen the evil consequences of *doubling* on the enemy, especially in a night action, had differed with the admiral in that plan of attack, saying that 'it never required two English ships to capture one French, and that the damage which they must necessarily do each other might render them both unable to fight an enemy's ship that had not been engaged; and, as in this case two ships could be spared to the three-decker, everyone might have his opponent.'

Inasmuch as Nelson, in pursuance of his previously announced idea, had himself in the flag-ship—the sixth to enter action—set the example of *doubling*, by anchoring on the side of the enemy's line opposite to that of his first five ships, and in doing so had deliberately taken position on one side of a French vessel already engaged on the other, Saumarez's remark was substantially a censure, inopportune to a degree singular in a man of his kindly and generous temper; and its reception by Nelson is not a cause for surprise. On the other hand, as a matter of tactical criticism, based upon tactical conceptions previously adopted, if we assume it to be true that two British ships were not needed to capture one French, it may yet be confidently affirmed that to attack with decisively superior force a part of the enemy's order—to combine in short—is shown by experience to attain the same degree of success more certainly and at less cost than the simple distribution of effort advocated by Saumarez. To double, and to beat in detail, remained the ideal of Nelson, as it had been of Howe. It was by him applied then and afterwards to all cases, small or great, actual or supposed. To it he chiefly owed his dazzling successes, and this divergence of ideals marks the difference in professional insight which mainly determines the relative positions of Nelson and Saumarez in naval biography. It indicates the distinction between the great general officer and the accomplished and resolute division or corps commander.

At the Battle of the Nile Saumarez received the only wound that ever fell to him throughout his numerous meetings with the enemy, being struck on the thigh and side by a heavy splinter, which had killed two officers before reaching him. The total loss of his ship was forty-two killed and wounded, out of a crew of six hundred. Ten days after the action he was ordered to take charge of six of the prizes, which had been partly repaired, and with seven of the fleet to convoy them to Gibraltar. At the same time he was notified that the *Orion* was to go home as soon as this duty was performed. A more charming prospect can scarcely be imagined than this returning to his family after a long absence, fresh from the completest achievement ever wrought by the British navy; but even his tranquil temper, whose expressions never lapse into the complaints of Nelson or the querulousness of Collingwood, was tried by the slow progress of his battered and crippled squadron. "The prizes get on very slowly," he writes; "but I am endowed with unparalleled patience, having scarcely uttered a murmur at their tardiness, so perfectly satisfied am I with the prospect before me." Some time later he notes: "We have been three weeks effecting what might be accomplished in two days. This extraordinary delay makes me more fractious than can be imagined, and I begin to lose the character for patience which I had given myself, by so tiresome a situation." It was still the season of westerly winds, and the voyage from Alexandria to Gibraltar occupied sixty-nine days.

The *Orion* was now completely worn out, having been continuously in commission since the war began in 1793. Besides the three general actions in which Saumarez commanded her, she had borne a valiant part in Howe's great battle of the 1st of June. "This last business has so shattered the poor *Orion*" wrote Saumarez, "that she will not, without considerable repairs, be in a state for more service." On reaching England she was paid off; and in February, 1799, he was appointed to the *Caesar*, of eighty-four guns, one of the finest ships in the navy, which was to bear his flag in the last and most brilliant episode of his hard-fighting career.

A year later, Lord St. Vincent, having returned from the Mediterranean, took command of the Channel Fleet, and at once instituted in its methods, and particularly in the blockade of Brest, changes which gradually revolutionized the character of the general naval war; baffling beyond any other single cause the aims of Napoleon, and insuring the fall of his empire. One of the new requirements was the maintenance of a powerful advanced division of six or eight ships-of-the-line, within ten miles of the harbour's mouth. It was a duty singularly arduous, demanding neither dash nor genius, but calmness, steadiness, method, and seamanship of a high order, for all which Saumarez was conspicuous. From either side of the Bay of Brest a long line of reefs projects for fifteen miles to the westward. Far inside their outer limits, and therefore embayed by the westerly winds which blow at times with hurricane violence, was the station of the advanced squadron, off some well-marked rocks of the northern reef, known as the Black Rocks. On this spot, called Siberia by the seamen, during fifteen weeks, from August to December, Sir James Saumarez kept so close a watch that not a vessel of any force entered or left Brest. "With you there," wrote Earl St. Vincent, "I sleep as sound as if I had the key of Brest in my pocket." No work ever done by him was more meritorious or more useful. Near its expiration St. Vincent wrote to him, "The employment you have conducted is the most important of this war." He there demonstrated that what before had apparently been thought impossible could be done, though involving a degree of anxiety and peril far exceeding that of battle, while accompanied by none of the distinction, nor even recognition, which battle bestows. His biographer says with simple truth:

> None but professional men who have been on that service can have any idea of its difficulties,—surrounded by dangers of every kind, exposed to the violence of storms, sailing amidst a multitude of rocks and variable currents in the longest and darkest nights, and often on a lee shore on the enemy's coast, while the whole of their fleet is near, ready to take advantage of any disaster.

Collingwood, who in the next war succeeded to the same unenviable duty, wrote home that, even in the summer month of August—

> I bid adieu to comfortable naps at night, never lying down but in my clothes. An anxious time I have of it, what with tides and rocks, which have more of danger in them than a battle once a week.

In this laborious task Saumarez was the patient, unobserved pioneer.

There was one man, however, who could and did recognize to the full the quality of the work done by Saumarez, and its value to those sagacious plans which he himself had framed, and which in the future were to sap the foundations of the French power. That man was St. Vincent. "The merit of Sir James Saumarez," he said, "cannot be surpassed;" and again, to Saumarez himself, "The manner in which you have conducted the advanced squadron calls upon me to repeat my admiration of it." Succeeding soon after to the post of First Lord of the Admiralty, he gave him an opportunity for distinction, which resulted in an action of singular lustre and striking success.

Bonaparte, long before returned from Egypt, and now, as First Consul, practically the absolute ruler of France, had overthrown all enemies on the Continent. Peace with Austria, after her disasters of Marengo and Hohenlinden, had been signed in February, 1801. The great objects of the French ruler now were to compass a maritime peace and withal to retain Egypt, associated from far back with the traditional policies of France, and moreover a conquest in which his own reputation was peculiarly interested. To compel Great Britain to peace, he sought, by diplomacy or force, to exclude her commerce from the Continent, as well as to raise up maritime enemies against her. Thus he had fostered, if not actually engendered, the Baltic league of 1801, shattered by Nelson at Copenhagen; and for this purpose he intended to occupy both Portugal and the kingdom of Naples. A powerful British expedition against Egypt had entered the Mediterranean. It was essential either to attack this directly, or to cripple its communications. Unable to do the former, and persistently thwarted in his attempts to reinforce his own troops in that distant dependency by the close watch of the British navy, of which Saumarez gave so conspicuous an illustration before Brest, Napoleon resorted to the common and sound military expedient of collecting a threatening force upon the flank of his enemy's line of communications. He directed a concentration of the Spanish and French navies at Cadiz, which, by its nearness to the straits, met the desired requirement. Among others, three French ships were ordered thither from Toulon.

The British ministry was informed that at Cadiz were collecting Spanish vessels, said by report to be intended against Portugal. This is unlikely, as Bonaparte could have subdued that country from the land side by the assistance of Spain; moreover, the object of the concentration is stated in his letters. A squadron of five ships-of-the-line was accordingly formed, and placed under the command of Saumarez, who on the 1st of January, 1801, had been made a rear admiral. His orders were to go off Cadiz, where he would find two more vessels, and to prevent the enemies within the port from sailing, or from being joined by any from outside. Whatever Bonaparte's object, it would be thwarted by a force thus interposed, in a position to meet either one or the other of the converging detachments before they could unite.

Saumarez sailed on his mission June 16, 1801, and on the 28th arrived off Cadiz. On the 5th of July he was informed that three French ships had anchored off Algeciras, the Spanish port on the west side of Gibraltar Bay, confronting the British fortress on the east side. This was the division from Toulon, which upon reaching the straits first learned of the British squadron that effectually prevented its entrance to Cadiz.

Saumarez at once started for Algeciras with six of his ships-of-the-line, the seventh being out of recall to the northward. The following day, July 6th, he entered the bay, and found the French moored in a strong position, under cover of Spanish land batteries, and supported by a number of gunboats. Still, though difficult and doubtful, the enterprise was not hopeless; and, as the breeze allowed his vessels to head for the enemy, he steered to engage at once. Unfortunately, the wind fell as the squadron drew nigh, and only four ships were able to take their intended places; the other two had to anchor outside their consorts, and fire as they could through the intervals. This mishap lessened by one-third the fighting power of the British, and, coupled with the acknowledged superiority of guns on solid ground over those afloat, reduced them to inferiority. Their disadvantage was increased by the arrangements of the French admiral, carefully elaborated during the two preceding days. Had the preparations of Brueys at the Nile equalled those of Linois at Algeciras, Nelson's task must have been harder and his victory less complete. Nevertheless, after an engagement of an hour and a half, the British fire so far prevailed that the enemy resorted to a measure for which precautions had been taken beforehand. Lines had been run from each French ship to the shoal water lying close inside them; and by means of these they were warped away from their opponents until they took the ground. This increase of distance was in every way a gain to the party standing on the defensive, and a corresponding loss to the assailants. Saumarez ordered the cables cut and sail made to close once more; but the light and fickle airs both baffled this effort and further embarrassed the British, through the difficulty of keeping their broadsides in position. Here happened the great disaster of the day. One of the outer ships, the *Hannibal,* tried to pass inside the headmost of the French, not realizing that the latter had moved. In so doing she ran aground close under a battery, to whose fire she could make no reply. After a brave and prolonged resistance, in which she lost seventy-five killed and seventy wounded out of a crew of six hundred, and had many of her guns dismounted, she hauled down her flag. By this time another ship, the *Pompée,* was dismasted, and success was plainly hopeless. The British admiral, therefore, ordered the action discontinued, and withdrew to the Gibraltar side; the *Pompée* having to be towed away by the boats of the squadron.

Saumarez had failed, and failure, however explained, can hardly be carried to a man's credit; but his after course, by wresting success out of seemingly irretrievable disaster, has merited the highest eulogium. Maintaining both courage and energy unimpaired, every effort was instantly made to get the ships once more into fighting condition, that the attack might be renewed. "Tell the Admiralty," said he to the bearer of his despatches, "that I feel confident I shall soon have an opportunity of attacking the enemy again, and that they may depend upon my availing myself of it."

The opportunity did come. On the morning of July 9th, the *Superb,* the seventh ship, which had not been in the action, was seen rounding the west point of the bay under all sail, with a signal flying that the enemy was in pursuit. A few moments later appeared five Spanish vessels, two of which, the *Real Carlos* and the *Hermenegildo,* carrying each one hundred and twelve guns, were among the largest then afloat. On board them had embarked a number of the *jeunesse dorée* of Cadiz, eager to join the triumphal procession which it was thought would soon enter the port, flushed with a victory considered by them to be rather Spanish than French, and escorting the rare trophy of a British ship-of-the-line that had struck to Spanish batteries. Besides the two giants, there were a ninety-gun ship and two seventy-fours; and the next day a French vessel of the latter class joined, making a total reinforcement of six heavy ships.

To these Saumarez could oppose but five. The *Hannibal* he had lost. The *Pompée* could not be repaired in time; her people were therefore distributed among the other vessels of the squadron. Even his own flag-ship, the *Caesar*, was so injured that he thought it impossible to refit her; but when her crew heard his decision, one cry arose,—to work all day and night till she was ready for battle. This was zeal not according to knowledge; but, upon the pleading of her captain in their name, it was agreed that they should work all day, and by watches at night. So it happened, by systematic distribution of effort and enthusiastic labour, that the *Caesar*, whose mainmast on the 9th was out and her rigging cut to pieces, was on the 12th able to sail in pursuit of the foe.

During the forenoon of the latter day the combined squadron was seen getting under way. The wind, being easterly, was fair for the British, and, besides, compelled the enemy to make some tacks to clear the land. This delay was invaluable to Saumarez, whose preparations, rapid as they had been, were still far from complete. Not till one in the afternoon did the headmost Spaniards reach the straits, and there they had to await their companions. The *Hannibal* was unable to join them, and re-anchored at Algeciras. At half-past two the *Caesar* hauled out from Gibraltar mole, her band playing, "Cheer up, my lads, 't is to glory we steer!" which was answered from the mole-head with "Britons, strike home!" At the same moment Saumarez's flag, provisionally shifted to another vessel, was re-hoisted at her masthead. The rugged flanks of the rock and the shores of Algeciras were crowded with eager and cheering sight-seers, whose shouts echoed back the hurrahs of the seamen. Rarely, indeed, is so much of the pride and circumstance, if not of the pomp, of war rehearsed before an audience which, breathless with expectation, has in it no part save to admire and applaud.

Off Europa Point, on the Gibraltar side, there clustered round the *Caesar* her four consorts, all but one bearing, like herself, the still fresh wounds of the recent conflict. Four miles away, off Cabrita Point, assembled the three French of Linois's division, having like honourable marks, together with the six new unscarred arrivals. At 8 p.m. of the summer evening the allies kept away for Cadiz; Linois's division leading, the other six interposing between them and the five ships of Saumarez, which followed at once. It was a singular sight, this pursuit of nine ships by five, suggestive of much of the fatal difference, in ideals and efficiency, between the navies concerned. Towards nine o'clock Saumarez ordered the *Superb*, whose condition alone was unimpaired by battle, to press ahead and bring the rear of the enemy to action. The wind was blowing strong from the east, with a heavy sea. At half-past eleven the *Superb* overtook the *Real Carlos*, and opened fire. Abreast the Spanish vessel, on her other side, was the *Hermenegildo*. The latter, probably through receiving some of the *Superb*'s shot, fancied the ship nearest her to be an enemy, and replied. In the confusion, one of them caught fire, the other ran on board her, and in a few moments there was presented to the oncoming British the tremendous sight of these two huge ships, with their twenty hundred men, locked in a fast embrace and blazing together. At half-past two in the morning, having by that time drifted apart, they blew up in quick succession.

Leaving them to their fate, the hostile squadron passed on. The *Superb* next encountered the *St. Antoine*, and forced her to strike. Soon afterwards the wind died away, and both fleets were much scattered. A British ship brought to action one of the French which had been in the first battle; indeed, the French accounts say that the latter had fought three enemies. However that may be, she was again severely mauled; but the English vessel opposed to her ran on a shoal, and lost all her masts. With this ended the events of that awful night.

The net results of this stirring week completely relieved the fears of the British ministers. Whatever the objects of the concentration at Cadiz, they were necessarily frustrated. Though the first attack was repulsed, the three French ships had been very roughly handled; and, of the relieving force, three out of six were now lost to the enemy. "Sir James Saumarez's action has put us upon velvet," wrote St. Vincent, then head of the Admiralty; and in the House of Peers he highly eulogized the admiral's conduct, as also did Nelson. The former declared that "this gallant achievement surpassed everything he had ever met with in his reading or service," a statement sufficiently sweeping; while the praise of the hero of the Nile was the more to be prized because there never was cordial sympathy between him and Saumarez. Closely as they had been associated, Nelson's letters to his brother officer began always "My dear Sir James," not "My dear Saumarez."

In this blaze of triumph the story of Saumarez fitly terminates. He was never again engaged in serious encounter with the enemy. The first war with the French republic ended three months after the battle of Algeciras. After the second began, in 1803, he was, until 1807, commander-in-chief at the Channel Islands, watching the preparations for the invasion of England, and counteracting the efforts of cruisers against British commerce. In 1808, in consequence of the agreements of Tilsit between the Czar and Napoleon, affairs in the Baltic became such as to demand the presence of a large British fleet,—first to support Sweden, then at war with Russia, and later to protect the immense British trade, which, under neutral flags and by contraband methods, maintained by way of the northern sea the intercourse of Great Britain with the Continent. Of this trade Sweden was an important intermediary, and her practical neutrality was essential to its continuance. This was insured by the firm yet moderate attitude of Sir James Saumarez, even when she had been forced by France to declare war against Great Britain.

It may be said without exaggeration that from this time, and until the breach between Napoleon and Russia in 1812, the maritime interest of the war between Great Britain and France centred in the Baltic. Elsewhere the effective but monotonous blockade of the continental ports controlled by the French Emperor absorbed the attention of the British fleets. Of great battles there were none after Trafalgar. To Saumarez, therefore, fell the most distinctive, and probably also the most decisive, field of work open to the British navy. The importance of the Baltic was twofold. It was then the greatest source of materials essential to ship-building—commonly called naval stores; and further, the Russian part of its coast line, being independent of Napoleon's direct regulation, was the chief means of approach by which Great Britain maintained commercial intercourse with the Continent, to exclude her from which had become the leading object with the Emperor. The contravention of his policy in this way, in disregard, as he claimed, of the agreements existing between him and the Czar, led eventually to the Russian war, and so finally to his own overthrow and the deliverance of the Continent from his domination.

The historical significance of the position now occupied by Saumarez, and its importance to the great issues of the future, are thus manifest. It was a post that he was eminently qualified to fill. Firm, yet calm, sagacious, and moderate, he met with rare efficiency the varied and varying demands of those changeful times. The unremitting and well directed efforts of his cruisers broke up reciprocal commerce between the countries surrounding the narrow inland sea, so essential to their welfare while submitting to Napoleon; while the main fleet sustained the foreign trade with Russia and Sweden, carried on through neutral ships for the advantage of Great Britain. Two instances will illustrate his activities better than many words. In the year 1809 four hundred and thirty local vessels were captured, averaging the small size of sixty tons each, three hundred and forty of which belonged to Denmark, then under Napoleon's absolute sway. At the close of the open season of 1810, the merchant ships for England, which ordinarily were despatched under convoy in bodies of five hundred, numbered, according to Saumarez's flag-lieutenant and biographer, no less than one thousand vessels, gathered in one mass.

As long as Sweden remained friendly, the admiral's duties,

though weighty, did not differ materially from those usual to his profession; but when she was unwillingly forced into a declaration of war by Napoleon, his task became more complicated and more delicate. The British minister having to leave, Saumarez succeeded to a diplomatic situation, in which the problem was to support the interests and dignity of his own nation, without transforming the formal war into actual hostilities, and substituting embitterment for the secret good will of the Swedish government and people, who, in common with the Russian nobles and subjects, were alienated by the imperious and merciless exactions of the French demands. The secret aim of Great Britain was so to nourish this ill-will towards France, and so to avoid causes of offence by herself, as to convert covert hostility into open antagonism, and thus to reverse the political and military combinations of Europe. In the absence of regular accredited diplomatic representatives, Saumarez became at once the exponent and the minister of this vital policy. He had to avoid quarrels, and yet at the same time to restrain Sweden from acts of injury to which she was constantly impelled by the Emperor, whose purpose naturally was exactly the opposite of his; and who sought further to estrange all people from Great Britain.

In the performance of this task Saumarez's success was not only complete, but peculiarly his own. His temper was at times severely tried, but it never got beyond his control. He repressed injury, and demanded satisfaction for it, when committed; but, relying with good reason on the motives of the Swedish government, he contrived to secure redress without resorting to force, which, however understood by statesmen, would enrage the peoples he had to conciliate. After the ordeal was over, and Russia was at war with France, a leading Swedish statesman wrote to him:

> You have been the guardian angel of my country; by your wise, temperate, and loyal conduct, you have been the first cause of the plans which have been formed against the demon of the continent.... Once more I must tell you, that *you* were the first cause that Russia had dared to make

war against France; had you fired one shot when we declared war against England, all had been ended and Europe would have been enslaved.

Saumarez, an extremely religious man, may have reflected that "he who ruleth his spirit is greater than he that taketh a city."

Though in the strictest sense professional, the Baltic service of Saumarez involved little of purely military interest. Shortly after his assuming the command, in 1808, a Russian fleet which had been keeping the sea took refuge, on the approach of the allied British and Swedes, in a harbour on the Gulf of Finland. Saumarez followed close upon their heels, and after a consultation and reconnaissance of the position, which consumed two days, secured the co-operation of the Swedish admiral for an attack on the day following; an essential condition, for the Russian force was superior to his own in the proportion of eight to six. Unhappily, the wind shifted, and blew an adverse gale for eight days; at the end of which time the enemy had so far fortified the surroundings that Saumarez thought it inexpedient to attack. In this decision he was supported by the opinion of captains of such established reputation as, joined to his own brilliant record, must be taken to justify his action, which seems to have caused some dissatisfaction in England. On the face, it could not but be a disappointment to people accustomed to the brilliant victories of Nelson, and his apparent invincibility by obstacles; but in the end it was all for the best, for doubtless the mortifying destruction of a Russian fleet would not have furthered the reconciliation, which soon became a leading object with the British government and the great bulk of the Russian nation. It is, however, probable that to this frustration of public expectation, which had been vividly aroused by preceding accounts of the conditions, is to be attributed the delay in granting the peerage, eagerly desired by Saumarez in his later days,—not for itself merely, but as a recognition which he not unnaturally thought earned by his long and distinguished service. Saumarez held the Baltic command through five eventful years,—from 1808 to 1812. After Napoleon's disastrous Russian expedition, affairs in that sea no longer required a force adequate to his rank, and he then finally retired from service afloat, still in the full maturity of a healthy prime, at the age of fifty-five. The remainder of his life, with brief exception, was passed in his native island of Guernsey, amid those charms of family affection and general esteem which he had deserved by his fidelity to all the duties of the man and the citizen. Though so far removed from the active centres of life, he kept touch with it by the variety of his interests in all useful and benevolent undertakings, to which an ample fortune allowed him freely to contribute. "The hopes entertained of his assistance and sympathy," observes his biographer, "were never disappointed." Among naval biographies, there is none that presents a more pleasing picture of genial and dignified enjoyment of well-earned repose. In 1831, upon the accession of William IV., the Sailor King, the long-coveted peerage was at last bestowed. Lord de Saumarez died on the 9th of October, 1836, in his eightieth year. Feuis eui tatummod dit aci bla autpat diam, sisl ex ex eraesequat pratincilit lortis autat adionse quismolobor sed et irit wisismod eugait er sim estrud molobor sum irit aut lum dolore elit amcor sequam doloreet, quissim vulput lore consenisl dolorero odo odolort inciliquis ex enisisim vullam illandignis dolor iustrud diam, quis autat. Facipsu scilla feugait nostie te min ut irilla facipsum vullamet eum vullandigna facipismodip ex estrud tem ercilit wis ero et eugiamet wisim euiscinis nis diamet wisl del ipit adion velisim num del do odit pratue faciliqui bla facip et wissed tem zzrit aut aliquipis ea adip etue dolorerostie modit inis elit lutat venis ad eros acidui exerili quatin ulla feu feuguero erostie conullandre tetue dolore dolore feu faci blan ecte veliqui sseniam nismod te euis num iriuscipsum iriustie commy nim nonsed molor si.

Equatissit lamet, suscin eu feugue faccum quatet nonsequam quis nisci exer senim quis ametum ex euip essis dio od tatumsa ndiamco nsequat, velis am nim zzrillut ulla faccum volutpa tisiscilit, sumsandre mincilit aut dolor ip ent luptat luptat lore venit nulla faccummolum diam dolent lorperatue tat luptat, sum quamconse dolorem dolendigna feum nonsed del ing el ulput velestisl eugait dolesenisi bla facilissi.

Xeraese tis non utat nibh ercidunt nosto commy nim exer

Pellew: 1757-1833

CHAPTER 7

Pellew: 1757-1833

Like the English tongue itself, the names of British seamen show the composite origin of their nation. As the Danes after the day of Copenhagen, to them both glorious and disastrous, claimed that in Nelson they had been vanquished by a man of their own blood, descended from their Viking forefathers; as Collingwood and Troubridge indicate the English descent of the two closest associates of the victor of Trafalgar; so Saumarez and the hero of this sketch, whose family name was Pellew, represent that conquering Norman race which from the shores of the Northern ocean carried terror along the coasts of Europe and the Mediterranean, and as far inland as their light keels could enter. After the great wars of the French Revolution and the Battle of Algiers, when Lord Exmouth had won his renown and his position had been attained, kinship with him was claimed by a family still residing in Normandy, where the name was spelled "Pelleu." Proof of common origin was offered, not only in the name, but also in the coat of arms. In England, the Pellew family was settled in the extreme southwest, in Cornwall and *Devonshire*, counties whose nearness to the great Atlantic made them the source of so much of the maritime enterprise that marked the reign of Elizabeth. Lord Exmouth's grandfather was a man of wealth; but, as he left many children, the juniors had to shift for themselves, and the youngest son, Samuel Pellew, the father of the admiral, at the time of the latter's birth commanded a post-office packet on the Dover station. He accordingly made the town of that name the home of his wife and children; and there Edward, the second of his four sons, was born, April 19, 1757. Their mother was the daughter of a Jacobite gentleman, who had been out for the Pretender in 1715,—a fact which probably emphasized the strong Hanoverian sympathies of Samuel Pellew, whose habit was to make his children, every Sunday, drink King George's health upon their knees.

In 1765, when the future admiral was only eight years old, his father died, and the mother making an imprudent marriage three years later, the children were thrown upon the world with small provision and scanty care. The resolute, active, and courageous character of the lads, however, brought them well forward among their equals in age. At school Edward was especially distinguished for fearlessness. Of this he gave a marked instance, when not yet twelve, by entering a burning house where gunpowder was stored, which no other of the bystanders would approach. Alone and with his own hands the lad brought out the powder. A less commendable but very natural result of the same energetic spirit was shown in the numerous fighting matches in which he was engaged. Being threatened with a flogging for one of these, the circumstance became the immediate occasion of his going to sea. If flogged, he declared, he would run away; and as a decided taste for seafaring life had already manifested itself, his guardian thought better to embrace at once the more favourable alternative and enter him regularly in the navy. He thus went afloat towards the end of 1770, the date at which Nelson, also, though one year younger, began his career.

His first cruise was in the Mediterranean. It came to a premature end through a quarrel between the commander of the ship and one of the midshipmen. In this the captain was clearly and grossly in the wrong; yet nevertheless carried his resentment, and the power of oppression in his hands, then little restrained by law, so far as to expel the youngster from the ship and set him on shore in Marseilles. Pellew insisted upon accompanying his messmate, and the two lads of fourteen, aided by some of the lieutenants, secured a passage home. It shows a pleasing trait in our hero's character that, some years afterwards, he advanced materially the professional fortunes of the son of the officer who had thus abused his authority.

He next passed under the command of a Captain Pownoll, between whom and himself were established such warm relations, of affectionate interest on the one side and reverential regard on the other, that Pownoll became a family name among the descendants of the admiral. He himself gave it to his firstborn, and it still appears in the present generation. Under him, also, Pellew was brought into direct contact with the American Revolution; for on board the frigate *Blonde*, Pownoll's ship, General Burgoyne embarked in 1775 for Canada, there beginning the undertaking which ended so disastrously for him. It is told that when the distinguished passenger came on board, the yards being manned to receive him with the honours due to his rank, he was startled to see on one yardarm a midshipman standing on his head. Upon expressing alarm, he was laughingly reassured by the captain, who said that Pellew—for he it was who put this extra touch upon the general's reception—was quite capable of dropping from the yard, passing under the ship's bottom, and coming up on the other side. A few days later the young officer actually did leap from the yardarm, the ship going fast through the water—not, however, as bravado, but to aid a seaman who had fallen overboard, and whom he succeeded in saving.

Throughout his youth the exuberant vitality of the man delighted in these feats of wanton power. To overturn a boat by press of canvas, as a frolic, is not unexampled among lads of daring; but it is at least unusual, when a hat goes overboard, to follow it into the water, if alone in a boat under sail. This Pellew did, on one occasion, when he was old enough to know better; being at the moment in the open Channel, in a small punt, going from Falmouth to Plymouth. The freak nearly cost him his life; for, though he had lashed the helm down and hove-to the boat, she fell off and gathered way whenever he approached. When at last he laid hold of her rail, after an hour of this fooling, barely strength remained to drag himself on board, where he fell helpless, and waited long before his powers were restored. It is trite to note in such exhibitions of recklessness many of the qualities of the ideal seaman, though not so certainly those of the foreordained commander-in-chief. Pellew was a born frigate captain.

At the end of 1775 the Americans were still engaged in the enterprise against Quebec, the disastrous termination of which is familiarly known. After the fall of General Montgomery in the unsuccessful night assault of December 31, 1775, the American operations were reduced to a land blockade of the town, which was cut off from the sea by ice in the river. A close investment was thus maintained for five months, until the early part of May, 1776, when the place was relieved by the arrival of a small naval force, commanded by Captain Charles Douglas. Immediately upon its appearance the commanding British general Carleton, attacked the besiegers, who, already prostrated by disease and privation, abandoned their positions and fell back upon Sorel, at the mouth of the river Richelieu, the outlet from Lake Champlain to the St. Lawrence. Here they remained until June, when the enemy, who had received heavy reinforcements, advanced in overpowering numbers. The Americans again retired above the rapids of the Richelieu to St. Johns. Thence there is a clear channel southward; and embarking there, the retreating force without further molestation reached Crown Point, a fortified post a hundred miles distant, at the head of the lake, commanding the narrow stream to which it is reduced in its upper part. Twelve miles above Crown Point is Ticonderoga, the well-known border fortress of the Colonial and Revolutionary wars; and for fifteen or twenty miles farther the stream is navigable for boats of some size, thus affording an easy means of communication in those early days of impassable forests and scanty transport.

Though greatly superior on land, the British had now for a time to stay their pursuit; for the water highway essential to its continuance was controlled by the flotilla under the command of Benedict Arnold, forbidding further advance until it was subdued. The presence of these vessels, which, though few, were as yet unopposed, gained for the Americans, in this hour of extremity, the important respite from June to October, 1776; and then the lateness of the season compelled the postponement of the invasion to the following year. The toil with which this little force had been created, a few months before, was thus amply justified; for delay is ever to the advantage of the defence. In this case it also gave time for a change of commanders on the part of the enemy, from Carleton to Burgoyne, which not improbably had a decisive effect upon the fortunes of the next campaign.

As soon as established at St. Johns, the British took steps to place a naval force upon the lake, an undertaking involving trouble and delay, notwithstanding their greatly superior resources in men and material. Some thirty fighting vessels, suitable to the waters upon which they were to act, were required, and also four hundred bateaux for the transport of the troops. These had either to be built upon the spot, despite the lack of all dockyard facilities, or else to be brought bodily from the St. Lawrence, by road, or through the rapids of the Richelieu, until the deep water at St. Johns was reached. In this hardy, strenuous work, Pellew naturally was conspicuously active; and in its course he gained a particular professional accomplishment which afterwards stood him in good stead. Several vessels were built upon the shores of the stream; among others, one of one hundred and eighty tons, the *Inflexible*, whose heavier timbers were brought overland to St. Johns. The construction of these craft was superintended by a lieutenant—afterwards Admiral Schank—of scientific knowledge as a ship architect; and through close association with him Pellew's instinctive appreciation of all things nautical received an intelligent guidance, which gave him a quick insight into the probable behaviour of a ship from an examination of her build, and enabled him often to suggest a suitable remedy for dangerous faults. During this period of equipment occurred a characteristic incident which has only recently become public through a descendant.[15]

> On the day the *Inflexible* was launched, Pellew on the top of the sheers was trying to get in the mainmast. The machinery not being of the best gave way, and down came mainmast, Pellew, and all, into the lake. 'Poor Pellew,' exclaimed Schank, 'he is gone at last!' However, he speedily emerged and was the first man to mount the sheers again. 'Sir,' Admiral Schank used to conclude, 'he was like a squirrel.'

---

15. Fleetwood Hugo Pellew, in *Our Naval Heroes*.

Thirty days after the keel of the *Inflexible* was laid at St. Johns, the vessel herself not only was launched, but had set sail for the southward. She carried eighteen twelve-pounders, nine on a side, and was thus superior in power, not only to any one vessel of the Americans, but to their whole assembled flotilla on Lake Champlain. Except the principal pieces of her hull, the timber of which she was built was hewed in the neighbouring forest; and indeed, the whole story of the rapid equipment of this squadron recalls vividly the vigorous preparation of Commander Perry, of the United States navy, in 1813, for his successful attempt to control Lake Erie. The entire British force, land and naval, now moved toward Crown Point. On the 11th of October the American flotilla was discovered, a short distance above Plattsburg and about twenty miles from the foot of the lake, drawn up between Valcour Island and the western shore, which are from one-half to three-fourths of a mile apart. It lay there so snugly that the British, wafted by a northwest wind, had actually passed to the southward without seeing it, and the discovery was purely accidental,—a fact which suggests that Arnold, who must have felt the impossibility of a force so inferior as his own contesting, or even long delaying, the enemy's advance by direct opposition, may have entertained some purpose of operating in their rear, and thus causing a diversion which at this late season might effectually arrest their progress. It is true that such a stroke would frightfully imperil his little squadron; but, in circumstances of absolute inferiority, audacity, usually the best policy in war, offers the only chance of success. Mere retreat, however methodical, must end in final destruction. To act towards St. Johns, trusting to dexterity and to local knowledge of the network of islands at the foot of the lake to escape disaster, or at least to protract the issue, offered the best chance; and that the situation thus accepted would not be hopeless was proved by the subsequent temporary evasion of pursuit by the Americans, even in the open and narrow water of the middle lake.

The British moved to attack as soon as the hostile shipping was discovered. Pellew was second officer of the schooner *Carleton*, of twelve guns, the third vessel of the flotilla in point of force. The wind being contrary, and apparently light, the *Carleton* alone of the sailing vessels got into action; and although she was supported by a number of rowing gunboats, whose artillery was heavy, the match was unequal. According to Arnold's own account, he had disposed his gunboats and gondolas "on the west side of Valcour Island, as near together as possible, and in such a form that few vessels can attack us at the same time, and those will be exposed to the fire of the whole fleet." To this Captain Douglas, in his report of the occurrences, adds the suggestive particular that the *Carleton*, by a lucky slant of wind, fetched "nearly into the middle of the rebel half-moon, where she anchored with a spring on her cable." The position was one of honourable distinction, but likewise of great exposure. Her first officer lost an arm; her captain, Lieutenant Dacres, was so severely wounded that he was about to be thrown overboard as dead; and Pellew, thus left without a superior, fought the vessel through the engagement. When signal was at last made to withdraw, the *Carleton* was able to do so only by help of the gunboats, which towed her out of fire. On the other hand, Arnold's flag-ship, the schooner *Royal Savage*, which had fought in advance of her consorts and under canvas, fell to leeward, and came there under the distant fire of the *Inflexible*, by which she was badly crippled. She then was run ashore on the southern point of the island, where she fell momentarily into the hands of the British, who turned her guns on her former friends. Later in the day, it seeming probable that she might be retaken, she was set on fire and burned to the water's edge. Thus abandoned, she sank to the bottom, where her hull rests to this day. During the recent summer of 1901 some gun-carriages have been recovered from her, after lying for a century and a quarter beneath the surface of the lake.

Pellew's personal activity and strength enabled his gallantry to show to particular advantage in this sanguinary contest. When the *Carleton*, in her attempt to withdraw, hung in stays under the island, her decks swept by the bullets of the riflemen on shore, it was he who sprang out on the bowsprit to bear the jib over to windward. When the tow-rope was cut by a shot, it was Pellew again who exposed his person for the safety of the vessel. His two seniors being forced by their wounds to leave the schooner, he succeeded to the command, in which he was afterwards confirmed. In this sharp affair the *Carleton* lost eight killed and six wounded,—about half her crew,—and had two feet of water in her hold when she anchored out of range.

Towards evening the *Inflexible* succeeded in getting within point-blank range of the American flotilla, "when five broadsides," wrote Douglas, "silenced their whole line;" a sufficient testimony to the superiority of her concentrated battery over the dispersed force of all her numerous petty antagonists. The British then anchored to the southward of Arnold's little force; but that active and enterprising officer succeeded in stealing during the night between the enemy and the western shore, and retired towards Crown Point. The chase to windward continued during the next day, but a favourable shift of wind, to the north, reached the British first, and enabled them to close. Arnold again behaved with the extraordinary bravery and admirable conduct which distinguished him in battle. Sending on the bulk of the squadron, he took the rear with two galleys, covering the retreat. Fighting like a lion, he opposed the enemy's advance long enough to secure the escape of six of his vessels; and then, seeing his one consort forced to strike, he ran his own galley ashore and set her on fire. The naval historian Cooper says:

> Arnold covered himself with glory, and his example seems to have been nobly followed by most of his officers and men. The manner in which the Congress was fought until she had covered the retreat of the galleys, and the stubborn resolution with which she was defended until destroyed, converted the disasters of this part of the day into a species of triumph.

A contemporary British writer says:

> The Americans chiefly gloried in the dangerous attention paid by Arnold to a nice point of honour, in keeping his flag flying, and not quitting his galley till she was in flames, lest the enemy should have boarded and struck it.

Pellew received like recognition, not, perhaps, from the popular voice, but from his official superiors. Douglas, the senior naval officer at Quebec, who was made a baronet in reward of these operations, Lord Howe at New York, and the First Lord of the Admiralty in England, all sent him personal letters of commendation; and the two latter promised him promotion as soon as he came within their respective jurisdictions. His continuance at the front of operations during this and the following year therefore postponed his deserved advancement to a lieutenancy, by retaining him from the "jurisdiction" of those able to bestow it.

The two gallant enemies were soon again brought together in an incident which came near to change the career of one of them, and, in so doing, to modify seriously the fortunes of many others. Arnold having one day pulled out on the open lake, in his venturesome manner, Pellew gave chase in another boat. The Americans being hard pressed and capture probable, Arnold unbuckled his stock and himself took an oar. So nearly caught was he, that he had to escape into the bushes, leaving behind him stock and buckle; and these, as late as sixty years after, remained in the possession of Pellew's brother. Had he thus been deprived of the opportunity that Saratoga gave him the next year, Arnold's name might now be known to us only as that of the brave officer who kept his country's flag flying till his vessel was in flames.

On the 14th of October Carleton landed at Crown Point, which the Americans had abandoned; but the lateness of the season deterred him from advancing against Ticonderoga, and he soon afterwards returned to Canada. The full import of this halt is too easily overlooked, with consequent failure to appreciate the momentous influence exerted upon the course of the Revolutionary War by this naval campaign, in which Pellew bore so conspicuous a part. It has never been understood in America, where the smallness of the immediate scale has withdrawn attention from the greatness of the ultimate issue, in gaining time for the preparations which resulted in the admittedly decisive victories about Saratoga. "If we could have begun our expedition four weeks earlier," wrote a German general there present, "I am satisfied everything would have been ended this year; were our whole army here, it would be an easy matter to drive the enemy from their entrenchments at Ticonderoga." The delay, not of four weeks only, but of the whole summer, was obtained by the naval force organized upon Champlain by Arnold and his superior, General Schuyler. The following year the invasion was resumed, under General Burgoyne. Pellew accompanied him with a body of seamen, taking part in all the operations down to the final surrender. Burgoyne, indeed, afterwards chaffed him with being the cause of the disaster, by rebuilding the bridge which enabled the army to cross from the east bank of the Hudson to the west.

Returning to England in the early part of 1778, Pellew was made lieutenant, and in 1780 we find him again serving under Captain Pownoll, as first lieutenant of the *Apollo* frigate. On the 15th of June, in the same year, the *Apollo* met the French frigate *Stanislas*. A severe action followed, and at the end of an hour Pownoll was shot through the body. As his young friend raised him from the deck, he had barely time to say, "Pellew, I know you won't give his Majesty's ship away," and immediately expired. The engagement lasted an hour longer, when the enemy, which had all the time been standing in for the Belgian coast, took the ground, the most of her spars, already wounded, going overboard with the shock. The *Apollo* had hauled off a few moments before, finding that she had less than five feet of water under her keel.

Though unable again to attack the *Stanislas*, which claimed the protection of the neutral flag, the result was substantially a victory; but to Pellew's grief for the death of a tried friend was added the material loss of a powerful patron. Happily, however, his reputation was known to the head of the Admiralty, who not only promoted him for this action, but also gave him a ship, though a poor one. After a succession of small commands, he was fortunate enough again to distinguish himself,—driving ashore and destroying several French privateers, under circumstances of such danger and difficulty as to win him his next grade, post-captain. This step, which, so far as selection went, fixed his position in the navy, he received on the 25th of May, 1782.

The ten years of peace that shortly followed were passed by

many officers in retirement, which we have seen was contentedly accepted by his distinguished contemporary, Saumarez; but Pellew was a seaman to the marrow, and constantly sought employment afloat. When out of occupation, he for a while tried farming, the Utopian employment that most often beguiles the imagination of the inbred seaman in occasional weariness of salt water; but, as his biographer justly remarks, his mind, which allowed him to be happy only when active, could ill accommodate itself to pursuits that almost forbade exertion. "To have an object in view, yet to be unable to advance it by any exertions of his own, was to him a source of constant irritation. He was wearied with the imperceptible growth of his crops, and complained that he made his eyes ache by watching their daily progress."

His assiduous applications, however, were not wholly unavailing to obtain him the professional employments usually so hard to get in times of peace. For five of the ten years, 1783-1793, he commanded frigates, chiefly on the Newfoundland station; and in them, though now turning thirty, he displayed the superabundant vitality and restless activity that had characterized his early youth. "Whenever there was exertion required aloft," wrote a midshipman who served with him at this period, "to preserve a sail or a mast, the captain was foremost in the work, apparently as a mere matter of amusement, and there was not a man in the ship that could equal him in personal activity. He appeared to play among the elements in the hardest storms. I remember once, in close-reefing the main topsail, the captain had given his orders from the quarter-deck and sent us aloft. On gaining the topsail yard, the most active and daring of our party hesitated to go upon it, as the sail was flapping violently, making it a service of great danger; but a voice was heard from the extreme end of the yard, calling upon us to exert ourselves to save the sail, which would otherwise beat to pieces. A man said, 'Why, that's the captain! How the——did he get there?' He had followed us up, and, clambering over the backs of the sailors, had reached the topmast head, above the yard, and thence descended by the lift,"—a feat unfortunately not easy to be explained to landsmen, but which will be allowed by seamen to demand great hardihood and address.

All this was the simple overflow of an animal energy not to be repressed, the exulting prowess of a giant delighting to run his course. It found expression also in joyous practical jests, like those of a big boy, which at times had ludicrous consequences. On one occasion of state ceremony, the king's birthday, Pellew had dressed in full uniform to attend a dinner on shore. The weather was hot, and the crew had been permitted an hour's swimming around the ship. While his boat was being manned, the captain stood by the frigate's rail watching the bathers, and near by him was one of the ship's boys. "I too shall have a good swim soon," called the latter to a comrade in the water. "The sooner, the better," said Pellew, coming behind him and tipping him overboard. No sooner had the lad risen to the surface from his plunge than it was plain that he could not swim; so in after him went the practical joker, with all his toggery. "If ever the captain was frightened," writes the officer just quoted, "it was then."

But along with all this physical exuberance and needless assumption of many of the duties of a foremast hand, Pellew possessed to a very remarkable extent that delicate art of seamanship which consists in so handling a ship as to make her do just what you want, and to put her just where she should be; making her, to use a common sea expression, do everything but talk. This is a faculty probably inborn, like most others that reach any great degree of perfection, and, while a very desirable gift, it is by no means indispensable to the highest order of naval excellence. Nelson did not at all equal Pellew in this respect, as is indicated by an amusing story transmitted by a Colonel Stewart, who served on board the great admiral's flag-ship during the expedition against Copenhagen:

> His lordship was rather too apt to interfere in the working of the ship, and not always with the best judgment or success. The wind, when off Dungeness, was scanty, and the ship was to be put about. Lord Nelson would give the orders, and caused her to miss stays. Upon this he said, rather peevishly, to the officer of the watch, 'Well, now see what we have done. Well, sir, what mean you to do now?' The officer saying, with hesitation, 'I don't exactly know,

my lord. I fear she won't do,' Lord Nelson turned sharply to the cabin, and replied, 'Well, I am sure if you do not know what to do with her, no more do I, either.' He went in, leaving the officer to work the ship as he liked.

Yet Nelson understood perfectly what ships could do, and what they could not; no one could better handle or take care of a fleet, or estimate the possibility of performing a given manoeuvre; and long before he was called to high command he was distinguished for a knowledge of naval tactics to which few, if any other, of his time attained. He was a great general officer; and whether he had the knack of himself making a ship go through all her paces without a fault mattered as little as whether he was a crack shot with a gun.

A ship is certainly the most beautiful and most graceful of machines; a machine, too, so varied in its movements and so instinct with life that the seaman affectionately transfers to her credit his own virtues in handling her. Pellew's capacity in this part of his profession was so remarkable that it is somewhat singular to find him, in his first frigate action, compelled to discard manoeuvring, and to rely for victory upon sheer pluck and luck. When war with the French republic began in 1793, his high reputation immediately insured him command of a frigate, the *Nymphe*. The strength of England as a naval power lay largely in the great reserve of able seamen manning her merchant ships; but as these were scattered in all quarters of the world, great embarrassment was commonly felt at the outbreak of a war, and especially when it came with the unexpected rapidity of the revolutionary fury. As the object of first importance was to get the fleets of ships-of-the-line to sea, Pellew had to depend chiefly upon his own indefatigable exertions to procure a crew for his vessel. Seamen being hard to find, he had on board a disproportionate number of landsmen when the *Nymphe*, on the 19th of June, 1793, encountered the French vessel *Cléopâtre*, of force slightly inferior, except in men, but not sufficiently so to deny the victor the claim of an even fight.

A peculiar incident preceding the action has interest, as showing the strong preoccupation of men's minds at the opening of war, before meetings with the enemy have lost novelty. Pellew's younger brother, Israel, a commander in the navy, being otherwise unemployed, had come out with him for the cruise. The *Cléopâtre* having been first seen in the early morning, Edward would not have him called till just as the *Nymphe* was closing. As he came on deck, the brother said affectionately, "Israel, you have no business here. We are too many eggs from one nest. I am sorry I brought you from your wife." But the other was unheeding, his eyes fixed upon the stranger. "That's the very frigate," he cried, "that I've been dreaming of all night! I dreamt that we shot away her wheel." And, hastening to the after-gun, he made the French ship's wheel the object of an unremitting fire.

By the way the enemy was handled it was evident that she was well manned and ably commanded. She had, in fact, been in commission for over a year. Great as was his own skill, Pellew could not venture upon manoeuvres with a green crew, untrained save at the guns, and only filled the night before by pressing from a merchant vessel. He therefore determined upon a simple artillery duel. The Frenchman waited under short canvas, while the *Nymphe*, with greater way, drew slowly up on his starboard, or right-hand side; both ships running nearly before the wind, but having it a little on the left side. Each captain stood uncovered, and as the bows of the *Nymphe* doubled upon the stern of the *Cléopâtre*, within three hundred feet, a French sailor was seen to run aloft and fasten a red cap of liberty to the mainmast head. The eyes of the British seamen were fastened upon their commander, awaiting the gesture which he had set, instead of word of mouth, for opening fire. At quarter-past six he gave it, raising his cap to his head. A furious cannonade at once began, and, the *Nymphe* shortening sail as soon as fairly abreast her antagonist, the two frigates continued on parallel lines, maintaining their relative positions as though at anchor, and rolling easily in the soft summer sea under the recoil of their guns. So nearly matched were the gunners that the conflict, unusually deadly though it was, might have lasted long, but at a little before seven Israel Pellew's dream was fulfilled. The Frenchman's wheel was shot away, and, the mizzenmast going overboard at the same time, the *Cléopâtre* yielded to the impulse of her forward sails, turned sharp round to the right, and ran perpendicularly into the *Nymphe*. The British boarded her, fixed in this disadvantageous position, fought their way aft, and, although the French crew was numerically superior, in ten minutes hauled down the colours. In this brief hour they had lost twenty-three killed and twenty-seven wounded, the enemy sixty-three killed and wounded, out of ships' companies numbering respectively two hundred and forty and three hundred and twenty.

This was the first decisive frigate action of the War of the French Revolution, and in consequence great was the enthusiasm aroused. Lord Howe wrote to Pellew, "The manner in which you have taken the enemy's ship will set an example for the war." In truth, however, while admitting the soundness of Pellew's judgment in adopting the course he did, the actual demand upon his personal skill was less, and in so far the credit due therefore less, than in the second successful frigate action, in the following October, in which Sir James Saumarez commanded. Not only was the French vessel's superiority in force more marked in the latter instance, but Saumarez's ship there met with an accident similar in character to that which befell the *Cléopâtre*, from the consequences of which she was extricated by his masterly seamanship. Still, it may with fairness be argued that, as the one action from its attendant circumstances evidenced the individual skill of the commander, so the other testified to the antecedent preparation and efficiency of the crew, which are always to be attributed to the care of the captain, especially under the conditions of Pellew's enlistments. Both captains fully deserved the reward of knighthood bestowed upon their success. Israel Pellew was promoted to post-captain.

During the first three years of this war British commerce in the neighbourhood of the Channel suffered most severely from French cruisers. The latter resumed the methods of Jean Bart and other celebrated privateers of the days of Louis XIV.; the essence of which was to prey upon the enemy's commerce, not by single vessels, but by small squadrons of from five to seven. Cruisers so combined, acting in mutual support, were far more efficient than the same number acting separately. Spreading like a fan, they commanded a wider expanse than a ship alone; if danger arose, they concentrated for mutual support; did opportunity offer, the work was cut out and distributed, thus insuring by co-operation more thorough results. At the suggestion of Sir Edward Pellew, the British Admiralty determined to oppose to these organized depredators a similar system. Groups of crack frigates were constituted, and sent to cruise within the limits of the Channel Fleet, but independent of its admiral. In these Pellew served for the next five years, much of the time as squadron commander; to him a period of incessant, untiring activity, and illustrated by many brilliant and exciting incidents, for which the limits of this sketch afford no space.

There are, however, two episodes in which he was so distinctly the central figure that they demand at least a brief narration. In January, 1796, while his ship was repairing, a large East Indiaman, the *Dutton*, carrying some six hundred troops and passengers, was by a series of mishaps driven ashore on the beach of Plymouth, then an unprotected sound. As she struck, all her masts went overboard, and she lay broadside to the waves, pounding heavily as they broke over her. Pellew was at this moment driving to a dinner with his wife. Seeing crowds running from various directions towards the same quarter, he asked the reason. Upon learning it, he left his carriage and hurried to the scene. When he arrived, he recognized, by the confusion on board, by the way the ship was labouring, by the poverty of the means that had been contrived for landing the imperilled souls,—only a single hawser having been run to the shore,—that the loss of nearly all on board was imminent. Night, too, was falling, as well as the destruction of the vessel impending. After vainly offering rewards to the hardy boatmen standing by, if they would board the wreck with a message from him, he said, "Then I must go myself." Though then close to forty years of age, his immense personal strength and activity enabled him, though sorely bruised thereby, to be hauled on board through the breakers by the hawser, which alternately slacked and then tightened with a jerk as the doomed ship rolled to and fro in the seas. Once on board, he assumed command, the want of which, through the absence of the proper captain, had until then hampered and well-nigh paralyzed all effectual effort. When his well-known name was spoken, three hearty cheers arose from the troops on board, echoed by the thousands of spectators on shore; and the hope that revived with the presence of a born leader of men showed itself at once in the renewed activity and intelligent direction of effort, on the decks and on the beach. The degree of the danger can be estimated from the fact that boats from the ships of war in port, his own included, tried in vain to approach and had to run for safety to the inner harbour. With sword drawn,—for many of the soldiers were drunk and riotous,—Pellew maintained order, guided with a seaman's readiness the preparations for landing, and saw the women, the children,—one child but three weeks old,—the sick, landed first, then the soldiers, lastly the seamen. When he himself was transferred to the beach by the same means that his skill had contrived for others, but three persons remained on board, officers of the ship, who eased him on shore. The injuries he had received in his perilous passage out, and which confined him to his bed for a week, forbade his being last. To the end of his life, this saving of the crew of the *Dutton* was the action in which he took most pride.

The year that opened with this magnificent act of self-devotion saw Pellew, at its close, bearing a seaman's part in the most serious crisis that befell his country during the wars of the French Revolution. The end of 1796 and the earlier months of 1797 marked the nadir of Great Britain's military fortunes. The successes of Bonaparte's Italian campaign were then culminating; Austria was on the point of making peace with France; England was about to find herself alone, and the discontent of the seamen of the navy, long smouldering, was soon to break out into the famous and threatening mutinies of the Channel Fleet and of the Nore. At the same time France, relieved on her eastern frontiers, felt able to devote seventeen ships-of-the-line and eighteen thousand troops to the invasion of Ireland.

Pellew, with two frigates besides his own, was stationed off the mouth of Brest harbour to watch the enemy's movements; the main British fleet being some fifty miles to seaward. To this emergency he brought not only the intrepidity of a great seaman and the ardour of an anxious patriot, but likewise the intense though narrow Protestant feeling transmitted from a past, then not so remote, when Romanism and enmity to England were almost synonymous. "How would you like," said he to an officer who shared Pitt's liberal tendencies, "to see Roman Catholic chaplains on board our ships?" and to the end of his life he opposed the political enfranchisement of persons of that creed.

The French expedition against Ireland sailed from Brest on the 16th of December, 1796. Having sent off successively each of his consorts with information for the fleet, Pellew remained with his own ship alone, the *Indefatigable*, at the moment of the final start. There are two principal channels by which Brest can be left, one leading to the south, the other due west. The French admiral had at first intended to use the former; but, the wind showing signs of an unfavourable shift, he endeavoured to change the orders just as night was falling. The weather being hazy, his signals were understood by but few of the forty-odd vessels composing the force. Eight or ten joined him; the remainder followed the original instructions and went out by the south. Pellew attached himself to the admiral's division, kept along with it just out of gun-shot, and by making false signals, burning blue lights and sending up rockets, introduced into the attempts to convey the wishes of the commander-in-chief such confusion as rendered them utterly futile. Having satisfied himself as to the general direction taken by the enemy, he left them, and made all sail for Falmouth, where he arrived on the 20th.

The general fortunes of the expedition do not belong to the present story. Suffice it to say that the greater part reached Ireland safely, but through stress of weather was unable to land the troops, and went back to France by detachments, in January, 1797. It is during this process of return that Sir Edward Pellew again appears, in perhaps the most dramatic incident of his stirring career.

On the afternoon of January 13th, being then in company

with the frigate *Amazon*, and about one hundred and twenty miles west of Brest, a French ship-of-the-line was discovered. The stranger, named the *Droits de l'Homme*, was returning from Ireland, and heading east. The frigates steered courses converging towards hers, seeking to cut her off from the land. The weather was thick and gloomy, with a strong west wind fast rising to a gale. At half-past four, as night was falling, the French ship carried away her fore and main topmasts in a heavy squall; and an hour later the *Indefatigable*, now under close reefs, passed across her stern, pouring in a broadside from so near that the French flag floated across her poop, where it was seized and torn away by some of the British seamen. The enemy, having on board nearly a thousand soldiers besides her crew, replied with rapid volleys of musketry, and, as the frigate passed ahead, sheered impetuously towards her, attempting to board, and in her turn grazing the stern of the *Indefatigable*. In another hour the *Amazon* drew up, and then the British vessels took their positions, one on either bow of the *Droits de l'Homme*, whence, by movements of the helm, they alternately raked her. The labour of the gunners, however, was arduous, due to the deep rolling of the ships, on board which, also, the seas poured in volumes through the gunports. On the main decks the men fought up to their middles in water, the heavy cannon broke away from the breechings, or ropes used to control them, and even iron bolts tore out from the ships' sides under the severe recoil of the guns. Thus through the long winter night the three ships rushed headlong before the gale towards the French coast, intent on mutual destruction; the constant storm of shot, though flying wild under the violent motions of the vessels, tearing through spars and rigging, and crippling them in much that was essential to their safety.

At four o'clock in the morning of the 14th, long before daybreak, land was sighted right ahead. The *Indefatigable* hauled at once to the southward, the *Amazon* to the northward; the enemy alone, seemingly unconscious of the danger, kept on, and as she passed Pellew's ship fired a broadside which severely wounded all the masts. The situation of the combatants was well-nigh desperate. They had reached the coast of France at a point where it forms a deep recess, called Audierne Bay, from either side of which project capes that must be cleared in order to gain once more the open sea. One only of the three escaped. The *Droits de l'Homme*, unmanageable for want of sail power, tried to anchor, but drove, and struck on a shoal some distance from the beach. Of sixteen hundred souls on board when the battle began, over one hundred had been killed; and of those who survived the fight three hundred perished in the wreck. The *Amazon*, likewise crippled, though not so badly, had gone ashore to the northward only ten minutes after she ceased firing. Of her people, but six were drowned. The *Indefatigable*, beating back and forth against the gale before the scene of the French disaster, upon which her crew gazed with the solemn feeling that such might soon be their own fate, succeeded at last in clearing the southern cape. At eleven o'clock, nearly twenty-four hours after first meeting the foe, and with six feet of water in her hold, she passed only three-quarters of a mile outside of the Penmarcks, a rocky promontory thirty miles south of Brest.

This remarkable encounter is said to have suggested to Marryat the vivid sea picture with which "The King's Own" ends. Pellew's unusual personal endurance was signally illustrated on the same day, very shortly after the safety of the ship from wreck was assured. Her principal sails had been so torn by shot as to require immediate renewing, and this had scarcely been done when two vessels were sighted, one of which was for the moment supposed to be the *Amazon*, whose fate was yet unknown. Pellew gave orders to chase, but his officers represented to him that, whatever he himself was capable of, the ship's company was too exhausted for present further exertion; and that, besides, the ammunition was very short, almost the last filled cartridge having been expended. Under these circumstances he was compelled to desist.

The interest of Pellew's career centres mainly in his command of frigates. This independent but yet restricted sphere afforded the fullest scope for a conspicuous display of those splendid qualities—fearlessness, enterprise, sound judgment, instant decision, and superb seamanship—which he so eminently possessed. He was, above all, the frigate captain. "Nothing like hesitation was ever seen in him. His first order was always his last; and he often declared of himself that he never had a second thought worth sixpence." In 1799, by a new Admiralty rule, he was transferred to the *Impétueux*, a ship-of-the-line, and thenceforth served in that class of vessel until his promotion to admiral.

As a general officer, Pellew had no opportunity to show whether he possessed ability of the highest order. For five years he held the command in India; and soon after Collingwood's death he was, in 1811, appointed commander-in-chief in the Mediterranean. On both stations he evinced that faculty for careful organization, systematic preparation, and sagacious distribution of force which carries success up to the point which administrative capacity can reach. His ability in planning, while yet a subordinate in command of squadrons, had been recognized by St. Vincent during his management of the Brest blockade.

The disposition made by Sir Edward Pellew for the descent on a certain point is the most masterly I have ever seen.... Although the naval command in Quiberon may appear too important for a captain, I shall not divest him of it, unless I am ordered to do so; feeling a thorough conviction that no man in His Majesty's Navy, be his rank ever so high, will fill it so well.

At the time this was written, June, 1800, he had seven ships-of-the-line under his orders. After the Peace of Amiens, when war again began in 1803, he commanded a similar division watching the Spanish port of Ferrol, in which, although formally neutral, a French division lay at anchor; and in discharge of this duty, both as a seaman and an administrator, he again justified the eulogium of the old Earl, now at the head of the navy as First Lord.

In 1804 he was promoted Rear-Admiral, and soon afterwards assigned to the East India Station, which he held from 1805 to 1809. Here no naval actions on the great scale were to be fought, but under his systematic organization of convoys and cruisers for the protection of commerce the insurance premium—the war risk—on the most exposed routes fell markedly,—for the port of Bombay fifty per cent less than at any former period of hostilities; while the losses by capture, when the merchants observed his instructions, amounted to but one per cent on the property insured, which was less than those caused by the dangers of the sea, and considerably less, also, than the average war losses in other parts of the world. All this shows great ability, carefully utilized in diligent preparation and efficient precaution; and the same characteristics are to be observed in his administration of the Mediterranean command, of wider scope and more purely military importance. Nevertheless, it gives no sure proof of the particular genius of a great captain. Whether, having forged his weapon, Pellew could also wield it; whether, having carefully sowed, he could also reap the harvest by large combinations on the battle-field, must remain uncertain, at least until probable demonstration of his conceptions is drawn from his papers. Nothing is as yet adduced to warrant positive inference.

Pellew's Mediterranean command coincided in time with the period of Napoleon's falling fortunes. After Trafalgar, the Emperor decided to increase his navy largely, but to keep it in port instead of at sea, forcing Great Britain also to maintain huge fleets, the expense of which, concurring with the commercial embarrassments that he sought to bring upon her, might exhaust her power to continue the war. In consequence of this policy, British military achievement on the grand scale was confined to the army in the Spanish peninsula; and in the bestowal of rewards, after Napoleon's first abdication, but one peerage was given to the navy. The great claims of Sir James Saumarez, who was the senior of the two, were disregarded on the ground that his flag was not flying at the moment, and Pellew was created Baron Exmouth.

During the process of settlement which succeeded the final fall of Napoleon at Waterloo, Lord Exmouth remained in the Mediterranean. In the early part of 1816 he was ordered to visit with his fleet the Barbary ports, and to compel the unconditional release of all slaves who were natives of the Ionian Islands; they having become subjects of Great Britain by the terms of the peace. For many years, while the powers of Europe were engrossed in the tremendous strife of the French Revolution, these piratical states, under pretence of regular hostilities, had preyed upon the coasts as well as upon the commerce of the weak Mediterranean countries, and captives taken by them were kept in bitter slavery. Nelson in his correspondence, in 1796, mentions a curious incident which sufficiently characterizes the general motives and policy of these barbarian Courts. He asked an Algerine official visiting his ship, why the Dey would not make peace with Genoa and Naples, for they would pay well for immunity, as the United States also at that time did. The reply was, "If we make peace with every one, what is the Dey to do with his ships?" In his later experience with the Mediterranean the great admiral realized yet more forcibly the crying shame of Great Britain's acquiescence.

> My blood boils that I cannot chastise these pirates. They could not show themselves in this sea did not our country permit. Never let us talk of the cruelty of the African slave trade, while we permit such a horrid war.

The United States alone, although then among the least of naval powers, had taken arms before 1805 to repress outrages that were the common reproach of all civilized nations,—a measure the success of which went far to establish the character of her navy and prepare it for 1812. Lord Exmouth was also directed to demand peace for Sardinia, as well as for any other state that should authorize him to act for it. Only Naples availed itself of this opportunity.

As far as his instructions went, his mission was successful, and, by a happy accident, he was able at Tunis and Tripoli to extort further from the rulers a promise that thereafter captives should be treated as in civilized countries; in other words, that they should no longer be reduced to slavery. Algiers refused this concession; and the admiral could not take steps to enforce it, because beyond his commission. The Dey, however, undertook to consult the Porte; and the fleet, with a few exceptions, returned to England, where it arrived towards the end of June.

Meanwhile British public feeling had become aroused; for men were saying that the outrages of the past had been rather welcome to the commercial selfishness of the country. The well-protected traders of Great Britain, shielded by her omnipotent navy, had profited by crimes which drove their weaker rivals from the sea. Just then news came that at the port of Bona, on the Algiers coast, where there was under the British flag an establishment for carrying on the coral fishery, a large number of the fishermen, mostly Italians, had been wantonly slaughtered by a band of Turkish troops. To insist, arms in hand, upon reparation for such an outrage, and upon guarantees for the future, would doubtless be condemned by some of our recent lights; but such was not then the temper of Great Britain. The government determined at once to send a fleet to the spot, and Lord Exmouth was chosen for the command, with such a force as he himself should designate. The gist of his instructions was to demand the release, without ransom, of *all* Christian slaves, and a solemn declaration from the Dey that, in future wars, prisoners should receive the usage accorded them by European states. Great Britain thus made herself, as befitted the obligation imposed by her supreme maritime power, the avenger of all those oppressed by these scourges of the sea. The times of the barbarians were fulfilled.

During a long career of successful piracy, the port of Algiers had accumulated an extensive and powerful system of defences. These had doubtless suffered in condition from the nonchalant fatalism of Turkish rule, encouraged by a long period of impunity; but they constituted still, and under all the shortcomings of the defenders, a most imposing menace to an attacking fleet. To convey a precise impression of them by detailed verbal description would be difficult, and the attempt probably confusing. It may be said, in brief, that the town faces easterly, rising abruptly up a steep hill; that from its front there then projected a pier, nearly a thousand feet long, at whose end was a circular fort, carrying seventy guns in three tiers; from that point a mole extended at right angles to the southward,—parallel, that is, in a general sense, to the town front, but curving inward through the southern half of its length, so as better to embrace and shelter the vessels inside. This mole was somewhat over a thousand feet in length, and had throughout two tiers of guns, linked at their northern extremity to the circular fort at the pier end. These principal works were flanked and covered, at either end and on the hillside, by others which it is unnecessary to particularize. The total number of guns bearing seaward numbered near three hundred, of very respectable size for that day. The basin formed by the pier and the mole constituted the port proper, and in it, at the time of the attack, was collected the entire Algerine navy, nine frigates and corvettes and thirty-seven gunboats, the paltry force that had so long terrorized the Mediterranean.

In prevision of his present enterprise, Lord Exmouth before leaving the Mediterranean had despatched a light cruiser to Algiers, on a casual visit similar to those continually made by ships of war to foreign ports. Her commander, Captain Charles Warde, received from him very precise and most secret instructions to examine closely into the defences and soundings; to do which it was necessary not only to observe every precaution of seeming indifference,—even to the extent of appearing engrossed with social duties,—but also to conduct under this cover measurements and observations of at least approximate correctness. This duty was performed with singular diligence and success, with the double result of revealing the hopeless inaccuracy of existing charts and of placing in Exmouth's hands a working plan of the ground, perfectly trustworthy for his tactical dispositions.

As before remarked, in the sketch of Lord St. Vincent, the defence and attack of seaports, involving as they do both occupation of permanent positions and the action of mobile bodies, are tactical questions. They differ much, though not radically, from operations in the open sea, or in the field, where positions may be taken incidentally, but where the movements of mobile bodies are the principal factor. In this way, though without using the word tactical, Exmouth treated the problem before him. Furnished, thanks to his own foresight and Warde's efficiency, with reliable information concerning the preparations of the enemy, he calculated the dispositions necessary to meet them and to crush their fire. Having assigned to the hostile works, severally and collectively, the force needed to overbear them, and having arranged the anchoring positions for the vessels of his command with reference to the especial task of each, as well as for mutual support, he had substantially his plan of battle, afterwards communicated to the fleet before going into action; and the same data afforded the foundation for his statement to the Government of the number and character of ships needed for success.

To the surprise of the Admiralty, Lord Exmouth asked for but five ships-of-the-line, five frigates, and five smaller vessels, to which were added four mortar boats to play upon the town and arsenal. When met with expressions of doubt, he replied, "I am satisfied, and take the responsibility entirely upon myself." To satisfy the hesitancy of the Government, he left with the Secretary to the Admiralty a written statement that his every requirement had been fulfilled, and that to him alone, therefore, would failure from deficient power be attributable. On the eve of departure he said to his brother Israel, "If they open fire when the ships are coming up, and cripple them in their masts, the difficulty and loss will be greater; but if they allow us to take our stations, I am sure of them, for I know that nothing can resist a line-of-battle ship's fire." He trusted to the extreme care of his preparations, which neglected no particular of equipment or organization, elaborating every detail of training and discipline, and providing, by the most diligent foresight and minute instruction, that each officer concerned should know exactly what was expected of him. In short, it was to perfection of quality, and not to an unwieldy bulk of superfluous quantity, that Exmouth confided his fortunes in this last hazard.

The fleet sailed from England on the 28th of July, 1816, was joined at Gibraltar by a Dutch squadron of five frigates, whose commander asked to share the coming contest, and on the 26th of August was off the north point of Algiers Bay, some twenty miles from the town. At daybreak the next morning, the weather being almost calm, a flag of truce was sent in, bearing the British demands. During its absence a breeze from the sea sprang up, and the fleet stood in to a mile from the works, where it stopped to await the reply. At two p.m. the boat was seen returning, with the signal that no answer had been given. The flag-ship queried, "Are you ready?"

Each ship at once replied, "Yes;" and all filling away together stood down to the attack, the admiral leading.

The Algerine batteries were fully manned; the mole, moreover, was crowded with troops. With singular temerity, they fired no gun as the ships came on, thus relieving the most anxious of Exmouth's preoccupations concerning the difficulties before him; fearing, seemingly, that, if otherwise received, the prey might turn and escape. The British, on their side, observed the utmost silence; not a gun, not a cheer, marred the solemn impression of the approach. The flag-ship, *Queen Charlotte*,[16] piloted by an officer who had served continuously with Exmouth since 1793, anchored by the stern across the mole head, at a distance of fifty yards, her starboard batteries pointing to sweep it from end to end. Still no sound of battle, as she proceeded to lash her bows to those of an Algerine brig lying just within the mole. This done, her crew gave three cheers, as well they might. Then the stolid, unaccountable apathy of the barbarians ceased, and three guns in quick succession were fired from the eastern battery. Stirred by a movement of compassion, Lord Exmouth, from the flag-ship's poop, seeing the Moorish soldiery clustered thick upon the parapets to watch the ships, waved to them with his hand to get down. At the first hostile gun he gave the order "Stand by!" at the second, "Fire!" and simultaneously with the third the *Queen Charlotte*'s broadside rang out, and the battle began.

The other vessels of the squadron were not all as successful as the flag-ship in taking the exact position assigned, and the admiral's plan thereby suffered some of that derangement to which every undertaking, especially military and naval, is liable. This, however, produced no effect upon the general result, except by increasing somewhat the lists of killed and wounded, through loss of advantageous offensive position, with consequent defect in mutual support. But the first broadside is proverbially

---

16. This *Queen Charlotte* was the successor of the ship which carried Howe's flag on the First of June, and which had been destroyed by fire off Leghorn in 1800.

half the battle. It was a saying of Collingwood to his crew, in a three-decker like the *Queen Charlotte*, that if they could deliver three effective fires in the first five minutes no vessel could resist them; and this was yet more certain when opposed to the semi-discipline of adversaries such as the Algerine pirates. Exmouth's general design was to concentrate his heavy ships at the southern end of the mole, whence the curve in the line of batteries would enable them to enfilade or take in reverse the works at the northern extremity. Here were to be the two three-deckers, with a seventy-four between them, all three in close order, stem to stern. The two-decker, however, anchored some seven hundred feet astern of the *Queen Charlotte*, the intervening space being left empty until filled by a thirty-six-gun frigate, upon whose captain St.Vincent passed the eulogium, "He seems to have felt Lord Nelson's eye upon him." The two remaining seventy-fours placed themselves successively close astern of the first, which was in accord with the original purpose, while the other three-decker took the right flank of the line, and somewhat too far out; in which exposed and unintended position, beyond the extreme north point contemplated for the British order, she underwent a very heavy loss.

In general summary, therefore, it may be said that the broadsides of the ships-of-the-line were opposed from end to end to the heavy central batteries on the mole, while the lighter vessels engaged the flanking works on the shore to the southward, thus diverting the fire which would have harassed the chief assailants,—a service in which the Dutch squadron, composed entirely of frigates, rendered important assistance. The bomb vessels from the rear threw their shells over the fighting ships into the town and arsenal, and in the admiral's report are credited with firing all the shipping in the harbour, except one frigate, creating a conflagration which spread over the arsenal and storehouses. Soon after the contest opened, the thirty-seven Algerine gunboats, crowded with troops, were seen advancing under cover of the smoke to board the flag-ship. The attempt, rash to insanity, met the fate it should have expected; thirty-three were sent to the bottom by the guns of the *Leander*, stationed ahead of the *Queen Charlotte*, and commanding the entrance to the port. An hour later, Lord Exmouth determined to set fire to the remaining frigate. The service was performed by an officer and boat's crew, with a steadiness which elicited from him such admiration that, on the return of the party, he stopped the working of the ship's upper battery to give them three cheers. As the hostile vessel burned, she drifted so near the *Queen Charlotte* as nearly to involve her in the same fate.

From three to ten p.m. the battle lasted, steady disciplined valour contending with a courage in no way inferior, absolutely insensible to danger, but devoid of that coherent, skilful direction which is to courage what the brain and eye are to the heart. Exmouth wrote to his brother:

> I never saw any set of men more obstinate at their guns, and it was superior fire only that could keep them back. To be sure, nothing could stand before the *Queen Charlotte*'s broadside. Everything fell before it, and the Swedish consul assures me we killed above five hundred at the very first fire, from the crowded way in which the troops were drawn up, four deep above the gunboats, which were also full of men. It was a glorious sight to see the *Charlotte* take her anchorage, and to see her flag towering on high, when she appeared to be in the flames of the mole itself; and never was a ship nearer burnt; it almost scorched me off the poop. We were obliged to haul in the ensign, or it would have caught fire.

He was himself struck thrice, though not seriously injured. A cannon-ball carried away the skirts of his coat, and one glass of the spectacles in his pocket was broken, and the frame bulged, by a shot.

At ten p.m., the ammunition of the fleet running short, and its work being substantially accomplished, the ships began to haul off. The sea defences and a great part of the town were in ruins. "To be again effective," wrote Exmouth, "the defences must be rebuilt from the foundation." The flanking batteries and the hill forts continued to annoy the vessels as they retired, but the spirit of the Dey was broken. Towards eleven a light air from the land sprang up, which freshened into a violent and prolonged thunderstorm, lasting for three hours; and the flashes of heaven's artillery combined with the glare of the burning town to illuminate the withdrawal of the ships.

The following morning the Dey signified his submission, and on the 30th of August Lord Exmouth made known to the fleet that all the terms of Great Britain had been yielded; that Christian slavery was forever abolished, and that by noon of the following day all slaves then in Algiers would be delivered to his flag. This was accordingly done, the whole number amounting to 1642; which, with those previously released at Tunis and Tripoli, raised to 3003 the human beings whom Exmouth had been the instrument of freeing from a fate worse than death. Of this total, but eighteen were English; the remainder were almost wholly from the Mediterranean countries. On the 3rd of September, just one week after the attack, the fleet sailed for England.

Profuse acknowledgment necessarily awaited the hero of a deed in which national exultation so happily blended with the sentiment of pity for the oppressed. The admiral was raised to the next rank in the peerage, and honours poured in upon him from every side,—from abroad as well as from his own countrymen. His personal sense of the privilege permitted him, thus to crown a life of strenuous exertion by a martial deed of far-reaching beneficence, was a reward passing all others. In the opening words of his official report he voices his thankfulness:

> In all the vicissitudes of a long life of public service, no circumstance has ever produced on my mind such impressions of gratitude and joy as the event of yesterday. To have been one of the humble instruments in the hands of Divine Providence for bringing to reason a ferocious Government, and destroying for ever the horrid system of Christian slavery, can never cease to be a source of delight and heartfelt comfort to every individual happy enough to be employed in it.

Here Lord Exmouth's career closes. Just forty years had elapsed since as a youth he had fought the *Carleton* on Lake Champlain, and he was yet to live sixteen in honoured retreat; bearing, however, the burden of those whose occupation is withdrawn at an age too advanced to form new interests. Though in vigorous health and with ample fortune, "he would sometimes confess," says his biographer, "that he was happier amid his early difficulties." The idea of retirement, indeed, does not readily associate itself with the impression of prodigious vitality, which from first to last is produced by the record of his varied activities. In this respect, as in others, the contrast is marked between him and Saumarez, the two who more particularly illustrate the complementary sides of the brilliant group of naval leaders, in the second rank of distinction, which clustered around the great names of Nelson, Howe, and Jervis. In the old age of Saumarez, the even, ordered tenor of his active military life is reflected in the peaceful, satisfied enjoyment of repose and home happiness, of the fruits of labours past, which Collingwood, probably without good reason, fancied to be characteristic of his own temperament. Lord Exmouth, compelled to be a passive spectator, saw with consequent increased apprehension the internal political troubles of Great Britain in his later days. Though not a party man, he was strongly conservative, so that the agitations of the Reform era concealed from him the advantages towards which it was tending, and filled him with forebodings for the future of his country.

Like his distinguished contemporary, Admiral Saumarez, and like many others of those lion-hearted, masculine men who had passed their lives amid the storms of the elements and of battle,—and like our own Farragut,—Lord Exmouth was a deeply religious man. Strong as was his self-reliance in war and tempest, he rested upon the Almighty with the dependence of a child upon its father. His noble brother, Sir Israel Pellew, who had followed Nelson into the fire at Trafalgar, departed with the words, "I know in Whom I have believed;" and of the admiral himself, an officer who was often with him during the closing scene said, "I have seen him great in battle, but never so great as on his deathbed."

Lord Exmouth died on January 23, 1833. He was at the time Vice-Admiral of England, that distinguished honorary rank having been conferred upon him but a few months before his death.

Postscript

Of the last four admirals whose careers have been here sketched, Howe alone inherited fortune and high social rank; but he also fought his way far beyond the modest position bequeathed to him by his brother. Eminent all, though in varying manner and degree, each illustrated a distinct type in the same noble profession. All were admirable officers, but they differed greatly in original endowments and consequent development. It was intuitive with St. Vincent to take wide and far-sighted views, and to embody them in sustained, relentless action. Endued by nature with invincible energy and determination, he moved spontaneously and easily along his difficult path. He approached, although he did not attain genius. In Howe is seen rather the result of conscientious painstaking acting upon excellent abilities, but struggling always against a native heaviness and a temper constitutionally both indolent and indulgent; a temper to which indeed he does not yield, over which he triumphs, but which nevertheless imposes itself upon his general course with all the force inseparable from hereditary disposition. A man of talent, he educates himself to acquirements which in his rival have the character of perception; and only under the spur of emergency does he rise to the height of greatness. Both were great general officers, a claim which can scarcely be advanced for Saumarez and Exmouth, able, brilliant, and devoted as they were. Saumarez was the steadfast, skilful, accomplished master of his profession, but one whose aptitudes and tastes placed him in the great organization of the fleet, as a principal subordinate rather than as head. Exmouth was the typical, innate seaman, intensely active, whose instincts are those of the partisan warrior, and who shines most in the freedom of detached service. All bore a conspicuous part in the greatest war of modern times, with honour such that their names will be remembered as long as naval history endures.

ALSO FROM LEONAUR
AVAILABLE IN SOFTCOVER OR HARDCOVER WITH DUST JACKET

CAPTAIN OF THE 95th (Rifles) by *Jonathan Leach*—An officer of Wellington's Sharpshooters during the Peninsular, South of France and Waterloo Campaigns of the Napoleonic Wars.

BUGLER AND OFFICER OF THE RIFLES by *William Green & Harry Smith* With the 95th (Rifles) during the Peninsular & Waterloo Campaigns of the Napoleonic Wars

BAYONETS, BUGLES AND BONNETS by *James 'Thomas' Todd*—Experiences of hard soldiering with the 71st Foot - the Highland Light Infantry - through many battles of the Napoleonic wars including the Peninsular & Waterloo Campaigns

THE ADVENTURES OF A LIGHT DRAGOON by *George Farmer & G.R. Gleig*—A cavalryman during the Peninsular & Waterloo Campaigns, in captivity & at the siege of Bhurtpore, India

THE COMPLEAT RIFLEMAN HARRIS by *Benjamin Harris as told to & transcribed by Captain Henry Curling*—The adventures of a soldier of the 95th (Rifles) during the Peninsular Campaign of the Napoleonic Wars

WITH WELLINGTON'S LIGHT CAVALRY by *William Tomkinson*—The Experiences of an officer of the 16th Light Dragoons in the Peninsular and Waterloo campaigns of the Napoleonic Wars.

SURTEES OF THE RIFLES by *William Surtees*—A Soldier of the 95th (Rifles) in the Peninsular campaign of the Napoleonic Wars.

ENSIGN BELL IN THE PENINSULAR WAR by *George Bell*—The Experiences of a young British Soldier of the 34th Regiment 'The Cumberland Gentlemen' in the Napoleonic wars.

WITH THE LIGHT DIVISION by *John H. Cooke*—The Experiences of an Officer of the 43rd Light Infantry in the Peninsula and South of France During the Napoleonic Wars

NAPOLEON'S IMPERIAL GUARD: FROM MARENGO TO WATERLOO by *J. T. Headley*—This is the story of Napoleon's Imperial Guard from the bearskin caps of the grenadiers to the flamboyance of their mounted chasseurs, their principal characters and the men who commanded them.

BATTLES & SIEGES OF THE PENINSULAR WAR by *W. H. Fitchett*—Corunna, Busaco, Albuera, Ciudad Rodrigo, Badajos, Salamanca, San Sebastian & Others

AVAILABLE ONLINE AT **www.leonaur.com**
AND OTHER GOOD BOOK STORES

ALSO FROM LEONAUR
AVAILABLE IN SOFTCOVER OR HARDCOVER WITH DUST JACKET

LIGHT BOB by *Robert Blakeney*—The experiences of a young officer in H.M 28th & 36th regiments of the British Infantry during the Peninsular Campaign of the Napoleonic Wars 1804 - 1814.

NAPOLEON'S RUSSIAN CAMPAIGN by *Philippe Henri de Segur*—The Invasion, Battles and Retreat by an Aide-de-Camp on the Emperor's Staff

SWORDS OF HONOUR by *Henry Newbolt & Stanley L. Wood*—The Careers of Six Outstanding Officers from the Napoleonic Wars, the Wars for India and the American Civil War. Illustrated.

HUSSAR IN WINTER by *Alexander Gordon*—A British Cavalry Officer during the retreat to Corunna in the Peninsular campaign of the Napoleonic Wars.

THE LIFE OF THE REAL BRIGADIER GERARD VOLUME 1 THE YOUNG HUSSAR 1782 - 1807 by *Jean-Baptiste De Marbot*—A French Cavalryman Of the Napoleonic Wars at Marengo, Austerlitz, Jena, Eylau & Friedland.

THE LIFE OF THE REAL BRIGADIER GERARD VOLUME 2 IMPERIAL AIDE-DE-CAMP 1807 - 1811 by *Jean-Baptiste De Marbot*—A French Cavalryman of the Napoleonic Wars at Saragossa, Landshut, Eckmuhl, Ratisbon, Aspern-Essling, Wagram, Busaco & Torres Vedras.

THE LIFE OF THE REAL BRIGADIER GERARD VOLUME 3 COLONEL OF CHASSEURS 1811 - 1815 by *Jean-Baptiste De Marbot*—A French Cavalryman in the retreat from Moscow, Lutzen, Bautzen, Katzbach, Leipzig, Hanau & Waterloo.

RIFLEMAN COSTELLO by *Edward Costello*—The adventures of a soldier of the 95th (Rifles) in the Peninsular & Waterloo Campaigns of the Napoleonic wars.

WITH THE LIGHT DIVISION by *John H. Cooke*—The Experiences of an Officer of the 43rd Light Infantry in the Peninsula and South of France During the Napoleonic Wars.

COLBORNE: A SINGULAR TALENT FOR WAR by *John Colborne*—The Napoleonic Wars Career of One of Wellington's Most Highly Valued Officers in Egypt, Holland, Italy, the Peninsula and at Waterloo.

A VOICE FROM WATERLOO by *Edward Cotton*—The Personal Experiences of a British Cavalryman Who Became a Battlefield Guide and Authority on the Campaign of 1815.

AVAILABLE ONLINE AT
www.leonaur.com
AND OTHER GOOD BOOK STORES

ALSO FROM LEONAUR
AVAILABLE IN SOFTCOVER OR HARDCOVER WITH DUST JACKET

THE JENA CAMPAIGN: 1806 by *F. N. Maude*—The Twin Battles of Jena & Auerstadt Between Napoleon's French and the Prussian Army.

PRIVATE O'NEIL by *Charles O'Neil*—The recollections of an Irish Rogue of H. M. 28th Regt.—The Slashers— during the Peninsula & Waterloo campaigns of the Napoleonic wars.

ROYAL HIGHLANDER by *James Anton*—A soldier of H.M 42nd (Royal) Highlanders during the Peninsular, South of France & Waterloo Campaigns of the Napoleonic Wars.

CAPTAIN BLAZE by *Elzéar Blaze*—Elzéar Blaze recounts his life and experiences in Napoleon's army in a well written, articulate and companionable style.

LEJEUNE VOLUME 1 by *Louis-François Lejeune*—The Napoleonic Wars through the Experiences of an Officer on Berthier's Staff.

LEJEUNE VOLUME 2 by *Louis-François Lejeune*—The Napoleonic Wars through the Experiences of an Officer on Berthier's Staff.

FUSILIER COOPER by *John S. Cooper*—Experiences in the 7th (Royal) Fusiliers During the Peninsular Campaign of the Napoleonic Wars and the American Campaign to New Orleans.

CAPTAIN COIGNET by *Jean-Roch Coignet*—A Soldier of Napoleon's Imperial Guard from the Italian Campaign to Russia and Waterloo.

FIGHTING NAPOLEON'S EMPIRE by *Joseph Anderson*—The Campaigns of a British Infantryman in Italy, Egypt, the Peninsular & the West Indies During the Napoleonic Wars.

CHASSEUR BARRES by *Jean-Baptiste Barres*—The experiences of a French Infantryman of the Imperial Guard at Austerlitz, Jena, Eylau, Friedland, in the Peninsular, Lutzen, Bautzen, Zinnwald and Hanau during the Napoleonic Wars.

MARINES TO 95TH (RIFLES) by *Thomas Fernyhough*—The military experiences of Robert Fernyhough during the Napoleonic Wars.

HUSSAR ROCCA by *Albert Jean Michel de Rocca*—A French cavalry officer's experiences of the Napoleonic Wars and his views on the Peninsular Campaigns against the Spanish, British And Guerilla Armies.

SERGEANT BOURGOGNE by *Adrien Bourgogne*—With Napoleon's Imperial Guard in the Russian Campaign and on the Retreat from Moscow 1812 - 13.

AVAILABLE ONLINE AT **www.leonaur.com**
AND OTHER GOOD BOOK STORES

www.ingramcontent.com/pod-product-compliance
Lightning Source LLC
Chambersburg PA
CBHW030227170426
43201CB00006B/140